International Trade
An essential guide to the principles and practice of export

Jonathan Reuvid and
Jim Sherlock

KoganPage

LONDON PHILADELPHIA NEW DELHI

First published in Great Britain and the United States in 2011 by Kogan Page Limited

Reprinted 2013 (three times), 2014, 2015

2nd Floor, 45 Gee Street	1518 Walnut Street, Suite 1100	4737/23 Ansari Road
London EC1V 3RS	Philadelphia PA 19102	Daryaganj
United Kingdom	USA	New Delhi 110002
www.koganpage.com		India

© Jonathan Reuvid and Jim Sherlock, 2011

ISBN   978 0 7494 6237 6
E-ISBN 978 0 7494 6238 3

British Library Cataloguing-in-Publication Data

A CIP record for this book is available from the British Library.

Library of Congress Cataloging-in-Publication Data

Reuvid, Jonathan.
    International trade : an essential guide to the principles and practice of export / Jonathan Reuvid, J. Sherlock.
        p. cm.
    ISBN 978-0-7494-6237-6 -- ISBN 978-0-7494-6238-3 (ebook)   1. International trade.
2. Export marketing.   I. Sherlock, Jim.   II. Title.
    HF1379.R485 2011
    382--dc22

                                                                                                                          2010031606

Typeset by Graphicraft Limited, Hong Kong
Printed and bound by CPI Group (UK) Ltd, Croydon, CR0 4YY

CONTENTS

LIST OF BOXES

LIST OF FIGURES

LIST OF TABLES

ABOUT THE AUTHORS

Jim Sherlock, Hon FIEx, Cert Ed

Jim is a full-time writer, trainer and consultant in international trade with extensive experience in the UK export manufacturing sector and 20 years as senior lecturer in international trade at Central Manchester College. He is currently senior tutor for the online qualification, certified international trade advisor (www.citaworld.co.uk) and a regular contributor to international trade publications including *Directions in International Marketing*, *Financial Management Handbook* and *The IoD Growing Business Handbook*.

Jonathan Reuvid, MA

Jonathan is the editor of *Managing Business Risk*, and the editor and part author of *The Business Guide to Credit Management*, *The Handbook of World Trade* and business guides to China, Morocco, and the 10 countries that joined the EU in 2004. Before taking up a second career in business publishing, he was sales and marketing director and then European operations director of the manufacturing subsidiaries of a Fortune 500 multinational. From 1984 until 2005 he engaged in joint venture development and start-ups in China.

FOREWORD

In 2010, ICC United Kingdom celebrates its 90th anniversary representing international business. The shared conviction of our members that international trade and investment is a strong and positive force that benefits people, companies, and countries around the world has underpinned the scope of ICC work throughout this time.

ICC's founders believed that increased trade and investment were integral to creating greater stability and interdependence between states, and that a multilateral, rules-based system to facilitate trade and investment flows would have a positive impact on the standard of living of millions of people worldwide – peace through prosperity. At the organization's conception, there were few working international structures and no global system of rules governing trade, investment, finance, or international commercial relations existed. ICC members gave their time and expertise to develop tools, rules and services to facilitate billions of dollars of trade worldwide each year.

Whilst the landscape in which business operates is different to that of the early 1920s, many of the challenges facing international trade today have merely taken on a new dimension. The dangers of financial crises, recession and protectionism that we have experienced over the past eighteen months, have been made more complex by issues such as dramatic technological advances, global imbalances, and the increasing appetite of states to apply domestic legislation on an extra-territorial basis.

Globalization itself has resulted in its own policy challenges. The economic downturn and financial crisis have necessitated a global and coherent response by governments. In this respect ICC has played a vital role in actively representing international business interests, based on an unrivalled legitimacy derived through our global network of ninety representative national committees across the world.

In 2009, we faced the deepest recession since the Second World War, bringing with it significant challenges to international trade and investment, and placing the role of business very much under the spotlight. There were real and understandable concerns that the crisis might trigger a beggar-thy-neighbour protectionist cycle, similar to that witnessed in the 1930s, which threatened to undo the consistent growth the world has experienced since the end of the 1950s.

Thankfully, the short-term temptations of protectionism have, in the main, been avoided by governments, in spite of an elusive conclusion to the Doha trade round and traders continue to experience considerable difficulties in accessing affordable trade finance. Whilst this is something to be grateful for, it is unfortunate that we continue to experience considerable instability in financial markets, along with growing global imbalances, and weak demand – particularly in developed economies. In this context, the role of organizations such as ICC in championing the freedom of movement of international trade and investment through providing business views, developing tools and services to facilitate trade, and protecting the positive contribution that international business can make to the international economy, is essential.

Our task in securing international trade is never quite complete. Against this backdrop, the International Chamber of Commerce and its members continue to play an essential role in championing international trade as a motor of economic recovery. We continue to communicate business views across issues ranging from the impact anti-money laundering legislation or international sanctions on international trade, competition law, as well as producing standard form international trade contracts and trade terms for business. These products, such as Incoterms® 2010, are underpinned by an unrivalled legitimacy derived through our global network of ninety representative national committees across the world.

In this connection, I am delighted to commend *International Trade – An essential guide to the principles and practices of export* to readers and all those who are involved in any aspect of the international trade supply chain, be they traders, freight and transport providers, trade finance professionals, or advisors. *International Trade* manages to cover and update readers on the wide array of developments in international trade practice from the fundamentals of international sales contracts to detailed requirements of customs controls and insurance. A clear and comprehensive review of the most recent developments assists those involved in international trade in navigating what can often seem to be complex legal and practical requirements. I am confident that users of the handbook will find it indispensable in their trade operations and welcome its publication as an excellent contribution to supporting international trade worldwide.

Tania Baumann
Acting Director
ICC United Kingdom

PART ONE
The global economy

01
The rationale for foreign trade and its organization

Why countries trade

There are two basic types of trade between countries: the first, in which the receiving country either cannot produce the goods or provide the services in question, or where it does not have enough; and the second, in which it has the capability of producing the goods or supplying the services, but still imports them.

The rationale for the first kind of trade is very clear. So long as the importing country can afford to buy the products or services, it is able to acquire things that it would otherwise have to do without. Examples of differing significance are the import of bananas into the UK in response to consumer demand, or iron ore and copper to China, essentials for Chinese manufacturing industry.

The second kind of trade is of greater interest because it accounts for a majority of world trade today, and the rationale is more complex. The UK imports motor cars, coal, oil, TV sets, clothing and many more products which it is well able to produce domestically. At first sight, it would seem a waste of resources to import from all over the world goods in which a country could be self-sufficient.

However, the reasons for importing this category of product generally fall into one of three classifications:

- The imported goods may be cheaper than those produced domestically.
- A greater variety of goods may be made available through imports.
- The imported goods may offer advantages other than lower prices over domestic production – better quality or design, higher status (eg prestige labelling), technical features.

Comparative advantage

The law of comparative advantage was first articulated by the 19th-century economist David Ricardo, who concluded that there was an economic benefit for a nation to specialize in producing those goods for which it had a relative advantage, and exchanging them for the products of the nations who had advantages in other kinds of product. An obvious example is coal, which can be mined in open-cast Australian mines or in China with low-cost labour and shipped more than 10,000 miles to the UK, where a dwindling supply of coal can be extracted only from high-cost deep mines. In coal, Australia and China have comparative advantages.

The theory of comparative advantage can be extended on a macro-economic scale. Not only will trade take place to satisfy conditions of comparative advantage; in principle the overall wealth of the world will increase if each country specializes in what it does best.

Stated at its most simplistic, of course the theory ignores many factors, of which the most important is that there may be limited international demand for some nations' specialized output. Nevertheless, the question arises why specialization has not occurred on a greater scale in the real world. The main reasons, all of them complex, may be summarized in order of significance, as follows:

- strategic defence and economic reasons (the need to produce goods for which there would be heavy demand in times of war);
- transport costs, which nullify the application of comparative cost advantage;
- artificial barriers to trade imposed to protect local industry, such as tariffs and quotas.

The evolution of world trade

In Chapter 3 the pattern of world trade over 140 years from 1870 to 2010 is discussed in detail. Overall, merchandise trade grew by an average of 3.4 per cent per annum from 1870 to 1913 in the period up to World War I. Two world wars interspersed by the depression and a world slump effectively reduced the annual rate of growth in international trade to less than 1 per cent in the period 1914 to 1950.

Then, as the international institutions which were established in the immediate post-1945 period began to introduce some financial stability and impact world trade, there followed a 23-year period of more buoyant growth averaging 7.9 per cent up to 1973. In the next 25 years to 1998, the average growth rate in merchandise trade fell back to 5.1 per cent. More recently, a less stable period of global economic slowdown saw the growth in merchandise exports fall to zero in 2001 after rising by an exceptional

13 per cent in 2000. Aside from the period between the two world wars and up to 2001, trade has continuously outstripped growth in the world economy as a whole.

From the low point of 2001 the annual growth of merchandise exports climbed back to 10 per cent in 2004. By 2008 growth had fallen back to the level of 2 per cent following the international financial crisis and as Western economies, particularly the USA and the EU, entered recession. The recessionary impacts on the trend and future pattern of international trade are identified and discussed in Chapter 30.

Protectionism

To analyse what happened in the interwar years of the 1920s and 1930s it is necessary to understand that the reaction of many governments to economic slump was to protect jobs at home by raising the protection against imports. The most common method of protection is the introduction or increase of tariffs on imported goods. In the 1920s and 1930s the widespread use of tariffs caused job losses, in turn, in other countries – an iterative process. In the second half of the 1930s the prolonged world slump was alleviated, particularly in Europe, by the heavy public spending on defence equipment and munitions in the lead-up to World War II.

After 1945, there were concerted international efforts to put in place organizations that would reduce the effects of trade protection and any future reductions in world economic activity. The first of these were the International Monetary Fund (IMF) and the International Bank for Reconstruction and Development (IBRD), now known as the World Bank, which were established by the Bretton Woods Agreement in 1947. These institutions, which have become the cornerstones of international macroeconomic management, were largely the brainchild of the British economist John Maynard Keynes, who was among the first to recognize that reductions in government spending and increases in protection had been major causes of the pre-war depression.

Methods of protection

The tools of protection may be categorized as either tariff or non-tariff barriers.

Tariffs

A tariff is a tax or import duty levied on goods or services entering a country. Tariffs can be fixed or percentage levies and serve the twin purposes of generating revenue for governments and making it more difficult for companies from other countries to do business in the protected market.

The 19th-century moves towards 'free trade' were largely offset by the reintroduction of tariffs in the early part of the 20th century at rates sometimes as high as 33 and 50 per cent. Since 1945 tariffs have been lowered significantly as a result of eight successive rounds of multilateral trade negotiations under the General Agreement on Tariffs and Trade (GATT), the third institution established following the Bretton Woods Agreement, and its successor the World Trade Organization (WTO).

Non-tariff barriers

Although progress was made in dismantling tariff barriers under GATT in the period up to 1995 when the WTO was established, the use of non-tariff protection increased during the 1980s, mostly as a substitute for the tariffs that were outlawed.

The following is a list of non-tariff measures that have been deployed by both developed and developing countries:

Quotas
A numerical limit in terms of value or volume imposed on the amount of a product that can be imported. French quotas on Japanese VHS equipment during the 1980s, Chinese quotas on imported automobiles and EU quotas on the import of shoes and textile clothing from China and other South-East Asian suppliers are well-known examples.

Voluntary export restraints
Agreed arrangements whereby an exporter agrees not to export more than a specific amount of a good to the importing country (usually to pre-empt the imposition of more stringent measures). Such agreements are common for automobiles and electronics but are also applied to steel and chemicals, as are the EU quotas referred to above.

Domestic subsidies
These are the provision of financial aid or preferential tax status to domestic manufacturers, which gives them an advantage over external suppliers or the local manufacturers in economies with which a given country trades. The most obvious examples are agriculture, where both the EU and USA have consistently employed subsidies to help domestic producers, or tax breaks for exporters.

Import deposits
This is the device of requiring the importer to make a deposit (usually a proportion of the value of the goods) with the government for a fixed period. The effect on cash flow is intended to discourage imports.

Safety and health standards; technical specifications
This more subtle form of deterrent requires importers to meet
stringent standards or to complete complicated and lengthy
formalities. The French bans on lamb and then beef imported
from the UK during the 1990s will be long remembered by the
British farming industry.

Exchange rate manipulation
Countries seeking to stimulate exports and/or dampen imports can
deliberately devalue their currencies. China has been accused of this
practice by pegging its currency (*renminbi*) to the US dollar.
Individual members of the European Monetary Union (EMU) are
denied the opportunity to devalue or revalue unilaterally.

Regions in world trade

Although the multilateral trading system promoted by the GATT and
now the WTO has been broadly successful in overcoming protectionist
regimes – at least up to the current Doha round – it has failed to prevent
the concomitant proliferation of regional pacts, regional trade agreements
(RTAs) and a multitude of bilateral agreements. Almost all major countries
have signed up to at least one RTA. In 2008, 72.8 per cent of the EU's trade
was between member states, and 49.8 per cent of North American trade
was between the three NAFTA countries. The jury is still out on whether
RTAs can be viewed as stepping stones towards multilateral integration or
as discriminatory arrangements that fracture the multilateral trading
system. The failure of successive WTO summit meetings during the
Doha round since 2003 to reach agreement suggests that the latter are
prevailing.

There are four basic models of trading block:

Free trade area
Members agree to reduce or abolish trade barriers such as tariffs and
quotas between themselves but retain their own individual tariffs
and quotas against non-members.

Customs union
Countries that belong to customs unions agree to reduce or abolish
trade barriers between themselves and agree to establish common
tariffs and quotas against outsiders.

Common market
Essentially, a common market is a customs union in which the members
also agree to reduce restrictions on the movement of factors of
production – such as people and finance – as well as reducing
barriers on the sale of goods.

Economic union

A common market that is taken further by agreeing to establish
common economic policies in areas such as taxation and interest
rates, and even a common currency, is described as an economic
union.

The original European Economic Community (EEC) in the mid-1950s,
comprising six members, was the forerunner of a number of such agreements.
In 2010 the European Union is still the most advanced economic grouping,
with its 27 existing members accounting for more than 38 per cent of world
trade in 2009. However, some of the more recent groupings, notably ASEAN
and NAFTA, having created regional trading agreements, account for
increasingly significant proportions of world trade.

Table 1.1 lists the principal trading blocks in date order of their formation together with details of their membership.

A new powerful free trade area came into operation on 1 January 2010
when China and the 10 ASEAN members combined to form the world's
third largest area, in trade volume ranking behind only the European
Economic Area (the EU plus EFTA) and NAFTA.

Regional arrangements are an important factor in the organization of
world trade. They are beneficial in allowing countries inside the arrangement to acquire some goods at lower prices through tariff reductions than
they could from the rest of the world. However, they may also cause trade
to be diverted away from efficient producers outside the arrangement and
towards less efficient sources within. A strong case can be made that the
proliferation of self-protecting trade blocks reduces the levels of potential
benefits to be gained from world trade.

The UK's changed status in world trade

The EU is now the most important market for most UK exporters, accounting for around two-thirds of the UK's trade. The ratio represents the most
dramatic difference between Britain in 1970 and Britain today.

In 1970, most of the UK's trade was with markets beyond Europe, mainly
Commonwealth countries including Australia, New Zealand, Canada, the
Caribbean, West and East Africa. Within the 20 years following, as a result
of the UK joining the then EEC, the situation was reversed, with UK trade
focused on Europe, and the Commonwealth countries becoming relatively
minor trading partners.

The consequences for both UK manufacturing industry and the Commonwealth have been far reaching:

- The countries of the Commonwealth had to make trading
  arrangements of their own, having lost previously captive UK
  markets.

TABLE 1.1   The principal regional trading blocks

European Union (EU)	1957	Austria, Belgium, Denmark[1], Finland, France, Germany, Greece, Ireland, Italy, Luxembourg, Netherlands, Portugal, Spain, Sweden[1], United Kingdom[1] ([1] not members of the eurozone)
		From 1 May 2004: Czech Republic, Cyprus[2], Estonia, Hungary, Latvia, Lithuania, Malta, Poland, Slovenia[2], Slovakia[2] ([2] members of the eurozone)
		From 1 January 2007: Bulgaria, Romania
European Free Trade Agreement (EFTA)	1960	Iceland, Liechtenstein, Norway, Switzerland
Central American Common Market (CACM)	1961	Belize, Costa Rica, El Salvador, Guatemala, Honduras, Nicaragua, Panama
Association of South-East Asian Nations (ASEAN)	1967	Brunei, Darussalem, Cambodia, Indonesia, Lao PDR, Malaysia, Myanmar, Philippines, Singapore, Thailand, Vietnam
Andean Pact	1969	Bolivia, Colombia, Ecuador, Peru, Venezuela
Economic Community of West African States (ECOWAS)	1975	Cape Verde, Gambia, Ghana, Guinea, Liberia, Nigeria, Sierra Leone
South African Development Commmunity (SADC)	1980	Angola, Botswana, Democratic Republic of Congo, Lesotho, Malawi, Mauritius, Mozambique, Namibia, Swaziland, Tanzania, Zambia, Zimbabwe, South Africa, Seychelles
South Asian Association for Regional Cooperation (SAARC)	1985	Afghanistan, Bangladesh, Bhutan, Maldives, Nepal, Pakistan, Sri Lanka
North American Free Trade Association (NAFTA)	1989	Canada, USA, with Mexico since 1993
Mercado Commun Del Sur (MERCOSUR)	1991	Argentina, Brazil, Paraguay, Uruguay, Venezuela (awaiting Paraguay ratification)

- Much of the agricultural produce previously imported by the UK from the Commonwealth is now sourced from within Europe.
- The UK has lost most of its markets for low-tech, low-cost goods.
- UK exports have tended to become higher tech and more expensive.
- UK exporters have had to learn to do business in foreign languages and, with the advent of the EU monetary union, in euros rather than sterling.

In fact, the UK has always experienced difficulties with trade in manufactured goods. Even during the halcyon British Empire days of the late 19th and early 20th centuries, the UK was heavily dependent on the import of cheap raw materials from the colonies and Commonwealth, in larger volume than the goods exported. However, throughout that period the UK continued to run substantial surpluses on its trade in services, which largely offset the deficits on merchandise trade. During the period 1816 to 1995, the UK registered surpluses on goods account in only six years and only three deficits on services and investments.

During the past 60 years the UK has drifted into deeper deficits in merchandise trade, alleviated to some extent by the production of North Sea oil and gas. At the same time, the City of London no longer dominates world financial markets and the 'invisible' earnings that it generates are no longer sufficient to offset the deficits in trade of goods. The advent of the eurozone and the installation of the European Central Bank (ECB) in Frankfurt has moved Europe's financial centre of gravity but, so far, London has maintained its dominant position in securities and money markets. However, it is significant that the traditional UK investment banks and brokerage houses are now mostly in foreign ownership.

Of course, commercial services comprise much more than banking, insurance and other financial services. They also include:

- the tourist trade: UK expenditure by foreign visitors less spending abroad;
- shipping and aviation freight services;
- communication services (telecommunications, postal and courier);
- computer and information services;
- royalties and licence fees;
- personal, cultural and recreational services;
- other business services.

In arriving at the net effect of 'invisible' transactions on the balance of payments, government disbursements, interest and profits earned abroad and emigrants' remittances are also taken into account. Their role is referred to again in Chapter 2.

The interplay of the deficits on merchandise trade and surpluses on commercial services since 1990 is identified in Chapter 3.

Organizations in world trade

Earlier in this chapter the significance of three international organizations of key importance formed in the immediate post-World War II period was discussed in the context of the campaign against protectionism. The aim of all three organizations was to attempt to establish international approaches to trade and to economic development that would enhance world wealth while helping countries to adjust to economic fluctuations.

The International Monetary Fund

The IMF's prime task is to try to regulate the way in which countries adjust to fluctuations in exchange rates. The IMF was set up to provide a way in which countries experiencing trade deficits could borrow funds to pay their debts from a central source. Member countries subscribe amounts of their own currencies and gold, which are used, in theory, to assist deficit nations. For that purpose the IMF also established a regime of currency rates and a form of 'world money' called 'Special Drawing Rights'.

Over the last 60 years the IMF has undoubtedly contributed significantly to the way in which world trade has been able to expand. It has also played a crucial role in helping to rescue the economies of countries from bankruptcy through external debt. Indeed, it is difficult to imagine how Argentina or Brazil could have survived their post-millennium financial crises without continuing IMF intervention. Most recently, in May 2010, the IMF, in association with governments of the eurozone, has provided a rescue loan of €110 billion (£95 billion) to Greece.

The World Bank

The World Bank was established – as its original title implies – to help with post-war reconstruction. It was initially known as the 'International Bank for Reconstruction and Development'. Since 1945 the World Bank has taken on the role of providing loans at preferential rates mostly to developing countries for projects that will assist and accelerate their economic development. Typical projects are irrigation and hydro-electricity schemes, roads and power supply.

From the 1980s onwards the World Bank has taken on a new role supporting the IMF in 'debt relief'. Between 1960 and 1980 many countries, particularly in South America and Africa, had accumulated substantial external debt on which the annual interest alone was creating real hardship. The scale of the debt was also creating the risk that a country would simply renege on its debt, which would create a domino effect as others followed suit. The IMF and the World Bank jointly have been active in negotiating a long series of agreements with debtor countries, which have allowed them to restructure their debt and pay less interest. (In some cases the wealthier creditor countries of the G20 have forgiven large amounts of debt altogether.)

The General Agreement on Tariffs and Trade (GATT)

GATT, which was superseded by the World Trade Organization (WTO) on 1 January 1995, was set up to try to avoid the competitive tariff wars of the 1930s. GATT was signed at Geneva in 1947 and came into operation in 1948.

Over a series of protracted negotiations, known as 'rounds', from 1945 onwards GATT established binding agreements on its members to reduce tariffs. Each round reduced general tariffs further, thereby creating the conditions for steady increases in world trade. Under the GATT arrangements any proposal to impose a new tariff had to be submitted to GATT and any disputes between members were, in theory, to be settled by reference to GATT.

GATT rules for preventing infringements of tariff concessions and keeping the channels of trade open are based on two principles:

- most-favoured nation treatment for members; and
- non-discrimination.

However, many exceptions are allowed. Controls in conflict with the rules are permitted if they were in operation when the General Agreement was concluded, or, in the case of new members, when they first enter into negotiations. New restrictive measures of a discriminatory nature are allowed under certain conditions, the most important being safeguarding the balance of payments.

Since the conclusion of the Uruguay round in December 1993, progress has been slower although WTO membership, currently 153, has continued to grow, with the important addition of China in December 2001, and more effective dispute-resolution procedures have been adopted. Of the major global economies, only the Russian Federation has yet to join.

The more recent problems of the WTO, which have been exposed during the current Doha development round, which commenced in 2001, have caused negotiations to stall since 2008 over a divide on major outstanding issues, such as agricultural subsidies, industrial tariffs and non-tariff barriers, as well as services and trade issues. These issued are discussed in Chapter 30.

02
Balance of payments: measurement and management

Measuring trade

In Chapter 1 we distinguished between international merchandise trade and trade in commercial services. The interplay between the two is the key element in national trade and balance of payments accounting, of which the main elements are illustrated in Table 2.1.

In the past it was common UK practice to distinguish between 'visible' and 'invisible' trade, meaning effectively the tangible items and the intangible items. The formal published trade figures now have the two headings: 'balance on goods' and 'balance on services' as in Table 2.1.

Other items of what used to be part of the invisibles account are now treated under the new heading of 'UK assets and liabilities'.

International balance of payments ratios

There are three yardsticks of international trade that are quoted commonly by economists and others seeking to compare trade performance between countries relative to their economies:

- Ratio of trade at market prices to gross domestic product (GDP): for example, China now has a surprisingly open economy with a ratio of 45 per cent in 2009, while Japan's ratio of trade to GDP was only 20 per cent.

- Ratio of current account balance to GDP: the ratios of the UK's and USA's deficits to GDP were 1.6 per cent and 3 per cent for 2009 against 0.7 per cent for the EU, while China and Japan registered surpluses of 5.8 per cent and 2.8 per cent.

TABLE 2.1 Balance of payments accounting

Balance on goods	The account for trade in manufactured goods and raw materials
Balance on services	The account showing balances on trade in services
Current account	The account that includes virtually everything that would be recognized as trade as well as some other things such as net investment income. Included are: balance on goods; balance on services; balance on investment income; balance on Government transfers.
UK assets and liabilities account	A new account introduced in the mid-1990s to show the UK's net earnings or net payments in respect of what it owns in the rest of the world
Balance of payments	The overall accounts for the UK's trade with the rest of the world

- Terms of trade: this more sophisticated measurement is the ratio of a country's prices of exports to those of its imports, and is an indicator of competitiveness.

Imbalances in trading accounts

The surplus or deficit resulting from the sum of the balance on goods and the balance on services is known as the 'balance of trade'.

The ultimate result of the collection of UK trade figures is a net total known as 'balance of payments'. This figure represents formally the final surplus or debt resulting from all UK transactions with the rest of the world in any given year.

It is customary to apply the term 'current account balance' to the reported net surplus or deficit for a given period or the current year to date.

The objective for trade balances is to achieve 'equilibrium' or sufficient surpluses to pay off a country's debts but not over such a period as to damage trade by affecting the exchange rate. A country whose balance of payments shows consistent deficits is said to be in 'disequilibrium'. Technically, the term 'disequilibrium' applies equally where consistent surpluses are experienced, but this is a more desirable result and is rarely referred to under the heading of disequilibrium.

Managing disequilibrium

A country with a surplus in its balance of payments is said to be a 'creditor nation'. It can add this surplus to its reserves or lend it to other nations to enable them to improve their economies.

Conversely, if a country incurs a deficit in its balance of payments, it is said to be a 'debtor nation' because it has spent more than it has earned. It must finance this deficit either by drawing upon its reserves or borrowing externally.

Clearly, a country's reserves of gold and foreign currencies are not inexhaustible, and sooner or later it would have to negotiate loans and eventually repay them. We have already mentioned the role of the IMF as a provider of loans for this purpose. IMF loans are generally granted with stringent conditions attached relating to the management of the borrowing country's economy. In the 1970s the UK negotiated significant loans from the IMF in order to cover accumulated deficits. Changes in domestic economic policy, in agreement with the IMF, enabled the loans to be repaid quite soon. The stringent conditions of the 2010 rescue loans imposed on Greece are already causing political unrest internally.

A country with a persistent balance of payments deficit must take appropriate measures to rectify the situation; these would depend upon the causes of the deficit. If it is due to imports, measures must be taken to restrict imports while stimulating exports. If it has been caused by an excessive outflow of capital, then measures must be taken to control overseas investment.

As we shall discuss in Chapter 30, both the UK and the USA are in deficit in 2010, as well as some other Western economies, and remedial action will become necessary in some cases.

Some of the measures that a country may take are summarized in the following sections.

Import controls

In theory, there are two methods of controlling imports, the protection tools described in Chapter 1, namely import quotas and import duties (tariffs).

Import quotas provide restrictions to the total number or value of goods that may be imported into the country during a specified period.

The imposition of import duties is intended to reduce demand for the commodities in question by increasing the price to the ultimate user.

As signatories to GATT and its successor the WTO, the boundaries within which the UK or the USA can impose import controls or tariffs, even to address disequilibrium, are severely restricted. As a full member of the EU, the UK can depart from the common external tariff only in the most exceptional circumstances.

Export incentives

A government might grant its exporters generally, or in specific industries, subsidies or taxation reductions to enable them to reduce their prices and undercut foreign competitors. Such incentives are also outlawed by the WTO and would certainly contravene EU agreements if applied to trade within Europe.

Monetary measures

Since the use of import controls and export incentives is constrained, the UK usually resorts to monetary measures when there is a balance of payments deficit.

Recognizing that the fundamental cause of current account deficits is usually excessive home demand for imported goods and the absorption of home-produced goods which may otherwise have been exported, the government may adopt one or more of the following measures:

- Increasing interest rates – thereby discouraging borrowing and consequently tightening and reducing spending power. Higher interest rates also attract foreign short-term capital.
- Open market operations – by selling securities in the open market, the government reduces the amount of money in circulation, which diminishes purchasing power.
- Special deposits – in the form of directives to the banks to deposit a certain proportion of their funds with the Bank of England, where they are frozen. This reduces the liquidity of the banks, which in turn restricts bank lending and diminishes purchasing power.

Fiscal measures

A government can also reduce spending power more directly by means of higher taxation, hire-purchase controls, etc.

Devaluation

The purpose of devaluing a currency is to make a country's exports cheaper to overseas buyers and, at the same time, its imports dearer. This method is applicable when a system of fixed exchange rates is in place, but is usually the measure of last resort.

Under a system of floating exchange rates, the exchange value of a currency will gradually depreciate if it is overvalued, which will have the same effect as a devaluation. The currencies of developing countries, which are 'pegged' by a fixed rate (or within a narrow fixed band) to a more stable 'hard' currency, such as the US dollar, are effectively insulated from the market forces related to their own national economies.

Managing exchange rates

The history of exchange rates is complex. In the early days of trade, exporters would accept payment only in commodities that were considered to have intrinsic value, such as gold, silver or jewels.

This approach continued until well into the 19th century, when certain currencies came into use for trade, notably the pound sterling, the Dutch guilder and the French franc, reflecting the growth of empires during that century.

The British Empire's wealth enabled the British government to back every single pound note with an equivalent amount of gold. The level of trust in paper currency became so great that large areas of the world traded and maintained reserves in sterling.

These territories became known collectively as 'the sterling area', a vast expanse of British government-backed paper that became a major embarrassment to successive governments of the 1950s and 1960s when countries began to convert their reserves to gold or US dollars.

In about 1873, the need to know the value of a trading currency led to the establishment of the 'gold standard', with currencies pegged in terms of their values in a specific weight of gold and each other. The gold standard created the first system of fixed exchange rates and provided the confidence required for a significant expansion in world trade. The standard began to break down after 1918 and disappeared during the 1930s. The lack of formal exchange rate mechanisms contributed to the collapse in world trade during that interwar period.

After World War II the IMF established a new system of fixed exchange rates, which were also fixed against gold but more remotely. Each country assigned a value to its currency in terms of an ounce of gold (which was valued then at $35). Nations were allowed to adjust their exchange significantly only in extreme circumstances but could make minor adjustments (up to 10 per cent) in circumstances that were described as 'fundamental disequilibrium'.

Few countries used this facility (only six between 1947 and 1971) and, by the 1960s, the system had become highly unstable. By 1971 continuing US difficulties caused the US government to announce that the dollar would no longer be convertible into gold. Soon afterwards the British and French governments also came off the gold standard.

Since that date the main system of exchange rate 'management' has been to allow currencies to float within reasonable limits against other currencies. In its European Community phase the EU operated several fixed and semi-fixed systems during the 1970s and 1980s, the last of which deteriorated into a smaller 'Deutsche Mark' area. However, the establishment of the European Monetary Union with the formation of the European Central Bank (ECB) and the launch of the euro currency from 1 January 1999 has put in place a single currency throughout the eurozone, which currently includes all members of the EU15 (member countries before the 2004 enlargement) except for Denmark, Sweden and the UK.

The UK retains the pound sterling, which the British government allows to float while monitoring its position closely. The 10 members of the eurozone have forgone the ability to devalue or revalue their national currencies individually.

03
Patterns of world trade

Trends and patterns of world trade have been disrupted in the first decade of the 21st century: in 2001 by the relatively mild cyclical recession that followed the 1998 Asian banking crisis and, more severely, in the latter part of 2008 and 2009 by the deep global recession that engulfed the developed economies of North America and Europe. This most recent recession, from which those economies are struggling to emerge in 2010 with varying degrees of success, was the direct result of the international banking crisis of 2008, which threatened the global financial system with collapse.

In order to provide readers with a more complete perspective, this chapter is divided into two parts: an overview of the evolution of international trade in the period 1870 to 2001; and a more detailed analysis of the period 2002 to 2009. In Chapter 30 the most recent WTO statistics and forecasts for international trade in 2010 are summarized.

International trade in the 20th century

The endeavours of participating nations in GATT and its successor, the WTO, to expand the free trade environment in the past 60 years may be appreciated best in the historical context of the growth in trade throughout the 20th century.

In Table 3.1 the rate of growth in the volume of merchandise exports for 11 countries and the world is summarized for the period from 1870 to 1998. In global terms, the annual average compound growth rate between 1913 and 1950 was less than 1 per cent, compared with pre-1913 growth of 3.4 per cent. The following 23-year period was one of strong international trade expansion, with annual compound growth averaging 7.9 per cent, which then eased off to 5.1 per cent over the 25-year period 1973 to 1998.

Comparing the latter two periods, among developed economies annual average growth fell back with the exception of the UK, where the growth rate increased from 3.9 to 4.4 per cent. In Europe, most striking was the fall

TABLE 3.1   Rate of growth (%) in volume of merchandise exports, 11 countries and world, 1870–1988 (annual average compound growth rates)

	1870–1913	1913–50	1950–73	1973–98
France	2.8	1.1	8.2	4.7
Germany	4.1	−2.8	12.4	4.4
Netherlands	2.3	1.5	10.4	4.1
United Kingdom	2.8	0.0	3.9	4.4
Spain	3.5	−1.6	9.2	9.0
United States	4.9	2.2	6.3	6.0
Mexico	5.4	−0.5	4.3	10.9
Brazil	1.9	1.7	4.7	6.6
China	2.6	1.1	2.7	11.8
India	2.4	−1.5	2.5	5.9
Japan	8.5	2.0	15.4	5.3
World	3.4	0.9	7.9	5.1

Derived from Appendix 1.6.1 of *A Handbook of World Trade*, 2nd edn (Reuvid, 2004), and 1950–98 IMF International Financial Statistics, supplemented by UN Yearbook of International Trade Statistics, various issues

in the growth rate of merchandise exports from Germany from 12.4 to 4.4 per cent as the post-war reconstruction period of German industry came to a close, while the annual growth in exports from the USA remained at the 6.0 per cent level. However, the fall in merchandise export growth has been most marked in the case of Japan, where the annual rate fell by almost two-thirds from 15.4 per cent over 1950–73 to almost European levels (5.3 per cent) during the 1973–98 period.

By contrast, the volume of merchandise exports from developing countries in Asia and Latin America soared. China's annual growth rate more than quadrupled from 2.7 to 11.8 per cent, while Mexican export growth rose from 4.3 per cent to 10.9 per cent.

The significance of merchandise exports to the economies of individual countries over the same time span of 130 years expressed as a percentage of GDP at 1990 prices grew for all major trading nations, although ratios fell back from 1929 as a result of the Great Depression and did not recover fully until after 1950. Globally, exports fell back from 9.0 per cent of GDP in 1929 to 5.5 per cent in 1950 before recovering to 10.5 per cent in 1973 and moving forward to 17.2 per cent in 1998.

Broadly, the developed countries conformed to this pattern, with much higher rates of export ratios in Europe and lower rates in the USA and

Japan. By 1998 the exports/GDP ratio had reached 25.0 per cent in the UK and 38.9 per cent in Germany. For the USA and Japan the ratios were 10.1 and 13.4 per cent respectively. The highest export/GDP ratio for 1998 among developed countries was recorded in the Netherlands at 61.2 per cent.

Among developing countries, in spite of their superior rates of export growth since 1973, export/GDP ratios are comparatively modest. In 1998 Mexico's merchandise exports represented 10.7 per cent of GDP, while China's export/GDP ratio was still only 4.9 per cent (up from 1.8 per cent in 1929), giving no more than a hint of the subsequent impact of Chinese exports on world trade as its per capita industrial output approached more developed economy levels.

Trends in merchandise trade and commercial services by region (1990–2001)

Merchandise trade

Global trade increased by 5 per cent between 1990 and 2001. Growth peaked in 2000 with an increase of 13 per cent before declining by 4 per cent in 2001 (the cyclical effect).

After increased exports of merchandise in all regions in 2000, of which the EU's increase of 3 per cent was lowest, all the groupings except for Central and Eastern Europe, the Baltic States and the CIS (5 per cent) and, in Asia, China (7 per cent) suffered export declines in 2001.

The EU

In terms of merchandise trade, the EU (within Western Europe) was the world's biggest grouping in 2001 in both exports ($2,291 billion) and imports ($2,334 billion), with imports marginally exceeding exports. The rate of growth of imports fell from 6 per cent in 2000 to just 1 per cent in 2001, while exports actually declined in 2001 by 1 per cent against 4 per cent growth the previous year.

Asia

Asia was the second largest exporting region ($1,497 billion), with exports exceeding imports by $122 billion in 2001. Following the 1997–8 Asian financial crisis, the annual growth in exports recovered from 6 per cent negative to 18 per cent positive in 2000 before falling back 9 per cent in 2001. The decline in 2001 was attributable to a reduction in Japanese exports of 16 per cent. Likewise, imports revived from 1998's decline of 18 per cent and peaked at 23 per cent growth in 2000.

North America

Conversely, North America (excluding Mexico) was the world's second largest importing region in 2001 ($1,408 billion), although only third in exports ($991 billion). However, export growth recovered by 4 per cent in 1999 (1998: 1 per cent decline) and peaked at 14 per cent growth in 2000 before declining 6 per cent in 2001. Imports achieved 14 per cent growth in 2000 against 5 per cent in 1998.

Central and Eastern Europe

Although exports from Central and Eastern Europe (CEE) had increased only marginally in 1999 – by 1 per cent against a 10-year average growth rate of 7 per cent – growth was more robust in 2000 and 2001 (11 per cent), to a total of $129 billion. Imports declined by 1 per cent in 1999 against 10 per cent average for the decade, but grew strongly in 2000 and 2001 to a total $159 billion. Thus, the annual trade deficit for the region was maintained at the level of $30 billion from 1999.

The Baltic States and CIS countries together achieved an export surplus of $31 billion in 1999, with exports slowing by 2 per cent and imports by 24 per cent; but in 2001 the trade surplus narrowed to $19 billion.

Middle East

The Middle East trade surplus in 2001 was $57 billion, with OPEC oil exports accounting for most of the export total of $237 billion. Although exports grew by 42 per cent in 2000, significantly higher than in other regions except the oil-producing Russian Federation (39 per cent), they fell away by 9 per cent in 2001.

Africa

African imports were at a similar level ($128 billion) to the CEE in 1999 but grew more modestly in 2000 and 2001 to $136 billion. Exports from Africa grew more rapidly from $117 billion (1999) to $141 billion (2001), thereby achieving a small trade surplus.

Latin America

Latin America's exports grew by a healthy 20 per cent in 2000 but fell back by 3 per cent in 2001 to $347 billion, resulting in a trade deficit of $3 billion.

Commercial services

The pattern of 2001 world trade in commercial services was rather different from that of merchandise trade. The world average annual growth rate in the value of commercial services exports over the 10-year period to 2001 was 6 per cent, similar to that for merchandise trade, but the decline in the export of commercial services in 2001 was less than 1 per cent, compared with 4 per cent in the case of merchandise. Among the regions, Western Europe and North America (excluding Mexico) were the only two net exporting regions of commercial services to the values of $70 billion and $32 billion respectively.

By contrast in 2001, Asia, by now the third-ranking region in commercial services, was a net importer to the value of $52 billion. Neither Central and Eastern Europe nor the Baltic States and the CIS registered a significant presence in commercial services world trade.

International trade in the 21st century

Between 2001 and 2008 world merchandise trade exports (excluding intra-EU trade) increased steadily from $4.7 trillion to $12.1 trillion (growth of 157 per cent), while trade in commercial services rose from $1.5 trillion to $3.8 trillion (growth of 153 per cent). However, the combined effects of the financial crisis and recession took their toll and in 2009, world trade in merchandise declined to $10.6 trillion and in commercial services to $2.8 trillion, registering falls of 12 per cent and 26 per cent respectively. Within the EU, intra-trade exports plummeted from approximately $4 trillion to $3 trillion, a fall of 25 per cent, compared with an increase in external merchandise exports of more than 100 per cent, up from $743 billion to $1.5 trillion and highlighting the comparison between recession-hit EU members and their trade with those regions of the world, notably Asia, who drew back first from the recessionary pit.

The impact of the 2008–10 recession

Merchandise trade

The relative experiences of the regions and leading trading nations in the period leading up to the current recession and in 2009 are detailed in Table 3.2.

The value of world trade in Table 3.2 includes EU intra-trade so that exports totalled $12.1 trillion against $16.1 trillion in 2008. While the growth in world trade was around 15 per cent in 2007 and 2008, the 24 per cent fall in 2009 brought growth for the period 2005 to 2009 down to only 4 per cent.

North America

The overall declines in NAFTA exports and imports of 21 and 25 per cent in 2009 caused export growth for the 2005–9 period to be limited to 2 per cent

TABLE 3.2 World merchandise trade by region and selected economy (2009)

	Exports		Imports	
	Value $ bn	% change year over year	Value $ bn	% change year over year
World	12,147	−23	12,385	−24
North America	1,602	−21	2,177	−25
USA	1,057	−18	1,604	−26
Canada	316	−31	330	−21
Mexico	230	−21	242	−24
South and Central America	461	−24	444	−25
Brazil	153	−23	134	−27
Others	308	−24	311	−25
Europe	4,995	−23	5,142	−25
EU (27)	4,567	−23	4,714	−25
Germany	1,121	−22	931	−21
France	475	−21	551	−22
Netherlands	499	−22	446	−23
UK	351	−24	480	−24
Italy	405	−25	410	−26
CIS	452	−36	332	−33
Russian Federation	304	−36	192	−34
Africa	379	−32	400	−16
South Africa	63	−22	72	−28
Africa less South Africa	317	−33	328	−13
Oil exporters	204	−40	129	−11
Non-oil exporters	113	−17	199	−14
Middle East	691	−33	499	−18
Asia	3,566	−18	3,397	−21
China	1,202	−16	1,006	−11
Japan	581	−26	551	−28
India	155	−20	244	−24
Newly industrialized economies (4)	853	−17	834	−24
Memorandum items				
Developing economies	4,697	−22	4,432	−20
MERCOSUR	217	−28	186	−28
ASEAN	814	−18	724	−23
EU 27 extra-trade	1,525	−21	1,672	−27
LDCs	125	−27	144	−11

WTO

and imports to decline by 1 per cent. In 2009 the USA suffered an 18 per cent fall in exports but reduced imports by 26 per cent, thereby moderating its chronic trade imbalance slightly. Conversely, Canadian imports were reduced by 21 per cent while exports fell by 31 per cent in 2009, so that its trade gap widened; over the five-year period Canada's exports actually fell by 3 per cent. With an experience more related to that of the USA, its principal trading partner, than to Canada's, Mexico's exports grew by 2 per cent and imports by just 1 per cent in the 2005–9 period (USA: –4 per cent and –2 per cent respectively).

South and Central America

With Brazil accounting for a third of regional exports and 30 per cent of imports, South and Central America overall suffered similar reductions in exports and imports of around 25 per cent, reducing net growth for the five years to 6 per cent in exports and 10 per cent in imports.

Europe

The EU now accounts for 91 per cent of European trade, of which exports fell by 23 per cent and imports by 25 per cent in 2009, bringing five-year growth in both down to a meagre 3 per cent. Performance in 2009 of the major trading economies among EU members, Germany, France, Italy, the Netherlands and the UK, was similar, with Italy's and the UK's trade declining rather more than that of the other three. Over the period 2005–9 only UK trade shrank, with falls registered in both exports and imports of 2 per cent.

Commonwealth of Independent States (CIS)

For the CIS, of whose trade the Russian Federation represents 67 per cent, the 2009 reductions in exports of 36 per cent and in imports of 33 per cent were steeper than any other region. Nevertheless, the net growth in trade from 2005 to 2009 of 7 per cent in exports and 11 per cent was exceeded only by China, India, the non-oil exporting countries of Africa and the Least Developed Countries (LDCs).

Africa

In sharp contrast to the North American and European regions, African countries were less involved in the global financial crisis but weathered the recession no better. Including the many African LDCs, their exports were both reduced by 32 per cent in 2009, while imports fell by 16 per cent, dampening five-year growth to 5 and 12 per cent respectively. South Africa, the continent's largest economy, lost 22 per cent in 2009 exports and reduced imports by 28 per cent. Of the remainder, the 10 oil-producing countries together lost 40 per cent of their exports in 2009, while exports of the remainder were depressed by only 17 per cent.

Middle East

In 2009, exports from the Middle East countries were together reduced by 33 per cent and imports by 18 per cent, causing five-year growth to be limited to 6 per cent and 10 per cent respectively.

Asia

The Asian region as a whole did noticeably better in 2009 than the other regions, with exports declining by 18 per cent and imports by 21 per cent. Although the region's international trade grew by only 6 per cent over five years, with Japan's exports declining by 1 per cent and imports growing 2 per cent, China and India performed better than any other economy, each registering net 12 per cent growth from 2005 to 2009 in spite of reductions over 2009 of 18 per cent and 20 per cent.

Commercial services

The combined effect of the financial crisis and recession on exports and imports of commercial services among the regions and major economies in 2009 was generally less and more uniform than for merchandise trade, as Table 3.3 demonstrates. Overall, the 2009 decline in commercial services was 13 per cent.

Reductions in exports over 2009 ranged from 5 per cent in Morocco and 6 per cent in Hong Kong; through 9 per cent in the USA, Brazil, South Africa and Israel; to 11 to 16 per cent in the UK, Germany, Spain, Italy, Egypt, China and Japan; and up to 23 per cent for Ukraine and 25 per cent for South Korea.

Over the five-year period from 2005 to 2009, world trade in commercial services increased by 7 per cent. The most buoyant economies were Brazil and China (15 per cent), the Russian Federation (14 per cent) and Morocco (13 per cent). None of these faced a banking crisis in 2008, thanks to more conservative, closely controlled financial systems.

Leading exporters and importers in world trade

Merchandise trade

The rankings of the top 12 exporters and importers of merchandise trade for 2009 are displayed in Table 3.4, with their shares of world trade.

In terms of individual country trade, China climbed up the table during the decade, passing France, the UK, Japan and the USA in export value prior to 2008 and finally overtaking Germany in 2009 to take first place.

TABLE 3.3 World trade in commercial services by region and selected economy (2009)

	Exports		Imports	
	Value $ bn	% change year over year	Value $ bn	% change year over year
World	3,310	−13	3,315	−12
North America	542	−10	430	−10
USA	470	−9	331	−9
South and Central America	100	−8	111	−8
Brazil	26	−9	44	−1
Europe	1,675	−14	1,428	13
EU (27)	1,513	−14	1,329	−13
UK	240	−16	160	−19
Germany	215	−11	255	−10
France	140	−14	124	−12
Spain	122	−14	87	−17
Italy	101	−15	114	−11
CIS	69	−18	91	−21
Russian Federation	42	−17	60	−19
Ukraine	13	−23	11	−32
Africa	78	−11	117	−11
Egypt	21	−15	14	−17
Morocco	12	−5	6	−13
South Africa	11	−9	14	−16
Middle East	96	−12	162	−13
Israel	22	−9	17	−12
Asia	751	−13	776	−11
China	129	−12	158	0
Japan	124	−15	146	−11
Hong Kong, China	86	−6	44	−6
India	86	—	74	—
Singapore	74	−11	74	−6
South Korea	56	−25	74	−19
Taiwan	31	−10	29	−15

WTO

TABLE 3.4 Merchandise trade: leading exporters and importers (2009)

| | Exports | | | Imports | |
	Value $ bn	% share world trade		Value $ bn	% share world trade
1. China	1,202	9.6	1. USA	1,604	12.7
2. Germany	1,121	9.0	2. China	1,066	8.0
3. USA	1,057	8.5	3. Germany	931	7.4
4. Japan	581	4.7	4. France	551	4.4
5. Netherlands	499	4.0	5. Japan	551	4.4
6. France	475	3.8	6. UK	480	3.8
7. Italy	405	3.2	7. Netherlands	445	3.5
8. Belgium	370	3.0	8. Italy	410	3.2
9. South Korea	364	2.9[1]	9. Hong Kong	353	2.8[2]
10. UK	351	2.8	10. Belgium	351	2.8
11. Hong Kong	319	2.6	11. Canada	330	2.6
12. Canada	316	2.5	12. South Korea	323	2.6

WTO

NOTES

1. includes re-exports of $314 billion
2. includes re-exports of $353 billion

Over the decade, the USA declined from second to third place in exports but maintained first place in imports. The chronic US deficit was more than $400 billion in 2001, adding to its massive indebtedness to China, which held dollar reserves in excess of $2.4 trillion at the end of 2009.

On a country-by-country breakdown of EU merchandise trade for 2009, UK exports ranked one place behind South Korea and in imports one place after Japan. In addition to Germany, the UK's merchandise exports were surpassed by the Netherlands, one place behind Japan, and then France, Italy and Belgium in that order.

Japan's ranking has declined by one place from third to fourth in exports and to fifth in imports. Canada has also lost export ranking between 2001 and 2009, declining from fifth to twelfth. Hong Kong has maintained its eleventh place in exports and ninth in imports.

Winner in the 2009 top twelve rankings was: South Korea (ninth in exports and twelfth in imports).

Commercial services

There were also significant shifts in the country rankings for trade in commercial services between 2001 and 2009, as Table 3.5 illustrates.

Exports

In exports, the USA and the UK continue to hold the two top positions while Germany has overtaken France for third place, with France now ranking fourth. In line with its dramatic advances in merchandise trade, China now ranks fifth in the export of commercial services compared with twelfth in 2001, causing Japan, Spain and Italy to each drop one place in the next three positions.

In the bottom part of the table, there were two winners: Ireland advanced from 21st to 9th place and India from 19th position to 12th. The two losers were the Netherlands, whose ranking fell from 8th to 10th, and Hong Kong, which declined from 10th to 11th.

Imports

There were similar movements in the ranking of importers. The USA and Germany retained the two top spots, while the UK advanced one place to third and Japan fell from third to fifth. China's ranking again soared from 10th to 4th and India's from 18th to 12th.

France and Italy were each driven down one place to sixth and seventh and the Netherlands down two places to ninth, as Ireland rose from 11th to 8th position. Spain improved its ranking by two places from 12th to 10th, but Canada was a loser again, declining from 8th to 11th.

TABLE 3.5 Commercial services: leading exporters and importers (2009)

	Exports		Imports	
	Value $ bn	% share world trade	Value $ bn	% share world trade
1. USA	470	14.2	1. USA — 331	10.6
2. UK	240	7.2	2. Germany — 255	8.2
3. Germany	215	6.5	3. UK — 160	5.1
4. France	140	4.2	4. China — 158	5.1
5. China	129	3.9	5. Japan — 146	4.7
6. Japan	124	3.8	6. France — 124	4.0
7. Spain	122	3.7	7. Italy — 114	3.6
8. Italy	101	3.0	8. Ireland — 104	3.3
9. Ireland	96	2.9	9. Netherlands — 87	2.8[2]
10. Netherlands	92	2.8	10. Spain — 87	2.8
11. Hong Kong	86	2.6	11. Canada — 77	2.5
12. India	86	2.6	12. India — 74	2.4

WTO

Conclusion

The two listings emphasize the rising significance of China and India in world trade. In 2009, China accounted for 9.6 per cent of merchandise exports and 3.9 per cent of exports of commercial services; India contributed a further 2.6 per cent and 2.6 per cent respectively. Their continuing rise for at least the next two or three generations seems more than likely, confirming that today we live in Asia's century.

PART TWO
International marketing: principles and practice

04
Principles

The marketing concept

There is no argument about the concept of marketing but there are constant arguments about the best way to define it. The consequence of this is that there are literally hundreds of definitions of marketing, all of which can claim to be correct. This does not mean that opinions differ about the essence of marketing, but that we can have different attitudes towards a single concept.

While we have the old cliché of 'Marketing is selling goods which don't come back to customers who do,' it is in fact possible to classify definitions into three basic attitudes.

Group one

This consists of definitions with the strong implication that a producer is doing something that involves consumers as nothing more significant than pawns in a game, with profit as the end goal:

The income-producing side of the business
McNair, Brown, Leighton and Englent

The process of determining consumer demand for a product or service, motivating its sale, and distributing it into ultimate consumption at a profit
L Brech

The planning, executing and evaluating of the external factors related to a company's profit objectives
G M E Ule in D W Ewing (ed)

The primary management function which organizes and directs the aggregate of business activities involved in converting customer purchasing power into effective demand for a specific product or service and in moving the product or service to the final customer or user so as to achieve company-set profit or other objectives
L W Rodger

Deciding what the customer wants; arranging to make it; distributing and selling it at the maximum profit

Durham University Careers Advisory Service

Group two

This consists of a number of definitions with the implications that the producer is doing something *for* consumers rather than *to* them, but still doing it to suit the producer's own purpose.

These definitions are, like those in group one, very much concerned with a means to a profitable end. They are completely company centred:

Getting the right goods to the right people in the right places at the right time and the right price

Anonymous

In a marketing company (as distinct from one which has simply accepted the marketing concept), all activities – from finance to production to marketing – should be geared to profitable consumer satisfaction.

R J Keith

Marketing development is systematic forward planning so as to ensure matching of resources to fit market trends and to ensure continued growth for the enterprise.

R Glasser

The total system of interacting business activities designed to plan, price, promote and distribute want-satisfying products and services to present and potential customers

W J Stanton

The activity that can keep in constant touch with an organization's consumers, read their needs and build a programme of communications to express the organization's purpose

Kotler and Levy

Group three

These definitions move us significantly forward by introducing the idea that there is an element of willingness on the part of consumers as well as producers to join in the process. The vital words 'transfer' and 'needs of consumers' appear in these definitions, although they remain company centred. Marketing is seen by these authors as a transaction of some kind:

The economic process by means of which goods and services are exchanged and their values determined in terms of money prices

Duddy and Revzan

Selling is preoccupied with the seller's need to convert their product into cash; marketing with the idea of satisfying the needs of the customer by means of the product and the whole cluster of things associated with creating, delivering and finally consuming it.

T Levitt

The business activities involved in the transfer of goods or the acquisition of services

R Webster

The organization and performance of those business activities that facilitate the exchange of goods and services between maker and user

L W Rodger

All activities intended to stimulate or serve demand

G A Fisk

To go just one stage further there are definitions that consolidate the tendency of group three to think in terms of transactions. They say that marketing can in fact be thought of as a social exchange process:

The medium through which the material goods and culture of a society are transmitted to its members

E J Kelley

The establishment of contact

P T Cherrington

The latter is included simply because it is probably the shortest definition you could find. However, these last two, while being interesting in their own right, have little practical value to the exporter.

The group that contains definitions which are most appropriate for international marketing is undoubtedly group three, in that its definitions not only contain a need for consumer satisfaction but also the need for the establishment of some sort of relationship or partnership with overseas buyers. This will have some resonance with most practising exporters.

The exchange process

The idea that international marketing can be seen as an exchange process can be broken down into its constituent elements in diagram form as in Figure 4.1.

This demonstrates the two sides of the exchange: the business on one side using its expertise and resources to offer products and services to a market made up of potential customers who have their own ideas about what they need and do not need. The business that most closely matches its products and services to the buyer's perceptions of their needs will be more likely to achieve its goal of profits and will be more likely to produce satisfied customers.

The other point about this diagram is that it is not a process with a start and a finish. Businesses should be constantly questioning what they do with

FIGURE 4.1 The exchange process

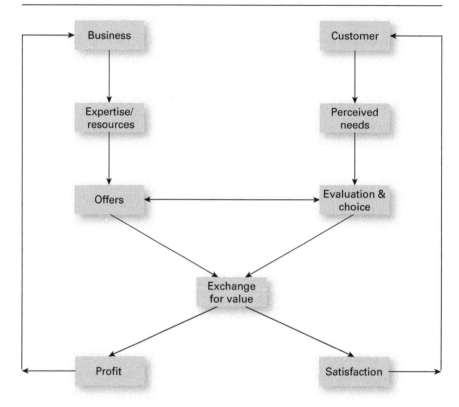

their expertise and resources in terms of offers to the market simply because the perceived needs of the customers are dynamic, that is, subject to change, and, in international trade, may be very volatile.

The marketing process

In fact we could take this a stage further. Perhaps the most important question any business should be continually asking itself is: 'What business are we in?'

You may think that this is a pointless question and that every business knows its business. But you could be wrong.

The fact is that many businesses can get so focused on their products and services that they can be very short-sighted regarding the actual expertise and resources that they possess. There are a number of case studies illustrating this, one of the more obvious ones being Bic who, when asked by consultants what business they were in, replied of course that they were in the 'pen business', more specifically the low-price pen business.

The consultants conducted a marketing audit, an in-depth investigation of the strengths and weaknesses of the marketing function of a business, and came back with their perception of Bic's business. They said that Bic's expertise and resources were in 'disposable plastic'. Not a very revolutionary statement but one that revolutionized Bic's attitude towards its business. It was not a pen manufacturer but a 'disposable plastic' manufacturer, more specifically extruded plastic containing metal inserts. What came next were the first disposable razors, to be followed by disposable lighters, disposable toothbrushes, disposable cologne dispensers and so on.

Simple questions can sometimes produce answers that fundamentally change the nature of a business.

Back to our marketing definitions. While there may be innumerable definitions of marketing, it is possible to pick out a couple of elements that are common to all of them, in fact the elements of a concept of marketing:

Customer orientation

Profit (or other objective)

That is to say that all of a marketing company's activities are centred around the needs of the consumer, and the whole process starts by finding out what the customer wants. This is the opposite of a product-orientated company, which attempts to produce what it chooses to produce and then sell it into the market.

Another cliché: 'Marketing is about making what we can sell, not selling what we can make.'

All of this is not because we like to please our customers, which of course we do, but primarily based on the fact that a satisfied customer is a more profitable customer.

However, it has to be said that definitions of words can help understanding but the more practical question concerns the *How* of marketing rather than the *What*.

That is, if a company were to accept the need to be responsive to market demand, to be 'customer orientated', as a means of becoming more successful in competitive markets, then how would it go about doing it? First, the difference between selling and marketing is important.

Figures 4.2 and 4.3 illustrate the basic difference in the processes, the major point being that selling starts with production, followed by the need to sell enough to make a profit, while marketing starts with market research in order to identify current market needs and profits from a satisfied customer.

FIGURE 4.2   The selling process

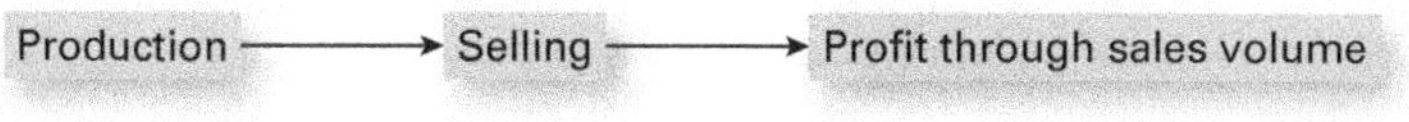

Production ⟶ Selling ⟶ Profit through sales volume

FIGURE 4.3 The marketing process (version 1)

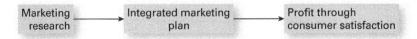

FIGURE 4.4 The marketing process (version 2)

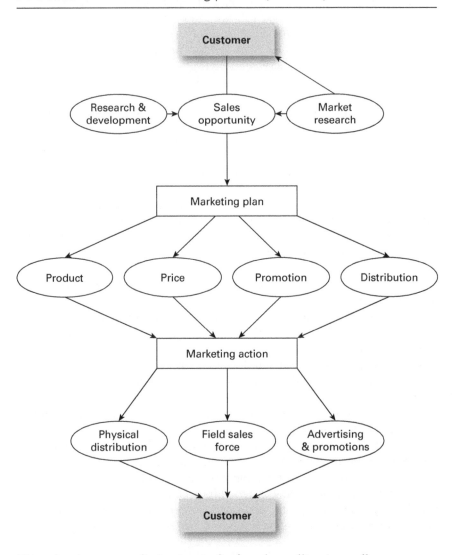

The other important distinction is the fact that selling is totally a one-way process while marketing is based on a continuous feedback from the customer and adaptation by the company to changes in consumer demand.

Figure 4.4 is perhaps more instructive as a more detailed overview of the marketing process, and helps us introduce physical distribution as a vital element of that process.

The beginning of this process is research carried out as a continuous activity in the marketplace, often underpinned by the internal research and development that improve a company's capability to produce. Once research has identified *Where* demand exists, and the company is capable of producing goods or services to meet that demand, then decisions need to be made as to *How* that demand might be serviced successfully.

The so-called 4 Ps approach is a simplistic, but nevertheless useful, interpretation of the basic decision-making areas of the marketing plan. All important strategic decisions that successful companies make can be categorized into the four elements of:

product;

price;

promotion;

place (or distribution: '3 Ps and a D' doesn't have the same ring to it!).

This is often referred to as the 'marketing mix', that is, a cluster of elements that all have to interact together in a cohesive plan. The right mix is the recipe for success!

There are other structures for the elements of the mix, notably the concept of the 7 Ps, which adds to the above and is particularly applicable to the supply of services:

people: considerations of the personnel involved and their responsibilities and needs;

process: administrative processes necessary for implementation;

physical: actual evidence of implementation, change and outcomes.

And a list of 12 elements produced by Professor Neil Borden of the Harvard Business School:

product planning;

pricing;

branding;

channels of distribution;

personal selling;

advertising;

promotion;

packaging;

display;

servicing;

physical handling;

marketing research.

All of which are contained within the more simplistic 4 Ps approach.

No amount of planning is beneficial without real implementation of the plan in practice, and Figure 4.4 illustrates the more obvious and visible activities of a company. Planning is not a process that can be seen but it does result in the high-profile activities of selling, promotion and physical distribution, which are clearly visible as the practical results of the planning.

Later in this chapter we will look a little more closely at the elements of the plan with specific reference to overseas markets, but first the point should be made that the process is the same whether we consider home or overseas trade. It is not the marketing process that changes from home to export markets, or even from one export market to another; it is the application of that process that will differ from one market to another.

The concept of market orientation, by definition, means that companies will attempt to discover the differences exhibited from one market to another and adapt to them in order to maximize profitable business. The differences encountered between the exporter's home market and overseas markets form a formidable list, and it is an ignorance of these differences that very often explains the failures of companies beginning to trade overseas.

The internationalization process

All trading organizations exist in a market environment that is always dynamic, that is, subject to change, and often volatile. In many cases these market movements are very unpredictable and adapting to them is a difficult task for even the most flexible of companies.

The market environment is made up of a whole range of *uncontrollables*, and the elements of the marketing plan, the *controllables*, represent the company's attempt to operate with maximum success in the face of the uncontrollable elements of the market.

A comprehensive list of the factors that may differ between the home market and overseas markets, and in fact between one overseas market and another, would occupy a disproportionate section of this book, but a brief list of the most obvious points is provided through a useful acronym, PEST:

Political/legal: leading to a wide variety of regulations and legislation. May also affect the stability, or otherwise, of the commercial environment.

Economic: type of economy – mixed private and public, state planned, etc. Level of economic development – primary, secondary, tertiary. Competition: the number, size and quality will vary.

Socio-cultural: cultural comprising many factors, eg religion, attitudes, opinions, morals and many more. They can lead to problems in

product design, packaging and promotion in particular.
Commercial practices: what is perceived as sharp, or even illegal,
practice is not the same in all markets. Taste: very few products
are sold in exactly the same form all over the world. Language:
totally innocent words in one language can be quite offensive in
another. Climate: there are obviously extreme differences from
one part of the world to another.

Technological: what is obsolete in one market may be state of the art
in another. The ways in which products are used may be not quite
as intended. Levels of maintenance will differ enormously.

Another version of the acronym is PESTLE, which lists 'Legal' as a distinct
category and adds 'Environment', which addresses things like green issues,
health and safety, levels of recycling.

While it could be argued that many of these distinctions could also apply
to the regions of a domestic market, there is little doubt that the extent
of the differentials is invariably far greater when operating in overseas
markets.

This is by no means a full list but does serve to illustrate the point that
the international trader is attempting to operate in a potentially infinite
number of differing commercial environments, each market segment requiring
individual approaches, which means that what is successful in one market is
by no means sure to work in others.

It is the company's ability to make the right decisions in those areas
within its control, in order to accommodate the differences in the range of
markets with which it deals, that makes the difference between success
and failure. One of the first things the exporter has to accept is the need to
differentiate from one market to another if profitable sales are to be
maximized.

It is the decisions made in the areas actually under the control of the
exporter that illustrate this differentiation in practice, that is, within the
areas identified as the 4 Ps earlier in this chapter. Of course, all of these
decisions should be based on a firm foundation of accurate and topical
market information.

Marketing research

Quality research underpins all successful export marketing and, if carried
out professionally, will always be cost effective in that any research costs
will be recouped by the benefits derived from the proper identification
of market potential, the maximum exploitation of that potential and the
avoidance of mistakes.

This and other basic questions regarding marketing research can be
illustrated in diagram form as in Figure 4.5.

FIGURE 4.5 The basics of market research

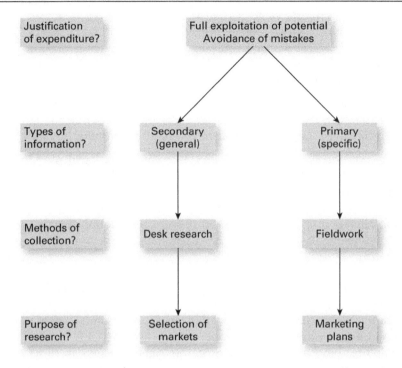

What is the purpose of market research? The simple answer is that it helps decide *Where* the company will operate, in terms of a logical market selection strategy, and then *How* those markets will be exploited for maximum returns.

Market selection

It is clearly important for exporters to develop a market selection strategy by which they choose the markets rather than the markets choosing them. But first we should ask the important question of whether we should in fact be exporting in the first place. This question might seem a little illogical in a book focused on international trade but there are situations in which many companies would do better if they did not export. One of the reasons for this is that many companies are actually exporting for the wrong reasons.

Bad reasons for exporting include:

Disposing of excess production
Not only does this devalue the potential of overseas markets but also evidences no permanent commitment to export, in that if and when

the home market takes up the excess, then the export markets are ignored. It is no surprise that such an attitude does nothing to develop overseas sales. A company with a permanent excess of production capacity should also be considering the efficiency of their capital investment. A permanent excess points to an underlying structural problem.

Marginal cost pricing

Sometimes linked with the above and based on the often incorrect assumption that sales in export markets have to be made at low prices. This process of pricing goods based on a recovery of direct costs only, and making no contribution to indirect costs, is one that can be legitimate as a short-term policy in markets quite separate from those paying the full price. In this respect, export markets are prime targets but too many companies simply adopt marginal pricing as a permanent policy, without considering the great potential for profitable sales overseas if they were only to approach the markets more professionally.

Prestige

Some companies operate under the misguided opinion that there is somehow great merit in dealing with a very large number of overseas markets. They appear to think that such a global image is evidence of their success. The truth is that in many cases they are trading badly in a large number of markets because the span of control is so wide. Such companies would often do much better if they were to be more selective about the markets with which they deal rather than adding new markets just because they are there.

Good reasons for exporting include:

Increased profits: either by an increase in volume sales based on the expansion of the size of a company's market network, or it may be possible to obtain better profit margins in export markets compared with home-market levels.

Spread of risk: a selective and controlled market expansion policy will decrease the company's dependence on, for example, its home market. Given the instability of most markets it is clearly preferable for a company to avoid having too many eggs in one basket, as it were.

Extension of the product life cycle: as is examined later in this chapter, there is often a situation in which the decline of the home market for a product, perhaps because of technical obsolescence, is not reflected in other markets. Because they are at a different stage of their economic development, they can often offer an expanding, as opposed to a declining market.

Even out seasonal fluctuations: products that have a seasonal demand can benefit from the fact that such a cycle is not the same in every part of the world. In simple terms it is always summer somewhere for the sunblock manufacturer.

National interest: it is in the interest of the home country's economy that companies should maximize their export business. OK, not much of a reason, except that most countries offer a variety of government services and incentives to the exporter, many of which are free, and that are specifically designed to encourage exports.

So the first decision a company should make is the conscious one to enter overseas markets. This should be based on a long-term commitment to export and a logical and informed market selection strategy.

Market selection criteria

Market research is essential if you are to take control and if *you* are to decide where to do business. Good-quality desk research will often supply sufficient secondary information to allow informed management decisions based on the following criteria:

Potential

The most obvious attraction of new markets is the potential they offer for increased business. This can be measured in a number of ways. The most obvious would be pure sales value, but also volume or profit or even market share could be of as much interest, depending on the company's particular requirements. For example, a company with a large production capacity would perhaps be more interested in the volume of units sold than the profit margin on each item. A company looking for control in a market may value a large market share, even if that means lower profit margins.

It should also be borne in mind that current market size is not necessarily guaranteed to remain unchanged and trends in the market must also be considered.

Accessibility

Not only must new markets offer current and future potential; that potential must also be accessible to the exporter. This is of very great importance in international trade, where barriers to trade exist that may make certain markets inaccessible to certain suppliers.

From the purely physical distribution point of view, there is hardly a place on earth to which an exporter could not physically deliver goods. The problem is the cost of such physical distribution, which is clearly not the same for every supplier in an overseas market.

The exporter has to compete with domestic suppliers in overseas markets and with competitors who are geographically closer, while facing greater physical distribution costs. It is no surprise that Canada's biggest single foreign supplier is the USA or that the Irish Republic's number one supplier is the UK. Even if this problem can be overcome, the exporter is still faced with a bewildering array of barriers to trade in the form of regulations that affect goods imported into a country.

Many of these rules and regulations are based on legislation in the country of destination and are often operated by the customs authorities of those countries. They can be broken down into two broad categories:

- Tariff barriers, comprising customs duties, levies, taxes, licensing, excise and quotas;
- Non-tariff barriers, comprising health, safety and technical standards (may be part of tariff controls), cultural considerations (eg taste, religion, language), national buying preferences and collaboration, eg cartels.

Many of these can simply bar entry into the market, as they are generally designed to do. It should also be noted that suppliers can also find that export controls in their own market impose significant barriers.

Similarity

Finally, given that the above requirements are met, the exporter would wish that any new markets are as similar to current markets as possible. There is no great merit in expansion into markets that exhibit totally different characteristics from current ones. The fewer changes that are necessary to the current marketing plan, the easier will be the market development.

The facts that almost 65 per cent of UK exports are to Western Europe and another 15 per cent or so to the USA, or that the USA's major markets are Canada and Mexico, followed by the EU and Japan, indicate that whether or not exporters actually apply the above criteria consciously, they do operate in practice.

It should be noted that it is a little simplistic to describe an overseas market purely in geographic terms. To identify a market simply by political boundaries, as in France or Germany, very rarely represents the actual nature of the market. What exporters must endeavour to do is define the segment of the market that contains their potential purchasers. This may be in terms of an end user profile describing the typical consumer or an identification of the industrial sector in which the consumer resides, which will give a very clear concept of the segment of the market that will be targeted in the marketing plan.

Managing the mess

The above is particularly and most obviously useful if you are in the position of a company about to start exporting and, of course, deciding to do it right. However, we have to accept that in many cases the damage has already been done. Historical accident has provided us with a range of overseas markets with which we now have to be deal.

Perhaps we can learn something from Pareto's law. More commonly known as the 80/20 rule, Pareto's law states that the typical situation for any company is that 80 per cent of its trade will come from 20 per cent of its customers. Illustrated on a graph, your sales profile is likely to look something like Figure 4.6.

FIGURE 4.6   Pareto's law: the 80/20 rule

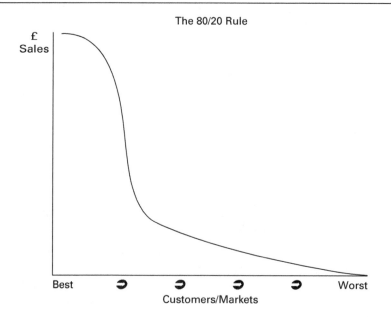

First it should be said that every company should know exactly what their version of the above graph looks like, that is, there should be a clear and quantitative measure of where the business is coming from.

Second, your customers can be categorized in accordance with how important they are to the business:

Class A: key markets that take priority over most of the others.

Class B: two types: some are declining Class A markets in which easy business can be taken without any effort; others are potential Class A markets – which is where your focus really should be.

Class C: no priority at all. Trading only at premium prices, or through local distributors, ensuring that a profit can still be taken on small orders. May require realistic minimum order values.

Where we are attempting to find new markets, it could be that a form of scoring chart might help to rate potential markets against each other. For example, rating a range of criteria from 1 to 10 (10 being the best) would at least start to provide an objective and quantifiable comparison. At the beginning of this process it may be that some boxes have to be left blank and others are just assumptions, but the closer we get to the identification of target markets the more information we should have collected. An example of such a scoring chart, which could be customized, is shown in Figure 4.7.

FIGURE 4.7 Classification of potential markets

	Potential markets			
	A	B	C	D
Market size				
Current/future demand				
Company potential				
Level of competition				
Transportation				
Product suitability				
Import restrictions				
Product protection				
Legal requirements				
Non-tariff barriers				
Pricing				
Exchange controls				
Business practices				
Local services				
Language				
Socio-cultural				

05
Methods of market research

The two basic reasons for market research, that is, market selection and market planning, do actually correlate with the two distinct methods for the collection of information.

Thus the process of market selection can often be achieved through the use of desk research, sometimes referred to as 'armchair research'. This involves the company in collecting information without actually venturing into the overseas market.

Such information will invariably be secondary information, in that we are secondary users and it is available to other companies. The sources of such information are very wide-ranging in a developed market.

Sources of information

Two main areas:

- material available within the company;
- independent external sources.

Within the company

Sales, production, cost, credit and customer information. Sales analysis is particularly important as it indicates:

- market share (% of total consumption/imports);
- rates of consumption;
- seasonal variations;
- long-term trends;
- price/volume relationships.

This information can be analysed by market, product or customer (or combinations of all three). But it must be systematically compiled and continually updated.

However, raw data, such as monthly sales figures, need to be processed into information that actually tells us something. It is also the case that much of the market information we can collect is quantitative. It is this area of marketing where statistical techniques become very useful. But first there are other secondary sources of information.

External sources (secondary)

Most developed countries offer a wide range of support to exporters, both financially and in the provision of information.

In the UK, for example, these are provided through the Business Links network comprising BERR/FCO and Chamber of Commerce services integrated as UK Trade and Investment (UKTI: **www.trade.uktradeinvest.gov.uk**), providing international trade advisors to SMEs and a range of web-based services, including (in their own words):

- Speak to your local expert. Our international trade teams are located in over 40 local offices around the country. Every UK region also has dedicated sector specialists who can provide support tailored to your industry.

- Passport to export. Our programme offers new and inexperienced exporters free capability assessments, support in visiting markets, mentoring from a local professional, action plans, customized and subsidized training and ongoing support once you've started to export.

- Access our market expertise. Each business and each market is unique. Our aim is to help you through research and advice, to make those initial approaches into new markets. We offer two key research and contact services:

  - OMIS (Overseas Market Introduction Service). OMIS puts you directly in touch with staff in our overseas offices, who are able to give you access to the best country- and sector-specific business advice, as well as offering support during your visits overseas. OMIS is available in the 99 UKTI markets overseas. It is delivered online, giving you a direct link to local experts overseas irrespective of their time zone or location, with fast access to reports and advice, and allowing you to keep in touch wherever you are.

  - EMRS (Export Marketing Research Scheme). Successful exporters consider their entry into new markets with care. You may wish to carry out export marketing research to obtain intelligence on topics such as:

- market size and segmentation;
- regulations and legislation;
- customer needs, usage and attitudes;
- distribution channels;
- trends;
- competitor activity, strategy and performance.

- UKTI provides a subsidized service for UK exporters. The British Chambers of Commerce administer EMRS on behalf of UKTI. Companies with fewer than 250 employees may be eligible for a grant of up to 50 per cent of the agreed cost of market research projects.

- Breaking down barriers. If you need help with linguistic and cultural aspects of doing business overseas, the Export Communications Review offers companies a variety of options and advice, including cultural awareness reviews and communications planning.

And a number of other services for experienced exporters:

- Global growth. A free service that offers a strategic review, planning and support to help grow business overseas. It offers a single route to a wide range of guidance and support from UKTI and other public and private sector organizations.

- Take part in our events. Why not test out a new market by taking part in an overseas event, such as a trade fair or mission?

While the above are UK government-specific, similar support is offered in many other developed countries:

- USA: **http://www.export.gov/about/index.asp**
- France: Ministry for Foreign Trade: **http://www.exporter.gouv.fr/exporter/**
- Germany: Trade and Invest: **http://www.gtai.de/**

An internet search for 'export promotion' would identify the equivalent government agencies in most countries in the world.

In addition to government services, there are many other organizations that offer support to exporters:

- Customs: import and export statistics, tariff levels, tariff and non-tariff barriers.
- Trade associations: specific product/market information.
- Banks: general economic and financial information; regular market reports.
- Business information organizations: eg Standard & Poor's, Dun & Bradstreet, credit, insurance companies, etc.

- Market research consultants: existing reports or original research.
- Bibliographic and ICT databases: very wide range of published/web-based information.

See also the list of useful websites in Appendix 1.

The general problem for exporters in developed countries is not a lack of secondary information but exactly the opposite. It is necessary to be as specific as possible about the objective of the research in order to pinpoint the relevant data.

Table 5.1 illustrates the relationship between the market selection criteria mentioned above and the appropriate types of secondary information.

TABLE 5.1   Information for selection criteria

Market selection criteria	Types of information
Potential	Statistical
Accessibility	Regulatory
Similarity	General Background

All the above types of information can be collected by desk research but it has to be accepted that as the questions become more specific, particularly in relation to the marketing plan, then the need for specialized fieldwork becomes more obvious. There is also the fact that, while secondary information is widely available and either free or relatively inexpensive, often problems arise because it is:

- generalized: does not relate to specific companies' needs;
- out of date: there is no guarantee that it will be topical;
- available to all: most information is not exclusive to the user.

To obtain original, specific and topical information it may be necessary to carry out some form of survey actually in the market. This is often referred to as fieldwork and requires more specialized methods of collection, the main methods being:

- observation;
- test marketing;
- interview;
- questionnaire.

All these methods require particular expertise and it may be that the typical exporter needs the assistance of consultants who specialize in this type of research.

Sampling

Before any of the above methods can be used, the researcher needs to be able to establish a small sample of the target population. It is clearly too expensive to ask the entire population about a given product or service, so the object is to select a small sample that will be held to represent that population.

Sampling is an important tool of market research used to collect, analyse and interpret market data. It involves the study of smaller representative groups taken from a larger population that cannot be completely covered by virtue of its size.

The theory of sampling is based on the study of relationships between a population (ie a group of individuals or objects that are similar and have characteristics that can be estimated and classified) and the samples drawn from it.

Using probability theory, certain conclusions can be drawn about a population from a study of samples drawn from it. Different types of sampling include:

- Random sampling: every unit in the population has an even chance of being selected. This is the simplest sampling technique.

- Systematic sampling: a set numerical routine is used to select the sample (eg every 20th passer-by or house, every 40th name in the telephone directory).

- Stratified sampling: this attempts to bring out the differences in particular strata or groups in the population. Quotas are often used by the researcher to achieve this (ie the fieldworker/interviewer is often given a quota of respondents in a group). This technique is applied to some product classes where innovators in the population are particularly important in new product acceptance.

- Cluster sampling: the respondents are selected on the basis of their grouping or clustering around a particular area or location within which they may be randomly selected. (Test market areas are sometimes examined in this way.)

In research, samples are generally used instead of a survey of the total group on the grounds of cost and speed. However, in some industrial markets the techniques of sampling would be inappropriate since the total population size is relatively small.

The skill employed in applying the sampling techniques determines to a large extent the accuracy of the results and the degree of confidence that can be placed in statements made about the total population. The two relevant concepts in this context are sample size and sample selection.

To arrive at the sample size the researcher will calculate on the basis of what constitutes an acceptable degree of accuracy, but the decision may need to be modified by cost considerations. It is dangerous to base decisions or findings on a sample that has little statistical validity since this would mean generalizing about the whole population on the basis of information about a very small group of individuals.

Conducting fieldwork

Observation

Any visitor to an overseas market, irrespective of the prime reason for the visit, is in a position to collect a wide range of topical information simply by keeping their eyes and ears open. This can produce very worthwhile information regarding distribution channels, infrastructure, consumer behaviour, etc, but we should always remain aware that such observation can be very subjective and should be supported by other, more objective, information.

To maximize the quantity and quality of such information it is important to establish a formal and structured means of collecting and recording what is perceived to be relevant.

A typical trip report could include:

- visits, enquiries, orders, etc;
- complaints and comments;
- market movements since last visit;
- competitors' activities;
- physical distribution, transport problems and developments;
- promotional activities and needs;
- economic developments;
- payment problems and changes;
- new regulations and legislation;
- technical developments;
- channel performance;
- future plans and developments;
- and any other specific areas thought to be relevant to the company's needs.

As long as personnel are aware before undertaking a visit of the form of the trip report, there is no reason why its completion should interfere with any prime purpose of the visit. It is particularly the case that personnel who consider that the only purpose of a visit is to sell should accept their responsibilities for information collection.

Test marketing

This involves the distribution, promotion and selling of a product or service in a selected sample territory on the assumption that we can infer from the market response in the test market area what the response of the whole market will be. This obviously requires the selection of a representative test market area and good control of the product distribution within the area. It can also allow an amount of experimentation regarding elements such as packaging, pricing, etc, which will not affect the whole market.

On a slightly larger scale there is an argument that the launch of a product into, for example, the European Union can greatly benefit from information collected by selling into the smaller markets, such as the Benelux countries, before a full-scale launch into the larger markets such as France and Germany. The use of the Benelux as a springboard into other EU markets is, in effect, a test marketing exercise.

In the same way a launch of a product into the USA might benefit from some test marketing in perhaps just two states.

While this method of fieldwork is common with consumer products, there is no reason why similar strategies cannot be applied to industrial goods.

Interview

Telephone interviews can cover a large number of respondents at the same time, but is expensive for large numbers over longer distances. Also, we must be aware that ownership of a telephone may not be general in some countries and there is therefore an immediate bias in the survey respondents.

Personal interviews can be one of the following or a combination of them:

- printed schedule of questions put or read to respondents;
- draft points for discussion, with some flexibility;
- free interview allowing a wide-ranging discussion (with prompting).

The last of these can be more expensive and time consuming than printed questionnaires but has the advantage of obtaining more accurate and detailed information.

Any personnel visiting a market will be conducting such interviews, often on an informal basis, and the structuring of such an interview should comply with their research responsibilities as mentioned above.

Where a formal interview campaign is proposed it may be the case that more specialized skills, particularly linguistic, are required, and the use of professional interviewers may be necessary.

The personal interview has some distinct advantages:

- High level of return: it is unlikely that we have many total refusals to supply information.

- Easier to select the sample: we can define the nature of the respondents likely to provide the most useful responses and specifically target them.

- Interviewer control: it is possible for the interviewer to elicit more detailed responses when needed or to return to topics that remain unclear. It is also possible for experienced interviewers to check early responses for veracity by returning to them with differently phrased questions.

- Allows use of visual material: a wide range of presentation materials can be used, including the actual products themselves.

- Makes delicate questions easier: experience shows that it is actually possible to elicit far more personal information from a face-to-face interview than from, for example, a written questionnaire.

However, we should be aware that there are some disadvantages:

- High cost: even if we do not use the services of professional consultants there are still the travel, subsistence and venue costs related to establishing the face-to-face situation.

- Interviewer bias: bad interviewers can lead or influence respondents or even misinterpret their responses. This may not be deliberate but be based on the subconscious perceptions of the interviewer.

- Time consuming: related to the cost issues is the fact that this process does take up a large amount of time for both interviewer and respondent. If a large number of interviews are conducted there could be a lengthy time gap from the first interview to the last.

- Need for close staff supervision: the completion of the planned interviews at the level of detail desired is to a great extent dependent on the conscientious work of the interviewers.

Questionnaire

This can be a very cost-effective way of obtaining good quality of information, but the information obtained is only as good as the questionnaire.

The mailed (or e-mailed) questionnaire has a number of advantages:

- Low cost: a large number of respondents can be targeted.

- Speed: over a relatively short period of time.

- No staff training or supervision: but the questionnaire itself may require a professional design input.

- Guarantees anonymity: which can help obtain information of a confidential nature.
- No interviewer bias or manipulation: any personal perceptions are removed from the process.

Of course, there are disadvantages:

- Low response rate: it is an inescapable fact that the great majority of mailed questionnaires end up in the wastepaper bin. A response rate of between 5 and 10 per cent should be seen as quite successful.
- 'Funny men': this refers to those respondents who will complete the questionnaire but not answer the questions in a serious or accurate manner.
- Limited to relatively simple questions: there is a limit to how complex and specific the questions can be.
- Needs accurate mailing list: the level and relevance of the responses are often dependent on the quality of the original mailing list.
- Problems with delicate questions: the fact is that the written, and therefore recorded, nature of the information may cause some reservations in the respondent. Anonymity can help to mitigate this.

The design of an effective questionnaire, particularly one that is to be used in an overseas market, requires a great deal of expertise. Most exporters would be well advised to consult professional market researchers to help in the design of such questionnaires.

Factors in questionnaire design

Closed or open questions. The majority of questions should be closed, ie avoid any actual writing by the respondent. Tick boxes or circled choices will increase the level and quality of response. Open questions can be included at the end, eg 'Do you have any other comments?' and as alternatives at the end of multiple-choice questions, eg 'other (please specify)'.

Layout. Begin with easy questions, gradually becoming more difficult. Look for a logical running order:

1 Classification questions: 'What are you?' eg name, age, job title, size of business.
2 Behavioural questions: 'What do you do?' eg buying habits, rate of consumption, products handled, main markets, sources of supply.
3 Attitudinal questions: 'What do you think?' eg opinions, attitudes, perceptions, preferences.

Questions on left, tick boxes on right (on the assumption that most people are right-handed). Do not forget that, if the questionnaire is translated into languages other than English, all languages do not read from top left to bottom right.

Question design

Avoid jargon, trade expressions, colloquialisms, slang and long words wherever possible. It may be the case that the respondent is using a second language, and common expressions in English may not transfer or translate. If technical language is necessary we must take extra care with the mailing list.

Types of questions

Dichotomous: only two possible answers, eg yes/no, male/female;

Multi-choice: provide a list of possible answers, eg current salary:

- up to £15k
- £15k or over but less than £25k
- £25k or over but less than £50k
- over £50k

Remember to ensure that the classes do not overlap, eg £15k to £25k, £25k to £50k would not work because £25k is correct for both.

Remember also to ensure that both nil and larger figures are available if appropriate.

- Where did you hear about our products?
  - recommendation
  - trade press
  - exhibition
  - circular mailing
  - our personal visit
  - other (please specify).

The addition of 'other' is important as we often cannot cover all the possibilities.

Semantic scales: these allow an expression of opinion, eg:

- How would you rate the quality of service?
  Excellent, Good, Average, Poor, Very Poor
- Do you think that our price levels are:
  Very important, Quite important, Not important?

A whole range of criteria can be applied to such questions. They should be based on five or even seven categories as we should be happy to accept a noncommittal response if that is more accurate. It is not constructive to force respondents to take sides.

It is also possible to ask respondents to rate or grade a list in order, eg number the following factors in order of importance to you (1 = most important; 5 = least important): price, quality, delivery, product range, reliability.

Open questions: these should be used very selectively. Towards the end of a questionnaire general questions requiring a written response can be included, eg What is your general experience in dealing with UK suppliers? Do you have any other comments?

Rubric and close

It is important to have clear instructions at the beginning of the question-naire, eg Please tick the appropriate box or make a brief comment; you may tick more than one answer if appropriate.

It may also increase the level of response to describe the purpose of the research and to be particularly grateful for respondents' cooperation, per-haps by emphasizing how important their opinions are. In some cases an incentive might be included, such as participation in a prize draw, although we should be aware that this could be product demeaning.

The close should thank the respondent, refer to the e-mail or freepost address for the response and maybe ask if they are prepared to participate in follow-up personal interviews.

Statistics

As mentioned earlier, whatever the source or method of research used, much of the information generated is quantitative hard data and therefore often needs to be statistically processed and analysed to provide useful informa-tion. In the examples that follow, all figures used are fictitious.

Presentation of data

Tables may be used (see Table 5.2):

- for orderly presentation of the original figures;
- to show some identifiable pattern in the figures;
- to summarize the figures;
- to make public relevant data on which future statistical studies may be based (eg government departments and trade associations).

Diagrammatic presentation of data

Various alternatives may be grouped under this heading. They include:

- pictograms;
- statistical maps;
- bar charts (simple, component, percentage component and multiple);
- pie charts.

TABLE 5.2   Imports of cars by country of origin and year ($m)

	Japan	Germany	USA
2006	43	77	105
2007	67	82	125
2008	98	80	110
2009	123	85	102
2010	188	88	95

Pictograms

This term describes a method of presentation that uses pictures to represent data.

There are two basic types:

- pictograms where the picture is always the same size, and magnitude is shown by the number of pictures;
- pictograms where the size of the picture changes to indicate magnitude or value.

The problem with this type of presentation is that the size of the picture may deceive the eye, and visual comparison of the figures may become very difficult since the pictures will not show very slight differences in magnitude with any clarity.

Bar charts

In the simplest of these, data are presented by a series of bars, and the magnitude of the particular figure is represented by the height of each bar.

In their method of construction, bar charts are similar to graphs, which will be discussed later. They are preferable to pictograms, largely because of their greater accuracy and because they are easier to construct.

Simple bar charts

These may be used where changes only in the totals indicated by the bars are needed.

Component bar charts

These are applicable where it is necessary to indicate not only the changes in the totals, but also the size of each component part within a specific bar amount.

Percentage component bar charts

These are appropriate where the most important factor to be indicated is the relative size of the component parts.

Multiple bar charts

These may be used where there is a need to express changes in the actual values of the component figures, and the overall total is not important (see Figure 5.1).

FIGURE 5.1 Multiple bar chart

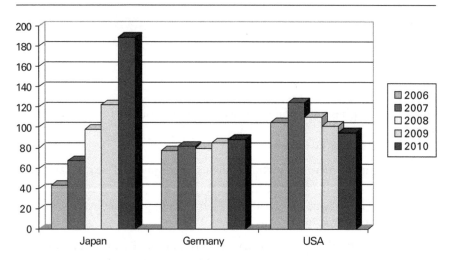

Pie charts

These may be defined as circles divided by lines radiating from the centre, much like the spokes of a wheel, or, rather like slices of cake or pie, from which the name derives. An example is shown in Figure 5.2.

FIGURE 5.2 Pie chart

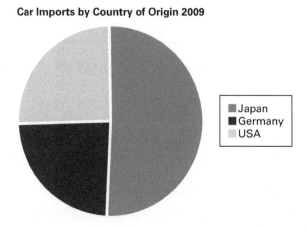

FIGURE 5.3 Mathematical graph

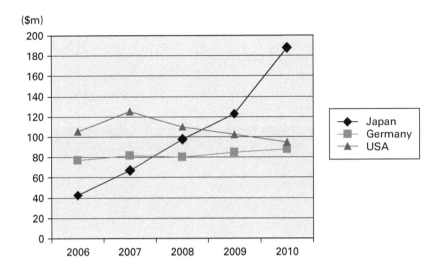

Graphs

In simple terms, a graph may be described as a representation of data by a continuous curve or straight line on squared paper. It is important to note that a line on a graph is always referred to as a *curve*, even though it may be a straight line. Some considerations to note when constructing graphs:

- Construct so as to provide an accurate and useful impression.
- The 'independent variable' is that which is unaffected by the other variables (sales volume, consumption, market size, etc); it is always located on the horizontal axis.
- The starting point for the vertical axis is always zero (0) to avoid giving the wrong impression (even if a 'break' is used to cut out unused amounts).
- The axes should be clearly labelled with both the nature of the variable (sales, distance, volume) and the units in which it is expressed ($, £m, kilometres, miles, etc).
- Curves drawn on the graph must be distinctive since the objective of the graph is to present the data and give an immediate visual impression of pattern, direction or trend in the figures (different colours, etc for different variables).
- It is important to indicate the source clearly.

Frequency distribution, measures of location and dispersion

In some instances, the data collected will be difficult to handle and comprehend in their original form. Consider the example below in Table 5.3 and try to draw some conclusions from them.

TABLE 5.3 Advertising expenditure by European pet food manufacturers in 2010

€000s				
307	322	361	345	357
319	311	387	335	372
309	312	382	370	351
348	339	364	373	369
340	367	388	378	412
322	401	351	365	355
323	339	354	306	396
316	392	343	390	317
300	301	319	354	303
353	378	326	341	352
333	349	303	386	357

Most of the figures are in the 300s with one or two 400s to be seen, but can you detect any pattern? In many instances it will be important to identify points of concentration since these may be of special significance.

Arrays

The figures in Table 5.3 represent a simple random listing of data as they were collected, and hence they are denoted 'raw data'. A usual first step would be to relist the figures in order of magnitude to present them more meaningfully, and such an ordered listing is known as an array (see Table 5.4).

It is possible to simplify this table one stage further. Since some of the figures repeat (303), it would be simpler to list each figure once, and in a second column to indicate the number of times it is repeated.

For statistical purposes, the number of times a figure occurs is called the frequency. Table 5.5 represents an *ungrouped frequency distribution*, ie a list of figures occurring in the raw data, together with the frequency of each figure. Note that the sum of the frequencies is expressed (Sf) and must equal the number of items making up the raw data.

It is possible to improve further still on Table 5.5 in terms of clarity and simplicity by condensing the information into a form that indicates more

TABLE 5.4 An array of the raw data in Table 5.3

€000s				
300	319	341	355	378
301	319	343	357	378
303	322	345	357	382
303	322	348	361	386
306	323	349	364	387
307	326	351	365	388
309	333	351	367	390
311	339	353	370	396
316	339	354	372	401
317	340	354	373	412

directly the significance of the data concerned. By grouping the figures into *classes*, we can reduce the number of figures considerably.

The information in Table 5.5 might therefore be re-presented as a *grouped frequency distribution*, as shown in Table 5.6.

It can be seen that, as an effect of grouping, some pattern can be detected in the figures. In Table 5.6 the expenditures cluster around 300 to under 320, and at 340 to under 380. The main drawback with such groupings is that although a pattern may emerge, the result is also a loss of information.

Means, medians and modes

In the field of statistics, we can identify three main types of *averages*. These are:

- the arithmetic mean (usually referred to for simplicity as the mean);
- the median;
- the mode.

The mean is the typical average: the numbers are added up and divided by the number of items.

The median can be defined as the middle value of a distribution, ie the middle item when the data are arranged from bottom to top (an array).

The mode is defined as the most frequently occurring value in the distribution. As the value that occurs most frequently, it is the most representative of the typical item.

In choosing an average, we might consider the following:

- The mean is most suitable if we wish to know what the consequence of an equal distribution would be: for example, per capita income (the total income of a nation, divided by the total population).

TABLE 5.5 Ungrouped frequency distribution constructed from the array in Table 5.4

€s	frequency	€s	frequency	€s	frequency	€s	frequency	€s	frequency
300	1	319	2	341	1	355	1	378	2
301	1	322	2	343	1	357	2	382	1
303	2	323	1	345	1	361	1	386	1
306	1	326	1	348	1	364	1	387	1
307	1	333	1	349	1	365	1	388	1
309	1	335	1	351	2	367	1	390	1
311	1	339	2	352	1	369	1	392	1
312	1	340	1	353	1	370	1	396	1
316	1	–	–	354	2	372	1	401	1
317	1	–	–	–	–	373	1	412	1

Total frequency (Sf) = 55

TABLE 5.6 Grouped frequency distribution

€s Expenditure		Frequency (f)
300	– under 320	13
320	– under 340	8
340	– under 360	15
360	– under 380	10
380	– under 400	7
400	– under 420	2
Total frequency (Sf) = 55		

- The mean, however, makes use of every value in the distribution and can, therefore, be distorted by extreme values.
- The median will be chosen if we wish to know the halfway value, with as many above as below (the average age of the population, for instance).
- The mode is the appropriate average to use where we want to find the most typical value of a series.

06
The marketing plan

The marketing plan is sometimes referred to as the marketing mix because it represents a mixture of decisions made in specific areas but which must blend together. The exporter has to make decisions designed to exploit to the full the potential identified in overseas markets. As we have seen, it is possible to rationalize these areas into the four broad categories of product, price, place and promotion.

Product

All exporters must accept the fact that most successful products are modified for sale in overseas markets, Very few products are sold in exactly the same form in all markets, and the reason for, and nature of, modifications will differ from one market to another. Illustrative of this point is the fact that most products that are thought to be the same throughout the world are, in many cases, not the same at all, eg Coca-Cola.

The reasons for such product modifications are numerous but include:

- Official regulations, trading standards, power supplies. Enormous differences exist in health, safety and technical standards, voltages, calibrations, fittings, controls, instructions, etc. A manufacturer of electric coffee percolators found that it could not export them to Canada unless they contained a form of electric wire made nowhere but in ... Canada!

  With no mains electricity how can we sell washing machines to African or Indian villagers? The answer is to de-invent, by producing special hand-driven machines.

- Size, weight and volume. French women tend to have bigger feet than English women, but the Japanese are even smaller. Many Finns sleep in smaller bedrooms than are usual here. The larger retail packages found in the USA are increasingly common in other developed countries.

- Colour. In some parts of the Far East, dentists often buy brown or black teeth for their patients' dentures because chewing betel nuts stains the teeth. Australians live in a country where eucalyptus trees dominate their rivals. Their colour key for green is in consequence the eucalyptus leaf, unlike a UK national where grass green is standard. Emerald green, the colour of the Muslim religion, is a favourite colour in Pakistan, where also saffron yellow, the colour of the robes of the Buddhist monks, is particularly disliked. White is associated with death in Malaysia, and purple with voodoo in parts of Africa (and even parts of the USA).

- Aesthetic features. Round or oval tables do not sell well in the Czech Republic, where nearly everyone prefers rectangular tables. Canadians, New Zealanders and Australians, like the British, prefer to buy bedroom, dining room and lounge suites, and are keen on matching kitchen cabinets. Elsewhere, for example in Holland, people enjoy bringing together a pleasant collection of odd pieces.

- Physical taste. Coca-Cola recipes vary from country to country, and across the world Nescafé has been offered in 40 different flavours. Equally, the British have their own distinctive taste in beer.

- Raw materials. In India, Hindus refused to buy British bone china as soon as they found that the ground bones mixed with the clay were those of their sacred animal, the cow. Pork products and derivatives find similar problems in Muslim countries.

- Method of use. In Holland, a bicycle is ridden by many to get them to and from work and to make trips to the shops. The Dutch, therefore, want a strong, reliable machine that can stand up to long years of constant use. In the USA bicycles are mostly bought as teenagers' toys or a piece of leisure or keep-fit equipment. Depilatory creams are used by men in West Africa as an alternative to shaving.

- Climate. In hot countries, cars need air-conditioning systems. In monsoon conditions, they require exceptionally effective and reliable windscreen wipers. Where winters are rugged, the starters must function in icy conditions and heaters must be powerful.

The above are just a small number of examples of product modifications, and reasons for them, from the many that exist in international trade. There are some products that are sold without modification throughout the world, for example Scotch whisky, and some, but only some, French perfumes, but even then certain brands will be more or less popular from one market to another. Also some products, usually high technology, which are used in the same way in all parts of the world, may not be modified, but even then other aspects of the marketing plan will almost certainly differ.

To be technically correct we should in fact refer to product/market strategies, as each product package should relate to a specific market segment. This process is known as *product positioning* and links in with the segmentation process mentioned as part of market selection.

Exporters must also realize that buyers are often not buying just the physical entity of the product, but a whole package of things that go with it. This is known as the *total product concept* and includes elements such as reliability, reputation, image and prestige as well as the more tangible parts of a package deal such as the packaging itself, credit terms, guarantees and warranties and pre- and after-sales service.

The role of marketing research

The value of marketing research is not only in ensuring that the product is suited to market requirements, but also that costly mistakes are avoided – like the UK company that produced a range of ladies' fashion garments for Scandinavian countries. Naturally they produced a winter range because it is often cold in that part of Europe. Unfortunately, they realized too late that the UK concept of a winter and summer range of clothes was of no relevance to Scandinavian countries, where the distinction between indoor and outdoor is far more important. The market is actually for lightweight, indoor clothes; functionality is more important than fashion for outdoor wear.

The list of expensive mistakes is almost endless. A bone-china dinner service specially designed for Italian taste did not sell at all due to the absence of a pickle bowl. White false teeth produced for the Far East did not match the betel-nut-stained teeth of the potential recipients, who objected to a mouth that resembled a piano keyboard.

Packaging may be more important than the product, as the company selling powdered milk into West Africa discovered. Their traditional metal container was replaced by a more cost-effective container but the customers found it difficult to carry water, and even more difficult to cook, with a cardboard box. The company totally misunderstood the usage of their product. As did the exporter of depilatory creams who discovered, too late, that the majority of their West African market was male, and not female, as men used the cream as an alternative to shaving.

Even when the product is right for the market, the name it is given can render it unsaleable. Some years ago, it is alleged, the Chevrolet Nova caused quite a stir in Latin American markets; *no va* is Spanish for 'won't go', and Toyota's competitor to the Mini would not have sold so well if they had persisted with the name 'Toyolet'. (Incidentally, the second example is true, the first just another urban myth.) It may therefore be necessary to sell the same product with a range of different names.

Basic market research could, and in some cases did, avoid the long-term cost of such mistakes.

Finally, exporters have to accept that even if current demand is being satisfied it is unlikely that the situation will never change. All products go through a *life cycle*, which begins with an *introduction* to the market, followed by a period of *growth* and then a *maturity* when the best returns are made, but this is eventually and inevitably followed by *decline*.

All products eventually decline; the problem is to determine the time scale (see Figure 6.1).

FIGURE 6.1   The product/sales cycle

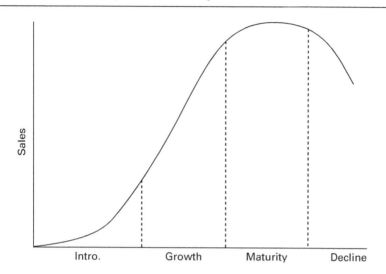

The profile will differ from product to product and, clearly, the timescale is the most difficult element to predict, although generally we would expect:

slow: chemicals, extractive industries, etc;

fast: clothing, electrical goods, etc.

In fact, fashion or fad products might have a very short life, as in Figure 6.2.

FIGURE 6.2   Fashion/fad product life

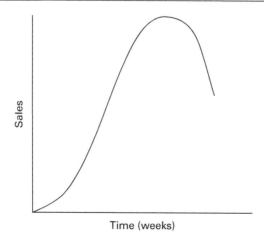

The application of the theory is essential to long-term product replacement and development strategies, as the development of replacement products must begin, at the latest, during the mature phase of current products.

However, it may be that we are not actually replacing a product but looking to extend its life through either modification (Figure 6.3) or a range of marketing activities (Figure 6.4).

FIGURE 6.3   Extended product life through modification

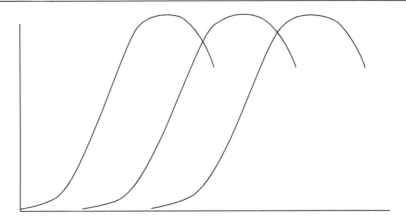

FIGURE 6.4   Extended product life through marketing activities

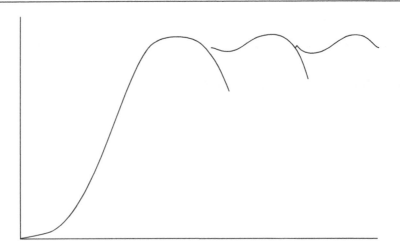

Activities designed to extend product life cycles can include:

- promotion, eg advertising campaign, exhibition, special offers, etc;
- repackaging;

- renaming/branding; and of course:
- expansion into new markets, ie exporting.

The Boston Matrix

This is an old concept but one that still has its uses in generating an objective view of what is sometimes a messy portfolio of products. Most companies will deal in a number, sometimes hundreds, of different products, and a method of taking an objective view of these is based on the concept that there are only four categories of product, illustrated in Figure 6.5.

FIGURE 6.5   The Boston Matrix

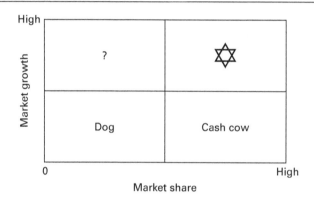

The stages in the Boston Matrix life cycle are shown in Table 6.1.

TABLE 6.1   Boston Matrix: stages in life cycle

?	High growth, low market share	Introduction
☆	High growth, high market share	Growth
Cash cow	Low growth, high market share	Maturity
Dog	Low growth, low market share	Decline

Good management is about maintaining a spread of products at different stages of their life cycles and avoiding the situation in which the portfolio is full of dogs or, almost as bad, full of question marks.

Price

Price, as an element of the marketing mix, may be designed to do more than just maximize profits. It may attempt to create a market share, generate early cash recovery, establish compatibility across a range of products (price lining), or generate a specific rate of return.

Basically the exporter has two choices in arriving at a selling price. The most common, because it is the easiest, is the least effective and that is *cost plus* pricing. The direct, and hopefully indirect, costs are calculated and a percentage profit margin is added. This produces the minimum price the company is prepared to accept, the same price for every customer and every market. The final delivered price may differ, because the physical distribution costs are different, but the bottom line EXW (Ex-works) price remains the same.

All companies should have a very clear idea of their minimum price levels but this strategy ignores the possibilities for more profitable sales should the buyer be prepared to pay more.

Sensible companies need to know the *price the market will bear* to complete the picture. Such information gathered from marketing research and, it has to be said, trial and error, will lead to an understanding of the maximum price the company can achieve. It will also naturally lead to a system of differentiated pricing in that the price obtainable from one market, and even one customer, will differ from place to place.

Between the two extremes it may be that companies can find compromises based on a variable add-on to a basic cost or in situations where it is simply a case of matching the main competitor's price in the market, as in Table 6.2.

The truth is often even more complex, as most products exhibit some sort of *price elasticity*. There is rarely a price the market will bear, but different prices will generate different sales volumes. The typical situation is that the lowest price will generate the highest volume sales, and vice versa. What exporters need to establish are the price–volume relationships that exist for their products in overseas markets (see Figure 6.6).

In practice the extremes of this curve are very unreliable and the exporter will attempt to define the range P1 to P2 and its relationship with V1 and V2 as being more predictable, as illustrated in Figure 6.7.

Many companies, knowing the minimum and maximum price parameters in their markets, are able to use price as a marketing tool. They may choose *skim* pricing strategies to take high-profit, low-volume sales, or use *penetration* pricing to take high-volume, low-profit sales. Or a range of options in between.

In extreme cases a company may even accept loss-making sales in the interest of long-term gains. All of these strategies will be supported by the other elements of the marketing plan.

TABLE 6.2 Pricing the product

Cost plus fixed %	Cost plus variable %	Match competition	Price the market will bear
Production costs plus % profit margin	Production costs plus % profit margin	Match established market price	Research must discover the optimum price; depends on next best, purchasing power; subjective value
Same price for all markets			Different price for all markets
Minimum we can obtain			Maximum we will accept

FIGURE 6.6 Export price–volume relationship

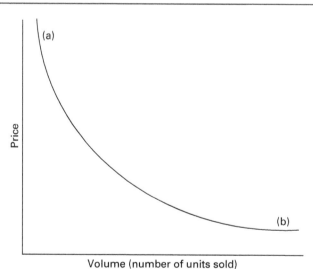

Volume (number of units sold)

a) The highest price will generate the lowest volume sales
b) The lowest price generates the highest volume sales

FIGURE 6.7   The reliable range of the price–volume curve

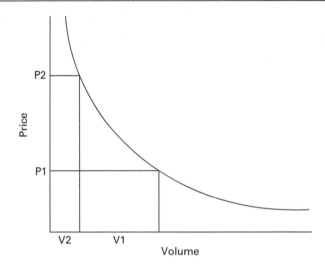

To operate successfully, the exporter must have a very clear understanding of all business costs, the margins necessary to achieve profit targets and the price–volume relationships available in each market.

Differential pricing

A range of different prices for different markets can lead to a number of practical problems in addition to the obvious one of a customer finding out that other buyers are obtaining the same products at lower prices. Specifically these are:

Parallel exports. This is a situation in which an exporter finds that exported products, sold at prices lower than, for example, their home sales price, actually find their way back into the home market and undercut their own home sales. This is a major problem with consumer products in general and branded products in particular but can affect any goods. The only way to control such movement of goods is to tie up the overseas buyer in contractual obligations that preclude re-exports or sales outside their own country. Appointing them as sole distributors may well be the only way to agree such a restriction. There is also, of course, the final censure: refusal to supply goods.

Anti-dumping legislation. A consequence of the situation described above may also be the accusation that the exporter is dumping products. The definition of dumping is quite specific; it is not to do with excess production or selling below cost but, specifically, if the export price is lower than the home price of a product (the current domestic value), then the exporter is dumping. This means that most exporters are dumping somewhere and some are dumping everywhere. In practice, while legislation exists, many countries do not use it extensively or even at all. The exceptions to this are the developed economies such as the EU and the USA. Where an exporter is building a significant market share, then an accusation of dumping can certainly slow down growth and may, if sustained, lead to an anti-dumping duty, which can price the product out of the market.

Promotion

All goods need promotion in order to sell. The type and extent depend on the products themselves, sales outlets, distribution channels and the end user. We must remember that home sales are to broadly similar users. Overseas markets present a far greater range of situations and require a clear policy of *differentiation* in all aspects of the marketing mix.

Most exporters are able to manage some aspects of promotional mix, such as personal selling or exhibitions, but for more specialized activities it is important to bring in specialist help. The complexity of the promotional mix can be simplified by identifying the four categories of promotional activity:

- advertising: any paid form of non-personal presentation and promotion of ideas, goods or services by an identified sponsor (media options: press, TV, radio, cinema, outdoor);
- publicity: non-personal and unpaid publication or broadcast;
- personal selling: oral presentation in conversation with one or more prospective purchasers for the purpose of making sales;
- sales promotion: those marketing activities, other than advertising, publicity and personal calling, that stimulate consumer purchasing and dealer effectiveness.

Objectives

It is important that some thought is given to the purpose of any promotional activities other than the obvious one of selling more goods or services. These objectives could include the following needs:

- to create awareness and knowledge of our goods;
- to establish a company image or brand name;
- to stimulate an interest and then a preference for our product.

Promotion budget

Since promotion involves expenditure, it is important to determine how much is to be spent. This can be done in two basic ways. The most common method is to allow a percentage in the selling price to cover promotional costs. See Table 6.3 for an example.

TABLE 6.3 Promotion budget

	$ per unit
Cost of raw materials	16
Direct costs	8
Indirect costs/overheads	18
Profit	12
Selling price	54
Promotion @ 10% of selling price	6 (ie 11.11% mark-up)
Final selling price	60

The advantages are that money spent does not affect profits, and the more units sold, the more money is available for promotion.

The disadvantage is that substantial sales have to be made before money is available. Ideally promotion should generate sales, not vice versa. This problem can be overcome by investing income at an early stage – based on sales forecasts rather than actual sales. This approach is sometimes referred to as an *investment budget* approach.

Also, there is an automatic increase in the promotional spend as sales increase, when in fact it might be more logical for the spend to reduce as the product becomes established in a market.

It should be noted that it would not be unusual for the local agent or distributor, if applicable, to make some contribution to promotional activities that will support their work in the territory. There is no harm in asking and ideally the company's agency agreement includes a clause formalizing such an arrangement (see Table 6.4).

TABLE 6.4 Promotion budget with agent's contribution

Sales forecast	$200,000
Promotion budget @ 5%	$10,000
Agent's contribution	$5,000
Promotion budget	$15,000

The alternative task method

The company decides the specific objective, eg a percentage increase in sales, and then attempts to calculate how much would need to be spent to achieve that objective. This is obviously more difficult to do, at least with any degree of accuracy, but it does mean that a clear relationship is established between the cost of promotion and the specific benefits. It may be that some experience needs to be established in particular markets before such a process achieves any degree of accuracy.

Only as a very general rule, the percentages spent on promotion would vary along the following lines:

- industrial/capital goods: 0.5% to 3%;
- consumer goods: 5% to 50%.

In the latter case it may be that a large part of the promotion budget is expended on the product's packaging, which should logically be perceived as part of the promotional costs.

Advertising

Press

Press media can be categorized into specific types:

- newspapers (local and national);
- magazines (general and specialized);
- trade publications.

In our home market, we often find regional divisions in the circulation of newspapers, and a political bias is common; but in overseas markets other factors can also distinguish one publication from another. Language, religion and race can often be more important, and local specialist advice is essential before choices are made regarding the location of advertisements. Similarly, magazines will often have a specific circulation. All publications should be able to supply quantitative information regarding their size and type of readership.

Trade publications are incredibly numerous, covering what might seem to be some very esoteric specialisms. The advantage is obviously that it is possible to hit the right type of buyer for your goods and it is possible to include technical details.

It is important to select the most appropriate outlet in line with cost, the object being to hit the maximum number of potential buyers at the minimum cost. In order to do this we must have a very clear idea of our end user in order to properly target all marketing activities, particularly promotion.

Television

Clearly, television represents a massive advance in mass communication media that is now being enhanced by the spread of electricity and increases in worldwide standards of living. It is, of course, expensive, but gives immediate impact and large coverage. However, it is difficult to be exact about the target market, although figures on audience composition are often available programme by programme. Therefore this medium tends to favour mass-market consumer goods rather than those with a more specialist market. Remember that commercial television is not always allowed overseas and the cost of the advertising slot may be much less than the cost of production.

Apart from the actual content of the ad, which requires professional advice and must consider the cultural mores of the market, we must also consider:

- running time;
- regional versus national;
- timing;
- colour or black and white;
- language;
- accents.

Radio

Television sells, radio reminds. There is invariably greater choice of outlets within radio and coverage of commercial stations has increased enormously over the last 20 years. The medium can be very useful in developing countries, particularly where there are high levels of illiteracy and areas of the population are isolated. The same rules apply as for TV but particular care should be taken with the voices used and especially the accents.

Remember that while commercial television and radio in the UK are based on the hire of a time slot, with advertisers having little influence on programme content, there are many other countries that follow the US model in which the advertisers actually sponsor the whole programme and thus have a far more direct control on content.

Cinema

TV did tend to reduce cinema attendance figures in developed countries but this trend is now reversing. However, in many developing markets, cinema can still be the main form of entertainment – or at least still attracts large audiences, eg Africa. There is still a provision by mobile cinemas of open-air shows, which can attract audiences of several thousands, and which incorporate short filmlets or slides. An advantage is that the shows can be localized rather than national.

Outdoor

Planning authorities may limit sites but they are usually associated with heavy concentrations of people, eg rail/bus stations. Be aware that hot climates may affect the life of billboard advertisements and it is not uncommon for a hand-painted hoarding to be used rather than paper posters. Their main purpose is to act as reminders and they do allow visual images to be used, which can be very effective. The organization of such advertisements will often be controlled by a local agent, in which case it is important to confirm that the posters do actually exist. Photographs can help but independent confirmation is preferable.

What all advertising is attempting to do is to generate AIDA:

Attention.

Interest.

Desire.

Action.

Advertising is distinctive because it is:

- public – which imparts legitimacy to the product;
- pervasive – repetitive and widespread;
- expressive – allows dramatization;
- impersonal – monologue, not dialogue.

Choosing advertising media

It is best to concentrate, as it is seldom possible to use all the media. We must:

- decide exactly the target audience and concentrate on the media that reach the greatest number at lowest cost;
- use the media constantly or not at all – repetition is essential;
- make sure that ads appear at the proper time;

- develop close working relationships between the campaign and sales staff, eg compel the distributor to build up stocks before the campaign begins;
- ensure that there is cooperation between promotion and sales production and dispatch.

Publicity

Some companies use professional public relations consultants or have a staff resource to prepare news stories and features. Without consultants' advice it is still possible in the UK to disseminate information overseas through the Central Office of Information and the BBC's external services. It is often necessary to create a newsworthy theme to generate widespread use. Press releases should be written not from the point of view of the company but from the point of view of the media that we hope will reproduce them. The less editing needed, the more likely they are to be used.

Newsworthy items are distinctive because they:

- have high veracity – accepted as (more) authentic than if sponsored by the seller;
- are off guard – hit those who otherwise avoid ads and salesmen;
- have dramatization – like advertising.

Always be careful with translations. Many mistakes originate from simple errors in the translation of advertising copy from one language to another. The Parker leak-proof fountain pen that prevented the embarrassment of ink-stained shirts found a totally new market when embarrassment was translated, in Spanish, as 'embarazada', which actually means 'pregnant'. Parker had apparently produced a new form of contraceptive...

Almost apocryphal, but true, is the case of the company who manufactured depilatory creams. They planned an expensive magazine promotion in the Middle East that involved the use of an advertisement that had been successful in a number of other areas. This involved two colour photographs depicting a pair of shapely legs before and after the application of the cream. The process was fluently described in the advertising copy below the illustrations.

This company was not caught out by a problem with the Arabic translation, because they had learnt that the only safe way to translate from one language to another is to have one translator handle the English to Arabic, and another then translate the Arabic back into English. In this way, any problems in interpretation are usually revealed. The problem in this case was not the quality of the Arabic but that they had not considered the fact that Arabic reads from right to left, and they had not reversed the photographs. They seemed to be promoting something that made hair grow.

As a final example, even the largest of companies can get caught in the language trap. Coca-Cola's famous global message that 'Coke gives life' was variously translated as 'Coke raises the dead' and 'Coke brings your ancestors back from the grave'.

Personal selling

Successful face-to-face selling in overseas markets requires a clear perception of the needs of the customer and an adaptation to the wide-ranging political, legal, economic, technical and cultural factors that will differ from one market to another. Face-to-face selling is distinctive because it involves:

- personal confrontation: immediate, interactive, flexible;
- cultivation: relationships may develop;
- response: buyer may feel under some obligation – greater need to attend and respond.

The selling concept

Wrong: the high-pressure approach (as in Figure 6.8). Right: the natural sales approach (as in Figure 6.9).

FIGURE 6.8　The high-pressure approach

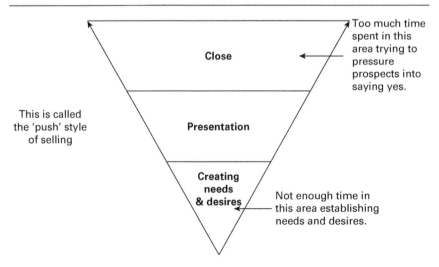

FIGURE 6.9   The natural sales approach

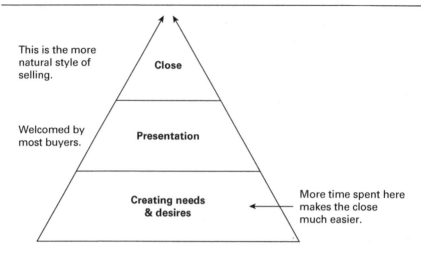

The sales interview

The bad salesperson sells product features. The better salesperson sells product benefits. The best salesperson satisfies needs.

Preparation for a sales interview

Be clear about your objectives, eg information gathering, information giving, action generating.

Once you have determined your objectives, you must ascertain the background information that you will require before the meeting can take place.

It will include the following:

- The prospect company:
    - possible requirements;
    - history of relationships between them and your company;
    - existing company and competitive product usage.
- The person:
    - their function and responsibilities;
    - their likely concerns and attitudes.
- Your company:
    - what are you able to commit to;
    - do you have sufficient product knowledge?
    - do you have sufficient authority?

Structure of a sales interview

Be clear in your own mind how you would like the meeting to go. What topics do you want to discuss, and in what order? When you are selling, remember the old communications maxim: Tell them what you are going to tell them. Tell them. Tell them what you have told them. (This is also a good maxim for any type of presentation.)

Sample structure of a sales interview: first visit

- Opening:
  - social: breaks the ice;
  - business: why you are there, present agenda;
  - check how much time is available.
- Create interest:
  - give them a reason to talk to you;
  - give a quick overview of your role.
- Explore needs:
  - get them talking;
  - qualify their requirement and your capability;
  - put them into their 'comfort zone'.
- Present your products:
  - total offering;
  - relate to their requirements;
  - *benefits* of using your company's products, not its *features*.
- Summary:
  - summarize what has been discussed and agreed;
  - highlight major reasons for using your company;
  - confirm next action.

As you depart, find a closing phrase that indicates how much you are looking forward to working with them.

Sample structure of a sales interview: further visits

For subsequent meetings the structure will vary depending on your objectives. As a guide, you should still follow the above rules for the opening and summary sections of the meeting and then remember the following sequence:

- past;
- present;
- future.

This will ensure that any suggestions for the future are clearly related to current and previous ways of working.

During the meeting

Spend more time questioning and listening than you do talking about yourself and your products. Take notes. It helps you to remember what was said and demonstrates interest in what your prospect is saying.

Use brochures to illustrate the points that you are making and, where appropriate, write comments on the brochure to personalize it to your prospect. However, remember to leave a spare copy for your prospect to pass to other people.

Take every opportunity to create or use visual aids.

Follow up

Always document *your* understanding of what has been agreed. Every meeting should be followed up in writing.

The objectives are to demonstrate your understanding of their present needs, act as a reminder of the agreed actions, assist in shutting out other suppliers and provide your prospect with as much justification as is necessary to assist them in presenting a persuasive argument within their own organization.

If the sale involves a series of meetings, the combined letters will form the basis of the persuasive argument within your offer document.

Handling objections

Question: to clarify understanding and regain control.

Answer: if true, agree, put into perspective, outweigh with other benefits, compensate with alternatives.

If untrue, you must protect your prospect's ego, explain the true picture, accept that you may have to offer proof, apologize for the misunderstanding.

If speculative, agree with the possibility, diminish probability.

Check, to confirm that they are happy with your answer.

Closing the sale

The request for the order should follow naturally. If you do not ask, you do not get!

Examples of closing questions:

Will you go ahead now?

Is there a reason for you not going ahead?

Would you like the agreement to start at the end of the month?

Suppose we were able to...? Would you go ahead then?

Is it that you don't want...?

You have agreed that you like... Should we start at the end of the month?

Nobody ever lost an order because they asked for it. Many people have lost orders because they did not ask for them!
Nobody will buy from you when they:

- do not understand *what* they are buying;
- do not understand *why* they are buying it;
- do not *want* the benefits;
- do not *trust* you to deliver the benefits.

Literature

It is important not to cut costs in this area, as the whole company may often be judged purely on the appearance of its literature. In overseas markets literature is often the first contact and may need to contain a range of relevant information. Consider:

- make-up: loose-leafed (to allow the replacement of pages), colour or black and white, paper quality, illustrations (often the greatest cost);
- inclusions: type and number of illustrations, company information, technical information, price lists, samples;
- language(s): which one(s), all in one brochure or separate brochures (other languages may require more copy space).

As literature can often be very expensive it is necessary to avoid wastage as much as possible. Ways to do this include making up selective brochures for individual enquirers, maximizing accuracy and topicality of the mailing lists used, mailshots with leaflets rather than full catalogues, ensuring that an agent uses them selectively, and even attempting to have them returned for reuse.
Where direct mailshots are to be used, consider:

- number of shots: it is often necessary to repeat with modified materials;
- accuracy of mailing lists: these can be derived from your own research (see sources of information earlier) or purchased from specialist organizations;
- recording systems: log all responses, follow up all replies with relevant copy;
- catching attention: without immediate impact the material is straight in the bin;
- generate an interest: use appropriate language and approach.

We must accept that the maximum direct response we are likely to receive may be as low as 10 per cent.

Sales promotion

This includes a wide variety of activities, other than advertising, publicity and personal selling, which have a particular application in overseas markets. These include, for example, exhibitions, trade fairs and displays, demonstrations, offers and merchandising (point-of-sale promotion).

How to exhibit

1 Selection of exhibition:
   - location: demand within the market, buyers from other markets;
   - content: specific trade sector and general fairs;
   - timing: in line with our marketing plans and budget; availability; production capacity;
   - cost: is there a better way to tap into customers' budget availability?
   - reputation: record of success, average attendance; our competitors present?
2 Schedule of events:
   - information-collecting exercise on market, customers, competition, etc;
   - obtain plans of hall (or visit if possible), deciding siting of stand (if we have a choice) and size;
   - finalize decisions regarding design of stand; consider: availability of electricity, water, lifting equipment; plans may need sending to organizers; information to our local agent; often beneficial to show products actually working;
   - approximately eight weeks before, invite all potential customers to stand;
   - decide staff; consider: language; range of skills required (sales, technical); need a team or can two suffice?
   - ensure stand materials are shipped in good time to arrive, and that no damage is evident on arrival;
   - staff arrive, ideally with enough time to acclimatize and also to manage: stand adjustments; literature and samples available (shipped with stand units); replacement equipment (if possible); incidentals, eg spare bulbs, refreshments, handouts, order forms, etc;

- day before: final check on working modals, incidentals, etc; maybe contacts with customers to ensure attendance, finalize attendance rotas;
- during exhibition make sure every visitor gets attention; maintain detailed contact records.

Some attempt must be made to collect and measure results of participation to facilitate a subsequent cost–benefit analysis.

It may be the case that all other promotional activities are linked to the timing of the exhibition, as this is the only activity over which we have little timing control . Other activities, such as mailshots, advertising, merchandising activities, personal visits, etc, must all be built around the exhibition.

07
Distribution

The final, and many would say most important, of the 4 Ps is the decision on the channels of distribution to be used. The fact is that most exporters feel the need, and often the necessity, to have intermediaries representing their interest and based in their overseas markets.

Consider what are the options:

- direct: which means direct to the end user;
- commission agent: sometimes referred to as broker;
- distributor: sometimes referred to as wholesalers, stockists, dealers, etc;
- retailer;
- local company: in many forms, eg sales office, stockist, assembly, manufacture;
- licence/franchise.

Their basic functions are described in the sections that follow.

Agent

Represents a number of principals for specific products in a specific territory. They are responsible for selling, promotion, order getting, debt collection, problem solving, etc; but they do not normally handle goods. They receive a commission payment on sales in that territory (usually between 5 and 10 per cent).

The commission may be:

- a standard rate for all sales;
- different rates for orders received through the agent and those received direct;
- different rates for different products;
- different rates for different customers;
- sliding scale based on order value or total turnover.

Agent's commission calculation

Common mistakes that many exporters make are to do with:

- The price basis on which commission is paid. We should pay commission only on the EXW (Ex-works) value of the goods. There is no justification for an agent to receive commission on the ancillary or third-party costs that may be included in an export price, eg freight, insurance, documentation. You are making no profit on them (or shouldn't be!) so why should they?

- The actual calculation of the commission amount. Hard as it might be to believe, many exporters do not calculate the commission that they pay to their agents correctly.

Let's look at the wrong way (with simple numbers).

Assume an agent is receiving 10 per cent commission on the EXW value of the goods and this is, say, $100 per unit, then add on the agent's commission at $10; the selling price to the buyer is $110 per unit.

Now assume the buyer pays on time (use your imagination!) and at the end of the month we pay our agent their commission, 10 per cent of the EXW selling price of $110, ie $11.

We have added on a cost of $10 per unit but are paying a commission of $11 per unit.

Multiply that by dozens of orders and thousands of units and the exporter is losing a significant amount of money.

So how do we do it right?

The mistake is to confuse the *mark-up* (added on to the basic EXW value) and the *margin* (percentage of the gross selling price that is paid to the agent).

The solution is this:

EXW value: $100 per unit;

mark-up for the agent's commission at 11.11 per cent: $11.11;

selling price to the buyer: $111.11 per unit;

we pay our agent 10 per cent of the EXW selling price of $111.11: $11.11.

The fact is that the mark-up has to be larger than the margin.

In round numbers:

To pay 5 per cent commission, add on 5.26 per cent (call it 5.5 per cent).

To pay 7.5 per cent commission, add on 8.11 per cent (call it 8.5 per cent).

To pay 10 per cent commission, add on 11.11 per cent (call it 11.5 per cent).

Distributor

Purchases goods from the manufacturer at a discounted price and resells into the specified territory at a profit.

Can be:

- sole distributor: no other distributors will be appointed in the territory but the manufacturer may also deal direct with buyers;
- exclusive distributor: no other distributors appointed and the manufacturer will not deal direct.

In addition to all the duties of the agent, distributors may also hold stock of finished goods, parts, components and repair materials and may provide pre- and after-sales service, maintenance, repair, etc.

Local company

Direct investment in the overseas market, possibly with other organizations (particularly local nationals) in the form of a joint venture, or as an independent project.

May be anything from a simple sales office to a stock holder to an assembly resource to a full-scale manufacturing unit.

Licence/franchise

Sale of 'intellectual property' such as know-how, patents, trade names or marks or copyright, in return for disclosure fees and royalties.

Selection of intermediaries

There are a multitude of factors to be taken into consideration in selecting intermediaries. In Table 7.1, a draft checklist is detailed to help you ensure that no important step in the selection process is omitted.

Choosing the method

All strategic decisions made in business, including the selection of the method of distribution, are based on three criteria:

TABLE 7.1 Checklist for selection of intermediaries

	✔
1. Ensure that the method chosen is suitable	
2. Draw up a clear job specification	
3. Conduct desk research to produce a long list of possibles	
4. Selection criteria	
a) Products currently handled	
b) Level of product knowledge	
c) Level of market knowledge	
d) Business acumen	
e) Reputation	
f) Marketing expertise	
g) Sales/promotional expertise	
h) Financial standing	
i) Facilities	
5. Compile short list and conduct further research if necessary	
6. Personal visit	
7. Appoint (trial period, eg 12 months?), with written agreement	

Product:

- consumer or industrial
- manufacturing patterns: one or multiple sources of manufacture;
- purchasing patterns: order values, product quality;
- product needs: lead time expectations, pre-sales service (advice, design, etc), installation, after-sales service, customer induction/ training, repair/replacement, specialized storage, security.

Market:

- physical distribution, delivery methods;
- activities of competition;
- availability;
- regulations, custom and practice;

- consumer practices;
- special arrangements (cartels?);
- economic/political stability.

Company:

- managerial resources and experience;
- financial resources;
- strategic organization: who makes the decisions?
- company policy: maintain brand name, licensing, etc;
- company image;
- existing arrangements.

There are also the overall considerations that the channel choice has to:

- fit into the overall marketing plan;
- operate within the desired time scales;
- allow freedom for future developments.

Job specification

It is essential that a clear picture of the role to be filled is decided and *then* to find the person or organization that 'fits the bill'. We do not appoint an intermediary and then see what they can do for us.

This is particularly the case if we are using third parties to research the market. Therefore, a pre-search requisite is the drafting of a job specification, as in Box 7.1.

Box 7.1 Draft job specification

A commission agent/distributor is sought in .... to act as a sole representative for the promotion and sale of the principal's products.

The intermediary will be required to:

- actively promote the principal's name and products;
- identify and actively pursue prospective customers;
- arrange and conduct personal sales interviews with such customers;
- negotiate sales orders with prospective customers;
- follow up all new and established contacts on a regular basis;

- manage a sales force of sufficient size and capabilities to adequately cover the territory;

- liaise between the principal and buyers with regard to orders, specifications, deliveries, payments, complaints and any other issues pertaining to the development of the principal's business in the territory.

Optionally:

- hold agreed levels of stock in the territory;

- provide agreed pre- and after-sales services;

- install, maintain, repair or replace all products in line with the principal's warranties;

- train new users where applicable;

- provide adequate showroom/demonstration facilities;

- make direct deliveries to buyers' premises.

The appropriate candidate would be required to meet the following criteria:

1 Product knowledge
   - a level of technical knowledge in ....;
   - specific knowledge of .... and .... industries;
   - appropriate qualifications and/or experience;
   - ability to absorb and understand the capabilities of the principal to produce;
   - ability to negotiate with technical specifiers.

2 Current principals
   - small number of current principals;
   - with compatible product ranges;
   - reputable principals;
   - sufficient length of representation;
   - no representation with directly competitive suppliers.

3 Market knowledge
   - general knowledge of the commercial practices of the market;
   - relevant linguistic abilities, both conversational and technical;
   - general knowledge of industrial infrastructures.

4 Sector knowledge
   - specific knowledge of practices in the targeted sectors;
   - specific knowledge of the main end users;
   - broad knowledge of competitors and their activities;
   - relevant personal contacts.

5   Facilities
   - adequate office premises and administrative systems;
   - appropriate location(s);
   - secretarial support;
   - installation and after-sales service;
   - e-mail capabilities;
   - transport;
   - storage.

6   Financial standing
   - corporate history;
   - adequate funds and capital base;
   - appropriate trading history.

7   Management expertise
   - appropriate management experience;
   - appropriate sales and marketing experience;
   - appropriate sales and marketing qualifications;
   - experience in appropriate exhibitions, presentations and other promotional activities.

8   Personal qualities
   - reputation in the industry;
   - willingness to develop technical knowledge;
   - willingness to provide market information;
   - keenness to develop greater market share;
   - straightforward and honest;
   - flexible and adaptable.

Sources of information

- UKTI (see Chapter 5).
- Databases and bibliographic.
- Trade associations.
- Marketing consultants.
- Chambers of Commerce (Joint Chambers).
- Foreign embassies.
- Customer's recommendation.

- Other exporter's recommendation.
- Direct approaches from overseas.

Selection criteria

- Products currently handled: compatible not competitive; reputation of current range; number of principals.
- Level of product knowledge: technical knowledge; staff qualifications; training facilities.
- Level of market knowledge: buyers, competition, conditions; personal contacts.
- Business acumen.
- Reputation.
- Financial standing: capital; balance sheet; trading history.
- Promotional expertise.
- Facilities: warehousing; showrooms; transport; assembly, manufacture.

Produce short list

Personal interview

- To confirm researched information, eg facilities, market knowledge, product knowledge.
- To assess personal qualities, eg keenness, selling ability, honesty, integrity, business acumen, sense of humour.

It is only at this stage that subjective criteria should apply.

In view of the protection that many agents and distributors may receive in law (particularly in the European Union), great care must be taken in their appointment.

In particular it is advisable to include measurable indicators of perform-ance, eg sales targets, and include a fixed duration for the agreement.

Motivation

One of the major problems for many exporters is motivation. You want to en-sure that your products receive a fair share of the agent's attention – preferably more. How can this be achieved?

The vital point is to accept that what motivates the agent is different, sometimes drastically, from what motivates you, the principal, as Table 7.2 illustrates.

TABLE 7.2 Motivations of principal and agent

Your needs	Agent/distributor needs
Volume/revenue	Profit
Small number of high market shares	Large number of small market shares
Small number of principals	Large number of principals
Brand awareness	Risk spreading
Ability to expand and develop	Security of tenure
Investment in development	Cost control
Commitment to you	Commitment to them

The fact is that the needs of the two parties involved in this arrangement are almost diametrically opposed.

The agent/distributor wants to make money by taking easy business for a large number of principals and keeping costs low. The principal wants a committed agent investing time and effort in achieving high market shares.

The trick to motivation is to address their needs and not your own. The only real way to do this is by providing them with added value through:

- staff training: not just on your company's products but including general management, administration, marketing, sales techniques, IT;
- management systems: develop their recording systems, accounting, cost controls, stock controls, profit management;
- resources updates: actual provision of hardware and software systems (at no cost to them);
- personnel: addressing their need for security, harmony, esteem and acceptance through regular contact, social relations and goodwill;
- and, of course, conspicuously honouring all your duties under the agreement.

Setting up a local company

A local company can be set up in a variety of forms:

Sales office: anything from one person working from home to a fully staffed sales department;

Stockist: in effect a wholly owned local distributor (which may still stock and sell compatible products);

Assembly: import of components and subassemblies to be assembled for the local market and possibly for export;

Manufacture: a full manufacturing facility using local or imported materials and labour, producing goods for the local market and export (the origins of the multinational company).

This can be done with a variety of ownership possibilities:

Wholly owned subsidiary;

Joint venture: invariably with a local national individual or company (in some countries a non-national can own no more than 49 per cent of the equity of a company).

The regulations governing the establishment of local companies vary from market to market. There are often limitations on the percentage of foreign ownership, the nationality of employees and the transfer (repatriation) of profits. They may be companies set up from scratch or by taking over national companies.

Why an exporter might set up a local company

- Sales volume too great for an agent/distributor to handle.
- Tariff barriers in the importer's country.
- Lower costs, eg labour, raw materials, transport.
- Springboard for local and surrounding markets.
- Restrictive purchasing policies in overseas market.
- Need for quality after-sales service.
- Releases production capacity.

Some markets actively encourage foreign investment, eg Eastern Europe, but exporters must be aware of any restrictions and of the potential danger of appropriation of foreign assets.

Setting up licensing

The licensing of 'intellectual property' includes one or more of:

- patents (design or process);
- trade and brand names;
- copyright;
- or simply know-how.

These will allow an overseas company to manufacture goods for sale in the local market.

Licensing agreements often involve 'disclosure payments' as lump sums following the provision of information and then regular payments of a share of the licensee's profits (known as 'royalties') during the period of the agreement (typically 10 years plus).

Why licences are granted

When appointing licensees the same reasons apply as for the formation of local companies plus:

- More control of selling operation (prevents cheap copies).
- Standard company policy, eg Coca-Cola.
- Royalties are often immune from exchange/transfer control.
- Local companies will develop eventually, anyway. Possibly by securing a licence from another licensor.

Licensing is actively encouraged by many developing countries, as their governments will have more control of the licensee than of a foreign-owned subsidiary – but the investment needed can be a problem.

An alternative arrangement may be part-ownership of the licensee, similar to a joint venture, where the exporter also finances the setting up of the licensee.

Conclusion

The selection of the correct marketing mix for a particular market is obviously not a simple thing for the average exporter. It requires quality research, an understanding of the options – and a little experience would not go amiss. But any planning is better than none and every company, including small ones, will benefit from any research and planning it is able to do, because the more a seller is able to identify and react to market demand, the more successful they will be.

Earlier we introduced the concept of customer orientation, emphasizing its importance in dynamic and competitive markets. This concept is important in home markets but becomes essential when the exporter is faced with the almost infinite variety of situations encountered in overseas markets. The more volatile the market, the more important it becomes for the seller to adapt and accommodate. The exporter that ventures into foreign markets thinking that these are simply extensions of their home market will invariably face a rude awakening.

PART THREE
The legal environment

08
An overview of UK law

The making of law

Law in the UK today is made by Acts of Parliament. These Acts must be passed by the House of Commons, the House of Lords, and finally signed by the Queen. (In practice, the Queen's seal is affixed for her by a committee and assent is never withheld.) Lawyers call Acts of Parliament 'statutes'.

One feature of English law that distinguishes it from the continental system is that, in addition to legislation passed by Parliament, the law is made and developed by the decisions of the courts. Court decisions not only establish the legal position between the parties to a legal dispute before the court, known as 'litigants', but also establish the law for the future by constituting 'precedents' that will be followed by judges in future cases. Nevertheless, as the highest authority in the land, Parliament can pass an Act to overrule a case if it so chooses.

The incidence of European Union law

European law now applies in the UK without being adopted by an Act of Parliament, following the European Communities Act 1972 5.2(1). The UK courts are bound to give effect to European law.

Occasionally, due to an oversight of Parliament, a statute is inconsistent with EU law, in which case the UK courts must follow EU law. On occasion, where Parliament has intended to pass a law inconsistent with EU law, the courts should uphold the statute.

Hierarchy of precedents

Precedent evolves as a result of the hierarchy of the courts, defined in Table 8.1, and efficient and accurate law reporting.

TABLE 8.1 Hierarchy of precedents

European Court of Justice	Binds all courts on points of EU law
House of Lords	Binds courts below but not itself
Court of Appeal Civil Division	Binds courts below and itself (unless an error of law is made)
High Court	Binds courts below but not itself
County Court	Does not bind any court

Over the centuries, precedent has allowed a uniform law to be moulded; the developing concept is referred to as *stare decisis* (which means 'let the decision stand'). Binding and persuasive precedent is very important to the English legal system and allows a degree of certainty and fairness. Since a higher court has greater jurisdiction than a lower court within the hierarchy, its decisions will be more authoritative in the interpretation of the law and its application to the facts of a dispute.

It follows that the decision of a higher court, and the reason or reasons for that decision (*ratio decidendi*), will be binding on a later hearing of a court lower in the hierarchy when it is asked to decide a case on similar facts. The reasons for deciding are the element of the judgement that is most important for the system of binding precedent.

However, decisions of courts lower in the hierarchy can be of only persuasive authority for higher courts. In the course of giving judgement, a judge may make comments not directly relevant to the dispute in question, which are described as *obiter dicta*. Such statements can only ever form persuasive precedent, no matter what the place in the hierarchy of the court in which they were made.

The application of higher court precedents is not entirely rigid. Judges will not always follow faithfully all decisions of the courts. They retain some discretion to develop the law, depending upon the individual circumstances of any particular case. In fact, when giving 'interpretations of the law', judges often change the law in very radical ways. A judge may have to decide what Parliament intended the law to be when it used certain words in a statute, and that interpretation will bind inferior courts as to the their meaning. Judges also have to apply or extend the law in cases that they adjudicate by deciding what exactly was decided in superior courts in similar past cases.

Sources of law

The main sources of law are therefore statutes and decided cases based on precedents. However, there are three further sources of law:

Delegated legislation

Parliament often passes an Act that is a general framework, giving government ministers or other bodies the power to fill in the details by making 'rules', 'orders', 'statutory instruments' or 'orders in Council', which are technically made by the Queen, although in practice made by the government.

Trade custom

A further source of law, of particular importance to the exporter, is how things are done in a particular trade, generally defined as 'trade custom'. Somewhat surprisingly, such practices can be adopted into law through common usage and frequently supersede the general rule of law in that trade. As an example, no one in their right mind would normally suggest that an insurance broker is responsible for the unpaid premiums of their clients, but by trade custom a marine insurance broker is held responsible.

EU law

When the UK joined the EU in 1973 it agreed to accept the European Communities Act 1972 and be bound by EC law, which would override any conflicting national law and be applied by the UK courts.

EU law is made by the European Commission, the Council of Ministers and the European Court of Justice. The legislative bodies, the Commission and the Council, make Regulations, which pass directly into the national law of member states, and issue Directives, which are binding on member states but leave each member state with a choice about the method used to achieve the directed result. A transitional period is allowed.

In summary, EU law takes the following four forms:

Treaties

Treaties are binding on member states and EU institutions. In certain circumstances, Treaties may create rights for individuals, which may be enforceable in national courts.

Regulations
Also binding on all member states without requiring any
    implementation or adoption by national parliaments, regulations
    apply directly and prevail over the national laws. They can also
    create rights enforceable by individuals in national courts.

Directives
These are binding but leave a member state a choice of the method by
    which the result required by the directive must be achieved. In the
    UK the alternative methods are an Act of Parliament or delegated
    legislation. A directive can also create rights for individuals
    enforceable in national courts.

Decisions of the European Court of Justice of the Communities
Such decisions are binding in their entirety on the highest courts in
    member states, the House of Lords in the case of the UK. Decisions
    are also binding on individuals or companies.

The Commission, among other public and private organizations (and even
citizens of EU states), can initiate proceedings against a member state if it
believes that steps taken to implement regulations and directives do not
achieve the desired results.

Types of law

Public law

By definition, public law is that law administered by and for the benefit of
the general public. The two most important branches are constitutional law
and criminal law.

Constitutional law is the law dealing with Parliament, government, elec-
tions to Parliament and the relationship between the individual and the state
or the country in which the individual lives.

Criminal law comprises the rules that tell us what we must not do.
Breaking these rules entails arrest, prosecution and punishment.

For the purposes of this handbook, the details of constitutional law and
criminal law have little relevance. Other branches of public law include
administrative law, which stems from the need for government to appoint
officials to administer various activities, and community law, which is
imposed by the European Union to achieve its aims. The aspects of community law that are relevant to international trade, notably competition law
and the law of agency, are dealt with in this chapter.

Private law

Otherwise called 'civil law', private law derives its name from the private decision of the individual whether or not to sue another. The outcome of a claim for breach of contract does not concern the nation as a whole, although it may provide a precedent for others in similar contractual circumstances.

Civil or private law is a wider area of law than public law and encompasses the following branches:

The law of contract
Chapter 9 discusses the law of contract and contractual disputes in some detail. The actual law of contract deals with claims by people for loss they have suffered as a result of breach of contract, which is the main area for disputes in international trade.

There is a popular misconception that a contract has to be written to have binding force. In practice, most everyday contracts are made verbally, eg when buying a train ticket or ordering a meal in a restaurant.

The law of tort
Derived from the French word meaning 'wrong', a tort is a wrong for which the wrongdoer can be sued for damages. The following are the main categories of tort:

– Negligence
Carelessness leading to injury. Motoring accidents caused by negligence are a common example.

– Trespass
Trespass generally means going on someone else's property without permission. More specifically, trespass to goods means damaging someone else's goods, and trespass to the person gives rise to claims for assault.

– Defamation
Saying things about someone else that are untrue and lower their reputation constitutes defamation. Defamation in writing is classified as 'libel' and often results in the award of damages.

– Nuisance
The tort of nuisance refers to the disturbance of a neighbour's enjoyment of and peace in their home.

Consumer credit and sale of goods
Personal transactions in goods or services on credit are covered by a range of legislation that gives the individual very considerable rights. Sale of goods law deals with the rights of consumers who buy defective goods and many other questions connected with sale of goods. See Chapter 10.

Agency law

Agents are people appointed by another to make contracts for them.
Agency law applicable to the use of agents in international trade is
dealt with in Chapter 12.

Other branches of private law that are not relevant to this book include:
the law of trusts, land law, law of landlord and tenant, law of succession and
family law.

09
The law of contract

Contract essentials

In essence a contract is an agreement between two or more people that is intended to have the force of law. It can be made in any of the following ways:

In writing. Some contracts, such as hire purchase agreements, must be in writing. Commercially, contracts involving large sums of money should be written, if only for the sake of clarity. Most large export transactions are the subject of a written contract.

Orally. The method for conducting everyday transactions such as buying food and transport services.

By conduct. Boarding a bus or buying goods from a vending machine are simple examples of contract by conduct.

By any combination of the above.

Essential ingredients

Certain ingredients are essential for there to be a valid contract. There must be an *offer* and *acceptance* that match. A verbal offer at a price of, say, £10 followed by an acceptance at £9 clearly does not signify an agreement between the parties. The response constitutes a *counter offer* and a rejection of the original offer, which is thereby terminated. An acceptance must exactly fit the offer and any attempt to accept on new terms amounts to a rejection of the original offer accompanied by a counter offer.

There must be *consideration* – something in return. No promise for which consideration in return is not given can be enforced in law. The only exception to this general rule is if a special legal document, called a *deed*, is drawn up.

Each party must have *capacity to contract* – in other words, the right to enter into legally binding contracts. Making a contract without capacity means that it cannot be enforced against the counter party. It does not mean that it is an offence or in any way illegal for them to make a contract.

The parties must be *ad idem*, which means that they must be making the same contract. Essentially the buyer and seller in a transaction must be intending to deal in the same product or service at the same price and on the same terms and conditions.

True consent: there must be an intention by both parties to create legal relations and for the contract to have the force of law. In commercial situations it is assumed that there is such an intention but an inclusion in the documentation of 'binding in honour only' would likely make the contract void.

There must be true *agreement* to the contract, which means an absence of the following:

- operative mistake;
- duress;
- misrepresentation;
- undue influence.

Illegality

The law may refuse to give effect to a contract on the grounds that it involves the execution of a legal wrong: a crime, a tort or a breach of contract. A statute may make the formation of certain kinds of contracts illegal.

Contracts contrary to public policy

Certain contracts, including those which are void for illegality, are regarded as injurious to society and therefore void. Contracts that restrain trade are an important category unless they can be regarded as reasonable between the parties or as regards the public interest when they were made. Figure 9.1 demonstrates the elements that create a simple contract.

FIGURE 9.1   Elements of a simple contract

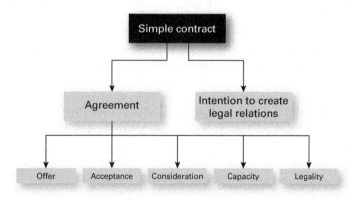

Breach of contract

The remedies for a breach of contract may be categorized as legal remedies and equitable remedies with the following sub-classifications.

Legal remedies

Termination   Where a breach of an important term of a contract has occurred, the innocent party may be entitled to bring the contract to an end, as well as to claim damages. The contract will then be terminated from the date of the breach and the parties will not have been bound by the contracts from that day forward.

Following termination, the innocent party cannot claim specific performance or an injunction.

Rescission and damages for misrepresentation   Effectively, rescission means cancelling the contract. After rescission for misrepresentation the contract is regarded as having been void from the beginning and the innocent party can be awarded damages for misrepresentation, which are assessed differently from damages for breach of contract.

Action for an agreed sum   An action for the price of goods or services sold when the purchaser does not pay is described as an action for an agreed sum. It is not an action for damages and is only available if the contract subsists. One cannot terminate for breach or rescind for misrepresentation and then sue for price.

Equitable remedies

Specific performance   In certain very limited circumstances where damages would not be enough to compensate the injured party, the court may award an order against the party in breach of a contract to carry it out.

Injunction   An injunction is a court order restraining a defendant from carrying out an act in breach of the contract.

Commercial considerations

Very often it is in the interests of a company that is a seller not to sue the buyer, because they are a regular customer. Litigation will have the inevitable consequence that goodwill will be lost and all future orders from the customer will cease. The use of legal remedies should be looked upon as a last resort where the prospects for future profitable business are dim.

Offer and acceptance

As already identified, the essential equation behind every contract is:

Offer + acceptance = contract

The realities behind each variable in the equation need to be spelt out.
    An offer must be distinguished from the following:

- a declaration of intention;
- a supply of information;
- an invitation to treat.

In the case of the last, goods displayed in shop windows with price tags attached are held to be invitations for offers, not offers themselves. Advertisements are also usually invitations to treat rather than offers.
    An offer must be communicated. This means that the other party must know of its existence. An offer can lapse. It can end after a certain time:

- by the death of either party before acceptance;
- by non-acceptance within any stated time;
- by non-acceptance within a reasonable time if no time is stated. (The definition of 'reasonable' depends on the facts of each individual case.)

An offer can be rejected directly or indirectly (by making a counter offer). An offer can be revoked (ie withdrawn) any time before it is accepted. If sent by post, revocation takes effect when the notification arrives.
    The requirements for a valid acceptance are similarly well defined. Acceptance must be unqualified. It must correspond exactly with the offer. (A counter offer at the same price but in instalments does not qualify as acceptance when the original offer was for 'cash'.)
    Acceptance must be communicated to the other party. Silence does not imply valid acceptance in the case of a seller writing, 'If I hear no more from you, I shall assume your acceptance.' Communication of acceptance must be actually received by the offeror and the contract will come into existence when and where acceptance is received. Any prescribed method of communicating acceptance must be followed if it is made clear that no other method will do.
    Acceptance subject to contract means that the contract does not become binding until certain formalities have been completed. An option to purchase where the buyer has given the seller something in exchange for keeping the offer open (ie provided consideration) is a contract. The seller will keep the offer open in exchange for the money.

Tenders

In addition to the standard commercial process of offer and acceptance, there is an alternative process called a 'tender', of which there are three types:

A request for offers
This kind of tender arises where an authority or state agency requests offers for the lowest price for doing a certain job (eg supplying a street lighting system to a town in a developing country). The tender is an invitation to treat, and the lowest offer will be accepted.

A standing offer to supply goods
A tender of this type is an arrangement whereby the buyer agrees to order goods from a supplier on a continual basis whenever they are wanted.

A promise by the buyer
An undertaking by the buyer to buy all the goods they need from the supplier is still not an obligation to order any. However, if supplies are ordered from elsewhere, the buyer can be restrained by injunction from doing so.

Standard form contract

Standard form contracts may be prepared for a business to cover all transactions of a particular type. Details about the particular transaction in hand are entered on the front of the standard form contract document. On the back is a list of terms that apply to that contract and will apply to all similar contracts made by each customer.

Theoretically customers agree to the terms, but they are usually in a 'take it or leave it' situation. The government eventually recognized that consumers were at the mercy of big business through such contracts and passed the Unfair Contract Terms Act and Supply Goods (Implied Terms) Act.

However, these statutes do not apply to international sales. Therefore the exporter must read the buyer's conditions very carefully and understand to what they are being asked to agree.

The battle of the forms

Most exporters insist on their terms of sale, and they must take particular care not to accept the buyer's terms by accident, which they will do if they:

- send out the goods on receipt of the buyer's order without countering it with their own terms; even if the buyer's order is not placed on special terms, accepting it without comment will still deny the seller the benefit of their own terms;
- allow the buyer to be the last party to send their standard form; in that event, dispatching the goods means accepting their orders by conduct;
- accept an order from a new customer, or from one who has dealt with the seller on a very few occasions, over the telephone without drawing attention to the fact that the terms exist.

In practice, a seller should consider varying or dropping some of their conditions only if the order they will gain is very substantial or their conditions are very harsh and they face the threat of adverse publicity concerning them.

Consideration

As noted earlier, all contracts must contain consideration except those made in a legal document called a deed. Consideration is defined as what each party puts into the contract.

The law of consideration refers to a 'promise' being made by one party (the 'promisor') to the other party (the 'promisee').

There are two types of consideration:

- Executory consideration is a promise of benefit to be given in the future (eg 'to be delivered tomorrow'). A promise can be consideration.
- Executed consideration is a benefit given at the time the contract is made.

Past consideration is not valid as consideration. The promise by one party of something already done is not sufficient to bind a promisee to perform their side of an agreement.

Consideration must be real but need not be adequate. In law it does not matter that a correct price has not been paid for an item sold, so long as some consideration has been paid. The law concerns itself with ensuring that some consideration is given – typically set at £1 in agreements concerning intangibles.

Composition with creditors

A composition with creditors is a particular form of agreement where the consideration is less than full value. It is an agreement made by a business or individual with all their creditors whereby each creditor agrees to take so much in the £ or $, ie less than the full debt. The creditors are legally bound by this contract because if any of them sued for the rest of the debt, the others would get less.

Part-payment by someone other than the debtor

If part-payment from a third party is accepted in full settlement, the debtor is released from the rest of the debt. Therefore, in business, whenever an offer of part-payment is received from someone other than the debtor, it is essential to write to them to state that it is accepted purely as part-payment and not to cash the cheque until they have agreed.

Terms of a contract

By definition, a 'term' is one of the promises made by one of the parties to the contract – ie it is what that party has agreed to do. It follows that the sum total of all the terms is the contract in its entirety.

Terms are classified into express and implied terms, and conditions, warranties and innominate terms.

Express and implied terms

An express term is one that is agreed orally or in writing between the parties. An implied term is one that is impliedly agreed between the parties without express words.

Terms can be implied into contracts in any of four ways:

By statute
Certain Acts of Parliament impose compulsory terms in all contracts of a certain type. Some are absolutely compulsory and cannot be excluded, whether the parties like it or not. Others can be excluded by mutual agreement between the parties.
For example, in the Sale of Goods Act (1979) the compulsory term that the seller must have the right to sell the goods cannot be excluded. But other terms, absolutely compulsory when a business sells goods to a consumer (eg satisfactory quality, correspondence to description and fitness for purpose), can be excluded by the parties in a contract of sale between two businesses having regard to the circumstances.

By the courts
The courts are reluctant to imply terms into contracts retrospectively. However, they are prepared to imply a term that is so obvious that no reasonable person would make the contract without it (eg the lease of a mooring in a harbour that is without water when the tide goes out).

From previous dealings

When the parties have made the same contract so many times that they must be taken to know what the terms are, the terms will apply to all future contracts of that type between them, whether they agreed to them or not when they made that future contract.

By trade custom

The courts will give the force of law to common practice if things are done in a certain way in a particular trade. In certain contracts in certain trade a term is always implied unless the parties agree otherwise.

Conditions, warranties and innominate terms

The courts have classified terms into either conditions or warranties since the 19th century. The distinction made is:

- A breach of condition gives the innocent party the right to terminate the contract from the date of the breach on the grounds that the contract has been repudiated by the other party. However, termination is not obligatory; the victim can affirm the contract despite the breach.

- A breach of warranty does not entitle the innocent party to terminate the contract; the victim may only claim damages. The logic is that a minor breach may be adequately remedied by money compensation.

An innominate term (sometimes called an 'intermediate term') is one that is neither exclusively a condition nor a warranty, but one that can be broken in either a minor or a major way. Depending on which kind of breach occurs, the courts will decide whether or not to allow the innocent party to terminate the contract.

If a term is classified as a condition, the innocent party can terminate the contract for breach even if the actual breach of that term is trivial, leading to the opportunity for an innocent party to terminate for a trivial breach of condition for reasons that have nothing to do with the occurrence of the breach. The possibility that a term described in the contract as a condition may be judged to be innominate and a breach of the term as minor when the issue is tried is plainly unsatisfactory from a commercial point of view.

The courts have therefore taken to 'recognizing' certain kinds of terms in advance as conditions so that the business community can rely on that knowledge. For example, time is particularly important in commerce and clauses specifying the time for performance of obligations under contracts are usually classified in advance as conditions.

Of course, the intention of the parties regarding the terms of the contract remains important. Contracting parties are advised to make certain that their intention is clear by expressly and unambiguously stating that the breach of a particular term will give the innocent party the right to terminate the contract. Mere description of a term as a condition is not conclusive and it is then open to a court to hold that the term is innominate, giving rise to an outcome that was not intended by the parties when entering into the contract. Figure 9.2 shows these basic terms of contract in diagram form.

FIGURE 9.2 The basic terms of contract

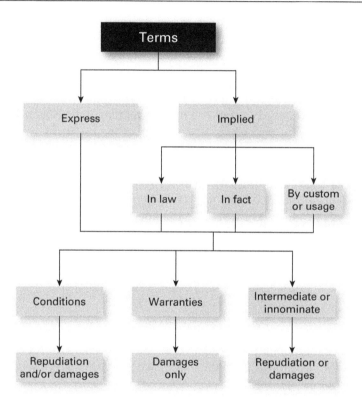

Duress

The law has generally ignored most of the pressures that may influence a person's decision to enter into a contract, including commercial pressures, economic pressures and social pressures. However, in recent years, the courts have showed an increased willingness to intervene, even in commercial contracts where people have entered into them without genuine consent because they were acting under duress or undue influence. Undue influence does not arise in commercial disputes and is therefore ignored here.

Duress, in order to affect a contract, must amount to a coercion of the will which vitiates (makes ineffective) consent. A contract affected by duress is voidable and can be avoided by the party claiming duress communicating their intention to the other party. The effect of avoidance is to nullify the contract completely.

Threats against the person or property clearly vitiate consent. The courts have also recognized that consent can be vitiated by economic duress, even in commercial contracts.

Mistake

Although the general rule is that it does not matter that there has been a mistake in a contract, there are a certain number of special mistakes, called 'operative mistakes' that do operate to make the contract void. Operative mistakes are categorized as common mistake and mutual mistake.

Mistake as to the nature of the contract

If someone signs a contract, the general rule is that they are bound by it whether they have read it or not. The only relief is a defence of '*non est factum*', where someone claims that the contract they signed was a of a totally different nature from that which they thought they were signing.

However, *non est factum* is no defence if the person signing is negligent and is therefore practically ineffective. There will be very few cases where a person signing a document that they have not read will not be negligent.

Unilateral mistake

This is where just one party makes a mistake. A unilateral mistake will seldom affect a contract, since the other party will not know about it, and has no reason to know about it.

Common mistake

This is where both parties make the same mistake. At common law, a common mistake by both parties will only render the contract void if it makes the contract impossible to carry out.

Mutual mistake

This is where the two parties make different mistakes. A mutual mistake will usually make the contract void because it will mean that the parties are not contracting the same thing.

The various form of mistake are illustrated in Figure 9.3.

FIGURE 9.3 Forms of mistake in contract law

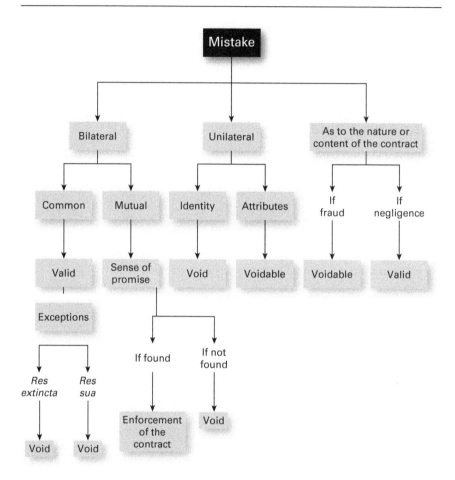

Misrepresentation

A misrepresentation that induced a party to enter into a contract has the effect of making the contract voidable (unless rescission is barred for some reason), not void as in mistake. Therefore the contract remains valid until it is rescinded by the innocent party, who must communicate the rescission to the other party. However, the innocent party is not obliged to rescind the contract.

In the Misrepresentation Act 1967, which gives the right to remedies in the event that a misrepresentation is proved, misrepresentation is defined as:

- A statement of fact,
- made by one party to the other before the contract is entered into,
- which is incorrect, and
- which is the reason (or one of the reasons) why the innocent party made the contract.

A misrepresentation is often something said about a product but it can also be an action that causes the innocent party to have a misleading impression of the product (eg turning back the mileage clock on a car offered for sale).

A statement of fact

Misrepresentations must be distinguished from:

- an opinion that is honestly held;
- a sales or trade 'puff'.

The law allows sellers some latitude to make claims about their products, such as a generalized claim about the product that does not say anything specific (eg 'the best on the market') or a claim that is obviously an advertising stunt that no reasonable person would ever believe.

A statement of law

If the seller of an item simply tells the buyer some incorrect information about the law, the buyer is deemed to know the law and cannot sue. Nevertheless, if the misrepresentation is deliberate it may constitute a criminal offence of obtaining the buyer's money by deception.

Types of misrepresentation

In civil law a misrepresentation need not be a deliberate lie. A person can sue if they have made a contract as a result of any of the following types of misrepresentation:

Fraudulent misrepresentation
Also known as deceit, fraudulent misrepresentation is a statement that the seller knows is untrue or suspects might be untrue but is unsure.

Negligent misrepresentation
This is a statement that the seller does not realize is incorrect, but which they ought to have realized was untrue.

Innocent misrepresentation
A statement that the seller believed, and a reasonable person would have believed, is considered neither negligent nor fraudulent and is classified as an innocent misrepresentation.

Misrepresentation and contract terms

A misrepresentation that induces someone to enter into a contract may have been made either by a person who is not a party to the contract or by a person who is.

If it was made by a person who became a party to the contract, the misrepresentation may become a term of the contract, depending on the intention of the parties at the time the contract was made.

A court would probably not hold the misrepresentation to be an express term of contract if:

- the person making the statement asks the other party to check or verify it;
- if the statement did not relate to an important aspect of the contractual deal;
- where the misrepresentor and misrepresentee were equally able, in terms of the necessary skill and knowledge, to verify the truth of the statement.

Remedies for misrepresentation

Remedies are available at common law, in equity or under statute. The Misrepresentation Act 1967 provides for damages in respect of negligent and innocent misrepresentation. Section 2(1) deals with negligent misrepresentation and Section 2(2) with innocent misrepresentation. A plaintiff can plead more than one cause of action in court in the alternative so that if they fail on one they may succeed on the other.

The remedies available for different types of misrepresentation are summarized in Table 9.1.

Criminal misrepresentations

There are three categories of criminal offence arising from misrepresentation:

Offences under the Trade Description Act (1968)
Selling goods under a false trade description is basically the same as misrepresentation. Curiously, there is no civil liability attaching to offences under the Act; a shopkeeper who displays at a false price cannot be forced to sell at that price.

Obtaining property by deception
Fraudulent misrepresentation made to the person who buys an item constitutes obtaining property by deception and enables the innocent party to sue.

TABLE 9.1 Remedies for misrepresentation

	Fraudulent misrepresentation	Negligent misrepresentation	Innocent misrepresentation
At common law	Damages in the tort of deceit	Damages in the tort of negligence, if a special relationship exists	
In equity	Rescission and damages. If the contract is executory, the fraud is a defence if the misrepresentor brings an action for specific performance.	Rescission	Rescission
Under the Misrepresentation Act 1967		In addition to rescission, or – at the court's discretion – damages under Section 2(1) if, as a result of the misrepresentation the injured party has suffered loss. Proof that the defendant believed, with reasonable cause, that the statements were true up to the time of the contract will be a defence.	

Obtaining a pecuniary advantage by deception
This offence is committed by a person who gets insurance without
disclosing all the facts. It carries a maximum custodial sentence of
five years.

Figure 9.4 shows in diagram form an overview of the elements of
misrepresentation.

FIGURE 9.4   The elements of misrepresentation

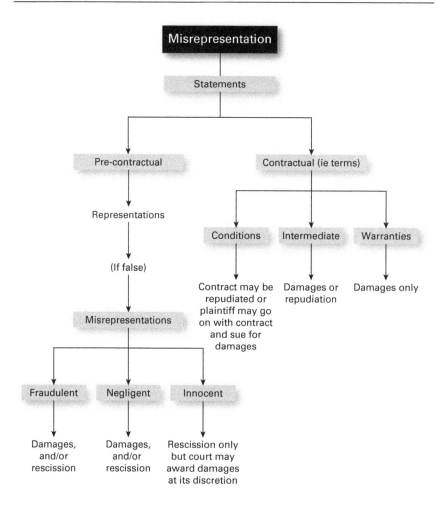

Discharge of contract

When a contract is discharged it comes to an end. A contract can be discharged by:

- performance;
- agreement;
- breach;
- frustration.

Frequently, the position of one party that has carried out the contract is of concern in terms of what benefits they can get for having done so.

Discharge by performance

Where one party has performed the contract they will look to the other party for performance. Before doing so, they must have completely carried out their side of the bargain.

This rule is subject to two exceptions:

- Where the agreement is so arranged that there is a series of small contracts, payment is due for each small contract completed.
- The doctrine of substantial performance states that if a person doing the work has completed it, but done it badly, they can claim the difference between the price of the finished job and what it costs to put that job right.

Time of performance

Common commercial clauses that relate the time of performance of duties under contract are often classified by the courts as conditions in the interests of certainty in commerce. The general rule in commercial contracts is that time is *prima facie* 'of the essence', provided that time for performance can be fixed with certainty, and that breach will be a breach of condition.

Therefore, where a specific date is fixed, failure to deliver on time will be a breach of condition entitling the buyer to reject the goods and terminate the contract. Conversely, where a commercial contract requires delivery 'within a reasonable time', time will not be of the essence; however, the buyer can make time of the essence by giving reasonable notice of a time for delivery. In the case of a dispute the court will have to decide when failure to deliver has been a total failure of consideration and the buyer can get their money back and terminate the contract.

In practice, the buyer will often prefer to accept late delivery rather than terminate in order to preserve good relations with a valued supplier, or because the terms are more advantageous than those offered by others, or because termination and placing an order with another supplier would involve greater delay. Perhaps the buyer will be able to negotiate a reduction in price in return for acceptance of late delivery.

However, the buyer should be aware that if they do not terminate the contract in response to delay but act in a way that leads the supplier to believe that they intend to continue to perform the contract (by continuing to press for delivery) a court will see this as a waiver of the right to terminate. The buyer should give reasonable notice of a new date on which delivery is expected and time will again be of the essence with respect to the adjusted date.

From the seller's standpoint, although the right to terminate may be waived in respect of any late delivery, the seller will still be liable in damages for loss arising from delay.

Discharge by agreement

If one party has completely carried out their side of a contract and is willing to release the other party, they can only discharge the other party by deed, because they will be getting no consideration for their agreement.

Novation

On the other hand, if both parties have duties left to perform, they can agree to cancel or revise these duties, because each party's promise to revise the duties will be consideration for the other party's promise to revise their duties. Where a contract is modified in this way, there is said to be a 'novation'.

Complete discharge by agreement

By the same principle, where both parties still have duties to perform under the contract, they can discharge each other entirely from the contract, the one's promise to release the other being consideration for the other's promise to release them.

Presumption of discharge by agreement

If a contract is made and remains unperformed for many years this will lead to a presumption that the parties have abandoned the contract.

Discharge by breach

Where one party announces their intention of not performing a contract that they are due to perform in the future, there is said to be an 'anticipatory breach'.

Discharge by frustration

The legal meaning of frustration may be defined as a totally unforeseen event that has the effect of making the contract either physically impossible, or such a different contract that the parties must be taken to have impliedly agreed that they would not go through with it under those circumstances.

Frustration is very much a last resort that the court is most reluctant to acknowledge. If the contract is still possible, the court will nearly always enforce it.

Events which do *not* frustrate the contract are increase in cost and absolute promise to perform, where one party has agreed to be bound by it 'come what may'.

However, a contract would be held to have been frustrated when it is made impossible by statute, eg government requisition under emergency powers for war use.

Frustration must not be self-induced

Where the event is caused by the negligence of the party who can no longer perform, the frustration is said to be self-induced, and a party that alleges that a contract has been frustrated must not have caused that frustration themselves.

The effect of frustration

Frustration discharges the parties from their obligation to perform the contract in the future. It is not declared void from its inception as in an operative mistake. This means that the rights and obligations of the parties prior to the frustrating event are preserved unless statute law intervenes.

Remedies for breach of contract

When the court has decided that one party is in breach of contract, it has to decide what action to enforce. Bearing in mind that the aim of the civil law is to compensate the plaintiff for their loss rather than punish the defendant for having broken the contract, the court can do one of the following.

Award damages

When awarding money compensation the court will bear in mind the following well-established principles:

- The aim of damages is purely to compensate. When there is no loss or minimal loss, the innocent party will only get nominal damages.
- In contracts for the sale of goods, damages are the difference between the contract price and the current market price of the goods. The test is 'What has the innocent party lost?'

- When assessing damages, liability to tax is taken into account. Where the party being awarded damages would have had to pay tax on what they lost due to the breach, then their loss should be assessed net of tax.

- The mere fact that damages are difficult to assess does not prevent the plaintiff from claiming them.

- In cases where the purpose of the contract was to provide enjoyment, relaxation or peace of mind, this principle has been extended to cover damages for injury to the innocent party's feelings, and their sense of disappointment and frustration as a result of the breach.

- Damages can be recovered for pecuniary loss resulting from loss of commercial reputation caused by a breach of contract but not for loss of commercial reputation itself.

- Damages will not be awarded if the damage is too remote. The 'remoteness of damage' rule is based on the principle that it would be unfair to make the defendant compensate the plaintiff for a never-ending series of losses consequent from the breach of contract.

- The plaintiff has a duty to mitigate their loss. This means that they must make their loss as small as possible. This is often an issue in cases of wrongful dismissal from work where a dismissed employee must make reasonable efforts to find themselves other work to mitigate the loss.

- There are cases in tort (though not for breach of contract) where it is possible for a court to award exemplary damages. In exceptional cases the aim of the award is to show that 'tort does not pay' when the defendant has deliberately committed a tort and they did so calculating that they would make a profit, after paying the necessary damages.

Allow a claim on 'quantum meruit'

'Quantum meruit' means 'as much as it is worth'. Such claims are put forward by persons seeking part-payment for work that they have done; for example:

- where the party paying for the work stops the work being carried out;

- where the contract to do work is void;

- where one person does work for another in circumstances where the parties do not actually agree on payment, but it is obvious that payment is expected.

With a quantum meruit all that the worker is entitled to is reasonable remuneration – not a proportion of the contract price.

Action for money had and received

If one party pays money to the other for which they receive absolutely no compensation, then the payer is entitled to its return under this action, which applies to any situation where one person comes into possession of another's money.

Award a decree of specific performance

Such an award is an order of the court to the guilty party to carry out the contract. If the guilty party refuses, they are in contempt of court and liable to imprisonment.

Award an injunction

There are two types of injunction: a prohibitory injunction, which orders the defendant not to do something, and a mandatory injunction, which orders them to do something. In the context of breach of contract a mandatory injunction is replaced by a decree of specific performance.

Acknowledgement

The authors would like to thank Nick Kouladis for giving permission to reproduce his figures in this chapter (Figures 9.1, 9.2, 9.3 and 9.4).

10
Sale of goods in international trade

U ntil 1893 a contract for the sale of goods was treated the same as any other contract, with the rules applying to it being developed by court decisions. The Sale of Goods Act 1893 was simply a 'codification' of the law, a statement of the rules that the courts had devised in the form of an Act of Parliament.

From then until 1973, aside from evolution through case law, the sale of goods law remained substantially as perceived by the 1893 legislators. However, as a result of the change in economic conditions, it was realized by 1973 that the protection given to the consumer, now a major aspect of sale of goods law, had become outdated. Following a general review of English law by the 1969 Law Commission, the Supply of Goods (Implied Terms) Act 1973 was passed, which stated that merchantable quality condition and certain other conditions could not be excluded in sales to customers (members of the public) and could be excluded only in sales to other businesses where considered reasonable.

The 1973 Act was followed by the Unfair Contract Terms Act 1977, which sought to extend consumer protection to all contracts entered into by members of the public. A new Sale of Goods Act combining the 1893 Act and the 1973 Act into a single Act was passed in 1979.

The 1979 Act has been amended further by:

- The Sale and Supply of Goods Act 1994.
- The Sale of Goods (Amendment) Act 1994.
- Sale and Supply of Goods to Consumers Regulations 2002.

The term 'merchantable quality', introduced as a qualifying condition for merchandise sold under the 1893 Act, was amended to 'satisfactory quality' in the former of the new Acts unless the parties to the sale agree otherwise.

Exporters should note that the protection given to consumers in England and Wales under these Acts is not extended to overseas buyers. Therefore the exporter need not be concerned about consumer protection legislation unless they sell to a merchant in this country who is going to resell abroad, in which case the protection will apply.

In the case of export sales through an agent, who never becomes the owner of the goods but is simply receiving commission for arranging the sale, the transaction remains an export sale and the protection does not apply.

The law relating to the sale of goods

The main elements of current sale of goods law and some of the reasons why the Sale of Goods Act 1979 was amended are discussed in this chapter.

Quality and suitability

Although merchantable quality and suitability (or fitness) for purpose were defined by statute in the 1979 Act, the following criticisms of the implied terms as to quality under Section 14 were identified by the subsequent Law Commission Report on the Sale and Supply of Goods (1987):

- The term 'merchantable' related to merchants and trade and was inappropriate to consumer transactions.
- There was some uncertainty about whether the 'suitability' test contained in the statutory definition covered minor defects that did not interfere with the use of the goods, eg a scratch on the paintwork of a new car.
- The standard of quality was linked to the expectation of the buyer. A fall in manufacturing standards could result in a fall in consumer expectations that would result in a lower legal standard of quality.
- No express reference was made to the qualities of durability or safety.

The implied terms of fitness for a particular purpose were not criticized.

The Law Commission recommended that the implied term of merchantable quality should be replaced by a new definition of quality expressed as a basic principle sufficiently general to apply to all goods and all transactions, and a non-exhaustive list of aspects of quality that would include fitness for purpose, safety, durability, etc. These recommendations are incorporated in the Sale and Supply of Goods Act 1994.

The new definition of quality applies to all contracts for the sale and supply of goods including agreements to transfer property in goods, such as barter, work and materials, hire purchase, hire and exchange of goods for trading stamps.

According to Section 14(2), goods are of satisfactory quality if they meet the standard that a reasonable person would regard as satisfactory, taking into account any description of the goods, the price (if relevant) and all other relevant circumstances.

There is an implied condition that the goods supplied are of satisfactory quality except to the extent of defects that:

- are brought specifically to the buyer's attention before the contract is made; or
- ought to have been noticed by the buyer if they have examined the goods.

In Section 14(2B), which explains that the quality of goods includes their state and condition, the following non-exhaustive aspects of quality are identified:

- fitness for all purposes for which goods of the kind in question are commonly supplied;
- appearance and finish;
- freedom from minor defects;
- safety;
- durability.

Section 14(2) does not impose absolute standards of quality with which all goods must comply. It recognizes that, from a practical point of view, it is likely that a reasonable person will find the quality of new goods satisfactory even if they have minor or cosmetic defects.

A buyer is not obliged to examine goods before they buy them and, if they choose not to do so, will still be entitled to protection under Section 14(2). A buyer's right to complain is lost in two situations:

- where the seller specifically points out that the goods are faulty;
- where they decide to check the goods but fail to notice an obvious defect.

Delivery of wrong quantity

Under Section 30, Sale of Goods Act 1979, the buyer has a number of choices open to them depending on whether the seller delivers more than ordered or less than ordered.

In non-consumer contracts the buyer is not entitled to reject the goods where the deviation is so slight that it would be unreasonable to reject the whole (Section 30(2A)).

Delivery by instalments

Unless otherwise agreed, the buyer is under no obligation to accept delivery by instalments (Section 31(1)). Their right to repudiate the contract will depend upon whether the contract is indivisible or severable.

Where a buyer has accepted some of the goods, they will not lose the right to reject the goods because of the acceptance where there is a breach in respect of some or all of the goods (Section 30(4)).

Acceptance of goods

Qualifications were added in the 1994 Acts to the three basic methods of acceptance:

- A consumer cannot lose their right to reject the goods by agreement unless they have had a reasonable opportunity to examine them. Therefore an acceptance note will not deprive a consumer of their right to examine the goods.
- A material factor in deciding whether goods have been accepted after the lapse of a reasonable time is whether the buyer has been given a reasonable opportunity to inspect the goods.
- A buyer is not deemed to have accepted the goods because they have asked for or agreed to a repair or where the goods have been sold or given to a third party.
- Where a buyer accepts goods that are part of a larger commercial unit, they are deemed to have accepted all the goods that make up the commercial unit.

Rejection of goods

Provided that the goods have not been accepted, the buyer has the right to reject the goods for any breach of the implied conditions, no matter how slight the breach may be.

This right is absolute for consumers but is subject to qualification in the case of a commercial buyer. The new Section 15A of the 1979 Act made a distinction between consumers and commercial buyers in relation to remedies. A consumer's right to reject goods is retained but a commercial buyer's right to reject is now subject to qualification.

Where a seller can show that the breach of Sections 13–15 Sale of Goods Act 1979 is so slight that it would be unreasonable for a non-consumer buyer to reject, the breach is to be treated as a breach of warranty and not as a breach of condition.

Other consumer protection aspects

Two other pieces of legislation, outlined below, relate to consumer protection and have a direct bearing on the supply of goods:

- General Product Safety Regulations 1994.
- Unfair Terms in Consumer Contract Regulations 1999.

General Product Safety Regulations 1994

The 1994 Regulations implement the provisions of the European Directive on General Product Safety, which was adopted by the Council of Ministers in 1992. The regulations that came into effect on 3 October 1994 imposed new requirements concerning the safety of products intended for consumers, or likely to be used by consumers, where such products are placed in the market by producers or supplied by distributors. A consumer is defined as a person who is not acting in the course of a commercial activity that in turn is defined as any business or trade.

The regulations apply whether the products are new, used or reconditioned. Products used exclusively in the context of a commercial activity, even if for or by a consumer, are not subject to the regulations.

Regulation 7 provides that a producer may not place a product on the market unless it is a safe product. It is an offence to fail to comply with the general safety requirement and for a producer or distributor to offer, agree to place or supply a dangerous product or expose or possess such a product for placing on the market.

Regulation 2 defines a 'safe product' as one for which, under normal conditions of use (including duration), there is no risk or the risk has been reduced to a minimum. The fact that higher levels of safety can be achieved or that there are less risky products available will not, of themselves, render a product unsafe.

Products that comply with UK legal requirements concerning health and safety are presumed to be safe products, but if no specific rules exist the safety of a product will be assessed according to:

- voluntary UK standards that give effect to a European standard; or
- EU technical specifications; or, in their absence,
- UK standards or industry codes of practice relating to health and safety, or the state of the art or technology, and the consumer's reasonable expectations in relation to safety.

Under Regulation 8, a producer is required to provide consumers with information so that they can assess inherent risks and take precautions, where the risks are not immediately obvious without adequate warnings.

A producer must also adopt measures to keep themselves informed of any risks that their products present and must take all appropriate action to avoid risk, which may include withdrawal of the product from the market.

A distributor will commit an offence if they supply dangerous products (Regulation 9(a)). They must also take part in monitoring the safety of products, including passing on information about product risks and cooperating in action to avoid them (Regulation 9(b)).

Regulation 15 provides a bypass provision to enable the prosecution of any person whose act or default, in the course of a commercial activity, causes another to commit an offence.

The penalties for offences under the regulations are a maximum period of imprisonment of three months and/or a maximum fine not exceeding £5,000 on conviction.

Unfair Terms in Consumer Contracts Regulations 1999

These regulations replaced the previous 1994 Act, which implemented a 1993 EU Directive on Unfair Terms in Consumer Contracts, and supplement the statutory restrictions on the use of exemption clauses contained in the Unfair Contract Terms Act 1977. There is some overlap between the 1977 Act and the regulations and similarity between the test of reasonableness within the Act and the test of fairness in the regulations. However, there are important differences between the two, illustrated in Table 10.1.

TABLE 10.1 Comparison of the Unfair Contract Terms Act 1977 and Consumer Contracts Regulations 1999

Unfair Contract Terms Act 1977	Unfair Terms in Consumer Contracts Regulations 1999
Mainly exemption clauses	All unfair terms
Business and consumer contracts	Only consumer contracts
Negotiated and non-negotiated contracts	Only non-negotiated contracts
Exemptions in contracts and notices	Only terms in consumer contracts
Exemptions are either automatically void or rendered void if unreasonable	Unfair terms are rendered voidable
Individual right of civil action	Individual right of civil action and administrative control by the D-G of Fair Trading, who may seek an injunction to prevent the continued general use of an unfair term

For the application of the regulations, a consumer is defined as a natural person who is acting for the purposes outside their trade, business or profession. A business includes a trade or a profession, or any government department and local and public authorities.

Contracts excluded from the scope of the regulations are those relating to:

- employment;
- succession rights;
- family law rights;
- the incorporation or organization of companies or partnerships.

Also excluded are terms that have been incorporated to comply with or reflect statutory or regulatory provisions of the UK or the provisions or principles of international conventions to which either the UK or the EU is a party.

Schedule 3 of the regulations sets out an indicative non-exhaustive list of terms that may be regarded as unfair. Terms that define the main subject matter of the contract or concern the adequacy of the price of the goods or services are not subject to an assessment of fairness, provided that they are in plain and intelligible language.

Where there is any doubt about the meaning of a term, the interpretation that is most favourable to the consumer must prevail.

The Unfair Terms in Consumer Contracts (Amendment) Regulations 2001 have also added references to external regulatory bodies, ie the Financial Services Authority.

Exclusion of liability

Sometimes referred to as an exemption clause, an exclusion clause in a contract is one that is designed to exclude, or cancel out, the liability to damages (civil liability) to which one party to the contract would otherwise be liable.

Up to 1973, all liability for almost any breach of contract could be excluded, following the logic that the buyer of the goods was deemed to have agreed to the conditions excluding liability by buying the goods. In practical terms, if the buyer did not agree to the conditions that were imposed on them, they did not get the goods. The more recent Acts have developed a number of rules to minimize the effect of exclusion clauses, but the courts have always been aware of their unfairness. There is a body of case law where the exclusion clauses in contracts were held to be unenforceable or void.

Exclusion clauses in sale of goods

The following rules apply to contracts for the Sale of Goods and no others (by virtue of the Unfair Contract Terms Act 1977):

- S12 (which states that the seller must have the right to sell) cannot be excluded in any contract of sale.
- S13–15 cannot be excluded in a consumer sale, but can be excluded in a non-consumer sale if the court thinks that the exclusion is reasonable.
- A consumer sale is:
  - one made by a seller in the course of a business;
  - sale of goods ordinarily bought for private use or consumption;
  - sale to a buyer who does not buy the goods for resale in a business, or make it look as if they are buying the goods for such a resale.
- A private sale is a sale by one individual to another, where neither person is in business or where only the buyer is a business. S14 of the Sale of Goods Act does not apply to private sales. There is no implied condition as to quality, although an express term as to quality will be effective and may be a warranty, condition or innominate term according to the court's construction of the contract. If there is no express term, a buyer may be able to rely on a misrepresentation made by the seller.

Other statutory implied terms do apply to private sales but can be excluded if the exclusion clause is reasonable.

Effect of guarantee periods

A guarantee period may be construed as an exclusion clause in the sense that the seller is stating that they will not be responsible for the goods after the period has expired. In a consumer sale, such a clause is void. The goods must serve their intended purpose for a reasonable period of time.

However, it may be costly to prove that the goods should have served their purpose for longer than they did and will involve calling outside experts. In the case of goods that develop a major fault after some time (not within the first few days of service), it will be very difficult for the buyer to prove that they were defective when they received them. Defects that arise after the sale do not count, but a buyer is entitled to have all their money back, and need not accept a credit note, if the breach of condition occurred before they accepted the goods.

Unfair Contract Terms Act (1977)

This act was passed to extend the consumer protection provided in the area of Sale of Goods to services also. The Act contains a number of provisions designed to strengthen consumer rights, of which the following two are the most important:

- Section 2 states that no person can exclude liability for death or personal injury caused by negligence. It also provides that a person cannot exclude liability for damage to property caused by negligence unless the court thinks that it is reasonable.
- Section 3 provides that if one party contracts as consumer or on the other party's standard terms of business, the other party cannot claim by virtue of a term of the contract:
  - to exclude liability for their own breach of contract; or
  - to be entitled to perform the contract in a way totally different from that expected; or
  - to render no performance at all, unless the court thinks that the terms in the contract are reasonable.

Non-application of the Unfair Terms Act 1977 to international sales

International supply contracts are exempted from the Act's provisions so that parties to such contracts must rely on the common law rules alone.

The Act defines an international supply contract as a contract for sale of the goods, or a contract under which the ownership of goods otherwise passes and that is made by parties whose places of business are in the territories of different states (the Channel Islands and the Isle of Man are treated as different states from the UK).

The contract must also satisfy one or more of the following criteria:

- contract goods are being carried or will be carried from the territory of one state to that of another; or
- the acts constituting the offer and acceptance have been done in the territories of different states; or
- the contract provides for the goods to be delivered to the territory of a state other than that within whose territory the acts of offer and acceptance were done.

Under this definition, the Act would apply where a company in the UK buys goods from a UK seller with the intention of reselling them to a foreign buyer. The Act would not apply where the UK company buying the goods is an agent of a foreign buyer and either or both of the first and third criteria above are satisfied.

A very important consequence of this for UK exporters is that the conditions implied by S12–15 of the Sale of Goods Act 1979 in all contracts of sale can be excluded by appropriately worded exclusion clauses where the contract is an international supply contract.

Supply of Goods to Consumer Regulations 2002

The above legislation has made a number of small amendments to the Sale of Goods Act 1979, particularly relating to the situations where the buyer also deals as consumer and where transferees are involved in the process. It has also added additional implied terms in relation to public statement not being the seller's responsibility.

The regulations have also made minor amendments to Section 9 of the Supply of Goods and Services Act 1982, the Supply Of Goods (Implied Terms) Act 1973 and the Unfair Contract Terms Act 1977, particularly in relation to consumer guarantees.

11
EU competition law

The European Economic Community came into being following the signing of the Treaty of Rome in 1957 by the then six member states of the European Coal and Steel Community, with the aim of creating a common market in Europe and, by thus pooling their resources, preserving and strengthening peace and liberty. The members were France, West Germany, Italy, Belgium, the Netherlands and Luxembourg.

The UK joined in 1972 with the passing of the European Communities Act of that year, together with Denmark and the Irish Republic. In 1981 Greece joined, in 1982 Spain and Portugal, and in 1995 Sweden, Austria and Finland, to make a then current European Union of 15 members.

An important development came in 1986 with the signing by the then 12 of the Single European Act (SEA). The aim of the SEA was to eliminate the remaining barriers to the single internal market within the deadline of 31 December 1992. The establishment of the 'Four Freedoms' – ie a free movement of goods, persons, services and capital – was achieved, in most areas, within the deadline.

The following articles of the Treaty of Rome were added by the SEA. The Treaty of European Union signed by the 12 at Maastricht in December 1991 should be distinguished from the SEA and was the next step towards full economic and political union involving in the economic sphere a single currency by 1999. By the same treaty the EEC was renamed the European Union (EU) in 1993.

The European Monetary Union duly came into being with effect from 1 January 1999, together with the European Central Bank (ECB) based in Frankfurt, and the launch of the new euro currency was executed smoothly with 12 of the 15 EU members joining. Only Denmark, Sweden and the UK have held back from joining. Denmark and Sweden have both rejected the euro for the time being through national referenda. There is no immediate prospect of the UK joining the eurozone.

In December 2002, after intensive preparation and negotiation, 10 further countries were judged to have made sufficient progress towards harmonization with the EU and were invited to join on 1 May 2004. The 10 admission candidates are the Czech Republic, Cyprus, Estonia, Hungary, Latvia, Lithuania, Malta, Poland, Slovakia and Slovenia.

During the first nine months of 2003 a national referendum was held in each country. All 10 countries voted in favour of entry on the terms negotiated and were admitted from 1 May 2004.

The most recent admissions of Bulgaria and Romania date from 1 January 2007. The Internal Market is defined in the Treaty of Rome as 'an area without internal frontiers in which the free movement of goods, persons, services and capital is ensured'.

To that end the completion of the internal market entails:

- Customs union, which involves the prohibition between member states of customs duties on imports and exports and of all charges having equivalent effect and the adoption of a common customs tariff in their relations with non-EU countries.

- The elimination of quantitative restrictions on imports and exports and all measures having equivalent effect.

- States are required to adjust any state monopolies of a commercial character so as to ensure that no discrimination, regarding the conditions under which goods are procured and marketed, exists between nationals of member states.

- States are prohibited from applying discriminatory taxation and from granting state aid that threatens or distorts competition.

Competition law consists of:

- EU Competition Law, principally Articles 81 and 82 of the Treaty of Rome;
- the English Common Law on contractual terms that restrain trade;
- the Fair Trading Act 1973;
- the Restrictive Trade Practices Act 1976;
- the Resale Prices Act 1976;
- the Competition Act 1980;
- the Competition Act 1998.

Just because a person is an exporter, they obviously cannot have better rights than anyone else, unless these are specifically provided for in legislation. Thus the exporter is prima facie just as subject to the legislation against anti-competitive practices as anyone else. Furthermore, they can only justify a restrictive practices agreement before the courts if a substantial volume of their business is export and likely to be affected if the restrictions they have agreed were not allowed.

But the exporter does have one very important concession in the Restrictive Practices legislation. Any agreement that contains restrictions that would otherwise be registrable is exempt from registration if the restrictions apply exclusively:

- to the supply of goods for export from the UK;
- to production or any process of manufacture outside the UK;

- to the acquisition of goods outside the UK for sale abroad;
- to any sales that take place wholly outside the UK (ie sales of goods purchased and sold abroad).

The only requirement regarding such agreements is that they be notified to the Director General of Fair Trading (but they do not have to be validated by the court). The exporter should study these exceptions carefully, because they may not cover all their trade. Thus although agreements governing the supply of goods by export from the UK are covered by the exemption, the acquisition of goods on the home market for export are not covered. Thus companies that buy up goods for resale abroad must comply with the domestic legislation. Further, even if the agreement is exempt, particulars of it must be furnished to the Director General.

Finally, if an exporter carries on some business in the home market and sells abroad as well, they should negotiate separate agreements: one for export sales, which will simply need to be notified to the Director General, and one for home sales, which will have to be registered and validated by the court.

EU competition law is contained in Articles 81 and 82 of the Treaty of Rome and is administered and enforced by the European Commission, which can impose fines and sanctions and has extensive investigatory powers. Decisions of the Commission can be challenged in the Court of First Instance of the European Courts of Justice (ECJ).

EU competition law has direct effect in the UK (and in other member states) and operates in parallel to UK competition law (with the exception of the 'merger regulation' examined below) so that both bodies of law may apply to an arrangement. Indeed, the UK's national competition authorities may take action under UK provisions while EU action is pending providing such action does not prejudice the effectiveness of the full application of EU law should it be applied.

EU competition law is an 'effects'-based system, which is triggered by an arrangement's effect on competition, while the UK legislation tends to looks to the form of an arrangement regardless of its actual effect. However, the Competition Act 1998 has effectively adopted EU competition law by banning any anti-competitive agreement and outlawing abuses of a dominant market position. The Director General of Fair Trading is empowered to police this legislation and to impose stiff financial penalties of up to 10 per cent of turnover.

EU competition law only applies to arrangements that 'may affect trade between member states'. Consequently, a body of English law is necessary to cover arrangements that cannot affect trade between member states.

Note the wording of Article 2 of the Treaty of Rome: 'The Community shall progressively bring about the conditions which will of themselves ensure the most rational distribution of production at the highest possible level of productivity, while safeguarding continuity of employment and taking care not to provoke fundamental persistent disturbances in the economies of Member States.' EU decisions on competition law must take this article into account. It may become more important as the inevitable political tensions caused by the effect of the single market emerge in the future.

Article 81 of the Treaty of Rome

This article is worded as follows:

1　'The following shall be prohibited as incompatible with the common market: All agreements between undertakings, decisions by associations of undertakings and concerted practices which may affect trade between Member States and which have as their objects or effect the prevention, restriction or distortion of competition within the common market and in particular those which:

- directly or indirectly fix purchase or selling prices or any other trading conditions;
- limit or control production, markets, technical development, or investment;
- share markets or sources of supply;
- apply dissimilar conditions to equivalent transactions with other trading parties, thereby placing them at a competitive disadvantage;
- make the conclusion of contracts subject to acceptance by the other parties of supplementary obligations which by their nature or according to commercial usage, have no connection with the subject of such contracts.

2　Any agreements or decisions prohibited pursuant to this Article shall be automatically void.

3　The provisions of paragraph 1 may, however, be declared inapplicable in the case of:

- any agreement or category of agreements between undertakings;
- any decision or category of decisions by associations of undertakings;
- any concerted practice or category of concerted practices which contributes to improving the production or distribution of goods or to promoting technical or economic progress, while allowing consumers a fair share of the resulting benefit and which does not:
  - impose on the undertaking concerned restrictions which are not indispensable to the attainment of these objectives;
  - afford such undertaking the possibility of eliminating competition in respect of a substantial part of the products in question'.

Article 81(1) defines what is prohibited and a number of examples (a) to (e) are given.

Article 81(2) provides that any agreement or decision in breach of Art. 81(1) is automatically void.

However, under Article 81(3), Article 81(1) may be declared inapplicable to agreements or decisions fulfilling a number of specified criteria.

Thus Article 81(1) provides a very broad base of liability subject to the possibility of exemption under Article 81(3).

The European Commission has the sole power to grant exemption under Article 81(3). To obtain exemption, parties must 'notify' their agreements or decisions to the Commission. Notification gives immunity from fines should the agreement or decision eventually be found to breach Article 81(1) and to be ineligible for exemption under Article 81(3). Notification cannot, however, prevent an agreement or decision from being void from its inception under Article 81(2). This could prove extremely expensive in lost expenditure. An agreement can be held partly void.

Alternatively or in addition to notification, parties can seek negative clearance from the Commission, ie a decision that their agreement or decision does not infringe Article 81(1) at all. It is common for parties to apply both for notification and negative clearance simultaneously. Both applications are made by completing and submitting the same form.

The combination of stiff penalties for breach and the breadth of Article 81(1) resulted in a heavy workload for the Commission and long delays. Delay had the tendency to deter business from entering into agreements beneficial to community goals for fear of the consequences. The Commission tackled this problem by: issuing 'Notices' providing non-binding guidelines as to the kinds of agreements that do not breach Article 81(1); enacting regulations creating 'block exemptions' on Article 81(3) grounds; and issuing 'comfort letters'.

What is the field of application of Article 81(1)?

Note the following points:

- Article 81(1) applies to agreements or decisions of associations or concerted practices that are 'vertical' arrangements (ie between manufacturer and dealer) as well as those that are 'horizontal' arrangements (ie between manufacturer and manufacturer). The undertakings must, however, be independent of each other. An agreement between a parent and its subsidiary will not be a breach of Article 81(1) unless the subsidiary enjoys full independence of action; otherwise they are not in competition with one another.

- The rules in the paragraph above apply to the relationship of principal and agent, so that an agent is not viewed as independent of its principal. The Commission will scrutinize the nature of a relationship in order to ascertain its true nature; the parties' use of the term 'agency' will not be conclusive.

- An undertaking or association of undertakings situated outside the EU may be liable under Article 81(1) provided that the agreement is implemented or partially implemented within the community.

What are the elements of an infringement of Article 81(1)?

There must be:

- an agreement between undertakings, or a decision by an association of undertakings or a concerted practice,
- that may affect trade between member states, and
- that must have as its object or effect the prevention, restriction or distortion of competition within the common market.

Agreements between undertakings

'Undertaking' is not defined but has been interpreted widely by the ECJ as including any legal or natural person engaged in some form of economic or commercial activity, whether the activity is pursued with a view to profit or not. A local authority acting commercially is acting as an undertaking but when acting executively in a governmental capacity it is not acting as an undertaking.

Such 'agreements' include non-binding 'gentlemen's agreements'.

Decisions by associations of undertakings

This applies to decisions of trade associations that may coordinate behaviour among undertakings without any need for actual agreement. A 'decision' need not be a binding decision of an association. A recommendation from an association to its members is considered to be a decision of an association of undertakings. Members of an association complying with an offending decision are liable for fines if they comply, whether willingly or unwillingly. Of course the association will also be liable.

Concerted practices

A concerted practice was defined in *Imperial Chemical Industries Ltd v Commission* (1969) as 'a form of cooperation between undertakings which, without having reached the stage where an agreement properly so called has been concluded, knowingly substitutes practical cooperation between them for the risks of competition'. A concerted practice does not require a concerted plan. It is sufficient that each party should have informed the other of the attitude they intended to take so that each could regulate their conduct safe in the knowledge that their competitors would act in the same way. Such practices are clearly harder to prove than agreements or decisions of associations.

The 'de minimis' rule

In *Volk v Etablissements Vervaecke sprl* (1969) the ECJ ruled that in order to come within Article 81(1), competition must be affected to a noticeable extent; there must be a sufficient degree of harmfulness. This involves consideration of the market for the product in question and the position of the parties to the agreement in that market. Thus even agreements that have as their object the prevention, restriction or distortion of trade entail some investigation of their potential or actual effect.

If the agreement is 'de minimis', then it will not be caught under Article 81(1) no matter how blatantly anti-competitive it is. The Commission has issued a *Notice on Agreements of Minor Importance* (1982), which states that as a general rule agreements between undertakings engaged in the production and distribution of goods and services that do not represent more than 5 per cent of the total market for such goods and services in the EU area affected by the agreement, and with an aggregate turnover of no more than 200 million euros, will not fall within Article 81(1). If, contrary to the notice, an agreement within the parameters of the notice is found not to be 'de minimis' and in breach of Article 81(1), then the parties will not be fined. The agreement will nevertheless be void from its inception effect.

Article 81(1) (a) to (e)

These cover agreements capable of preventing, restricting or distorting competition.

Paragraphs (a) to (e) comprise a non-exhaustive list of examples of the type of agreements *likely* to infringe Article 81(1). Provided that the other elements of Article 81(1) are infringed by an agreement, and the agreement is not 'de minimis', if it falls within (a) to (e), then it is very likely that the agreement is void.

From the cases it is possible to discern that the Commission's and the ECJ's approach is that restrictions are either inexcusable or excusable. Inexcusable restrictions always breach Article 81(1) and are not exempt under Article 81(3). Excusable restrictions either breach Article 81(1) but are exempt under Article 81(3) or do not breach Article 81(1).

'Agreements which directly or indirectly fix purchase or selling prices or other trading conditions'

Price fixing

This is almost always inexcusable.

Minimum price agreements

These are regarded in the same light as price fixing.

Maximum price agreements

Recommended maximum prices do not breach Article 81(1) since they do not affect competition.

Other trading conditions

These fall under two heads: agreements partitioning markets on national lines (dealt with above), which will always breach Article 81(1), and franchise agreements (franchising in distribution and services is the subject of a block exemption under Article 81(3), leaving only a few cases as relevant only to franchise agreements in manufacturing). In such cases it has been upheld that selective distribution systems will not breach Article 81(1) provided that franchisees are chosen on the basis of objective criteria of a qualitative nature relating to the technical qualifications of the franchisees' staff and suitability of their premises and that such conditions are laid down uniformly and not applied in a discriminatory manner. Such qualitative criteria must not go beyond what is necessary to protect the franchisees' intellectual property, name or trademark.

Article 81(1)(b) 'Agreements which control production, markets, technical developments or investments'

These are usually horizontal agreements and are always in breach of Article 81(1), but block exemptions operate where the agreement supplements an agreement on specialization or research and development.

Article 81(1)(c) 'Agreements to share markets or sources of supply'

These are horizontal agreements and are always in breach of Article 81(1).

Article 81(1)(d) 'Agreements which apply dissimilar conditions to equivalent transactions with other trading parties, thereby placing them at a competitive disadvantage'

These will only breach Article 81(1) if the transactions in question are 'equivalent'. Thus an agreement to charge different prices to different customers would not breach Article 81(1) if the prices genuinely reflected different (eg transport) costs; it would if they were based on what the market would bear. Similarly, discounts for bulk purchases will not breach Article 81(1) if they genuinely reflect cost savings, while 'loyalty rebates' that are tied to the volume of business transacted are a breach of Article 81(1).

Article 81(1)(e) 'Agreements which make the conclusion of contracts subject to acceptance by other parties of supplementary obligations which, by their nature and/or according to commercial usage, have no connection with the subject matter of such contracts'

These always breach Article 81(1) but exemptions are made under Article 81(3). If a clause has sufficient connection with the subject matter of the contract, then the clause is not one to which Article 81(1)(e) refers; though it may still be held to breach Article 81(1). Sufficient connection is a matter of judgement. Consider the following examples:

- Agreements within (a) to (e) which nevertheless are not found to breach Article 81(1) point to the use of the 'rule of reason' by the Commission and the ECJ at the initial stage of considering whether an agreement infringes Article 81(1). The rule of reason applied in this context allows those restrictions that constitute an essential element of the agreement, without which the agreement would be emptied of its substance, and which pose no real threat to competition or to the functioning of the common market. There must be some benefit to the common market in the agreement to justify its anti-competitive aspect.

- Of course, Article 81(3) enshrines the rule of reason in the Article itself at the exemption stage of deliberation. However, the existence of Article 81(3) means that the scope of the rule of reason in Article 81(1) deliberations is necessarily constricted and policy dependent.

Article 81(3): exemption

Only the Commission can grant exemptions. The phrase 'or category' allows the Commission to make block exemptions. An agreement *must* be notified if it is to be exempted. Therefore an agreement that is not notified risks losing the possibility of exemption. When the Commission decides that a particular agreement should be exempted it issues a decision to that effect. The parties concerned must be given an opportunity to be heard and the Commission will also hear people with a 'sufficient interest'. The decision must be published in the *Official Journal*. Appeal is to the Court of First Instance of the ECJ.

In order to gain exemption under Article 81(3), the agreement or decision must satisfy four criteria:

- It must 'contribute to improving the production or distribution of goods or to promoting technical or economic progress'. The agreement as a whole must show positive benefits of the above kind and one or more of the above kinds of benefit must be shown:

    - Production
    Benefits in production are most likely to accrue from specialization agreements. These are horizontal agreements. Specialization enables each party to concentrate its efforts on what it can do most efficiently and to achieve the benefits of economies of scale. These are now subject to block exemption.

    - Distribution
    Benefits in distribution occur mainly through vertical agreements in the form of exclusive supply or dealership or distribution agreements. The benefits result from the streamlining of the distribution process and concentration of activity on the part of the distributor, whether it be in the provision of publicity, technical expertise, after-sales service or simply the maintenance of adequate stocks. Exclusive distribution agreements are subject to block exemption.

    - Technical progress
    This benefit is most likely to result from specialization agreements, particularly those concerned with research and development. Research and development agreements are subject to block exemption.

    - Economic progress
    All the other heads are covered by this head. However, it serves as a catch-all to cover beneficial arrangements not covered by (a) to (c).

- 'While allowing consumers a fair share in the resulting benefit'
    Provided that there is sufficient inter-brand competition, ie from other producers in the relevant market, the improvements achieved will inevitably be passed on to the consumer in the form of a better

product or a better service or greater availability of supplies or a lower price. If the benefits are not passed on to consumers, the parties risk losing market share to their competitors. The Commission will therefore be interested in the parties' market share.

- The agreement must not 'impose on the undertakings concerned restrictions which are not indispensable to the attainment of these objectives'.

  This is the proportionality principle enshrined expressly within Article 81(3). The Commission will examine each offending clause in an agreement, to see if it is necessary, and no more than is necessary, to the objectives of the agreement as a whole. Where the economic benefits of an arrangement are great, even a clause preventing parallel imports may be justified. Price fixing will rarely be indispensable. If without the restriction the beneficial objectives of the agreement could not be obtained or would only partially be obtained, then the restriction is proportionate and should be exempted under Article 81(3).

- The agreement must not 'afford such undertakings the possibility of eliminating competition in respect of a substantial part of the products in question'.

  In all the cases in which exemption has been granted, the parties have been subject to a substantial inter-brand competition whether from producers inside the EU or from outside.

Block exemptions

Block exemptions are regulations made by the Commission to solve the twin problems of uncertainty (for business people) and excessive workload (for itself). If parties tailor their arrangements to fit one of the block exemptions, then there is no need to 'notify'. Because the block exemptions are regulations they can be applied in national courts. A complainant can bring an action in a national court and that court can decide whether the arrangement complained of is within a block exemption or not. This reduces the number of references to the ECJ from national courts (though the parties may appeal to the ECJ). However, parties should make sure they are within a block exemption and if in doubt they should 'notify'; if they do not and they are outside the relevant block exemption, they will be fined.

The areas selected for block exemption are those which, although restrictive of competition within Article 81(1), are on the whole economically beneficial and pose no real threat to competition. The regulations are technical and only general scope is dealt with here. Where a block exemption does not apply, individual exemption may be granted. The format of a regulation lays down a 'white list' of the kinds of restrictions that are permitted under it as essential to agreements of the type to which it applies, and this is followed by a 'black list' of the kinds of clauses not permitted. With the exception of Regulations (a), (b) and (f) below, the regulations also have a 'grey list' of restrictions that are subject to a special procedure known as the 'opposition procedure'. Grey restrictions must be 'notified' but if they are not opposed within six months they are deemed to be exempt.

The following are the most important block exemptions:

- exclusive distribution agreements;
- exclusive purchasing agreements;
- specialization agreements;
- research and development agreements;
- patent licensing agreements;
- motor vehicle distribution agreements;
- franchising agreements;
- know-how licensing agreements.

Comfort letters

The Commission has further attempted to reduce delays and its workload by the issuing of 'comfort letters'. These are letters from the Commission to the effect that in its opinion, the agreement either does not infringe Article 81(1) at all ('soft' negative clearance) or that it infringes Article 81(1) but is of a type that qualifies for exemption. Though these letters are not formal decisions, the file is normally closed. Authoritative legal opinion is that so long as parties act in good faith in reliance on a letter, then they would not be fined and would be compensated for any loss resulting from a contrary subsequent decision of the Commission.

Article 82 of the Treaty of Rome

This states: 'Any abuse by one or more undertakings of a dominant position within the Common Market or in a substantial part of it shall be prohibited as incompatible with the Common Market in so far as it may affect trade between Member States. Such abuse may, in particular, consist in:

- directly or indirectly imposing unfair purchase or selling prices or other unfair trading conditions;
- limiting production, markets or technical development to the prejudice of consumers;
- applying dissimilar conditions to equivalent transactions with other trading parties thereby placing them at a competitive disadvantage;

- making the conclusion of contracts subject to acceptance by the other parties of supplementary obligations which, by their nature or according to commercial usage, have no connection with the subject of such contracts'.

There is no provision for exemption from liability under Article 82, so that a party cannot notify and get exemption from fines. The difference between Article 82 and Article 81 is one of degree rather than kind. The existence of a dominant position makes the conduct more dangerous and that is why there is no possibility of exemption from Article 82. However, parties can apply for negative clearance in order to obtain a decision that their proposed action does not breach Article 82.

Article 82 contains a prohibition with three essential ingredients:

- There must be an abuse by one or more undertakings
- of a dominant position within the Common Market or a substantial part of it; and
- the abuse must affect trade between member states.

The prohibition is followed by a non-exhaustive list of examples of abuse.

Article 82 is aimed at the dangers to competition in the common market from individual undertakings and at the special problems raised by market power. 'Undertaking' has the same meaning as in Article 81(1).

The scope of Article 82 is not limited to monopolies enjoying substantial market power but covers groups of undertakings within the same corporate grouping and also parent companies acting in conjunction with their subsidiaries. Article 82 can also apply to the activities of undertakings that are independent of each other, though the degree of cooperation must be distinctively high. There is an overlap with Article 81(1).

This was defined in *United Brands Co. v Commission* (1976) as 'a position of economic strength enjoyed by an undertaking (or undertakings) which enables it to prevent effective competition being maintained on the relevant market by giving it the power to behave to an appreciable extent independently of its competitors, customers, and ultimately of its consumers'. In a subsequent case the Commission added that 'the power to exclude effective competition is not in all cases coterminous with independence from competitive factors but may also involve the ability to eliminate or seriously weaken existing competitors or to prevent potential competitors from entering the market'. Ascertaining whether an undertaking is dominant within this definition involves:

- identifying the relevant product market, which includes a temporal aspect (ie time period);
- ascertaining whether that market is geographically within the common market or a substantial part of it; and
- ascertaining whether the undertaking is dominant within that market.

The relevant product market

The relevant product market in any particular case is determined using the economists' notion of 'product substitution'. Seasonal considerations affecting opportunities for product substitution may be a factor in determining the relevant product market.

The relevant geographical market

To fall foul of Article 82 an undertaking must be dominant 'within the common market or in a substantial part of it'. Thus the 'relevant geographical market' must be determined so that it can be decided whether it is a substantial part of the common market.

Proof of dominance in the relevant product market

The question of dominance requires a wide-ranging economic analysis of the undertaking concerned and of the market in which it operates. The Commission thought in *United Brands* that an undertaking's market share, either in itself or when combined with its know-how, access to raw materials, capital or other major advantage such as trademark ownership, were the relevant considerations. Thus market share is not the only factor. From the decisions and case law the following guidance can be given:

Market share
This is the first consideration but a high figure is not essential. Where the market share is less than 50 per cent, the structure of the market will be important, particularly the market share of the next largest competitors. Where the market is highly fragmented, a 20 to 40 per cent share may constitute dominance.

Duration of market strength
A firm cannot be dominant unless it is dominant over time.

Financial and technological resources
These enable a firm to adapt its market strategy in order to drive out competition, for example by selling below cost in order to undercut rivals. Technological resources enable a firm to keep ahead of potential competitors.

Access to raw materials and outlets
The greater the degree of vertical integration, the greater a firm's power to act independently of the market.

Behaviour
If a firm acts independently of the market, then that is evidence of dominance. A discriminatory rebate system would be accepted by the Commission as evidence going to dominance.

Dominance must be accompanied by abuse if Article 82 is to be activated. Article 82 (a) to (d) is a non-exhaustive list of examples of abuse.

Abuse under Art. 82 can be divided into exploitative abuses and anti-competitive abuses.

Exploitative abuses

An exploitative abuse occurs when an undertaking seeks to take advantage of its position of dominance by imposing oppressive or unfair conditions on its trading partners, such as:

Unfair prices
The Commission has defined an excessive price as 'one which bears no reasonable relation to the economic value of the product'. Problems inevitably arise over the question of 'economic value'. Though economists and accountants do disagree on the principles to be applied in answering such a question, the courts take a practical common-sense approach, taking the arguments into account.

Discriminatory treatment
Charging different prices in different common market countries, not, apparently, according to objective criteria but according to what the market would bear, would constitute discriminatory treatment of trading partners.

Refusal to supply
A refusal to supply that was not retaliatory would fall into the category of anti-competitive abuses.

Anti-competitive abuse

This type of abuse is not in itself unfair or oppressive but is damaging because it reduces or eliminates competition. This arises under (b) and in some cases under (d) of the Article 82 list. The Commission takes a hard line on import and export bans.

An abuse must affect trade between member states

As with Article 81 there must be some effect on trade between member states for Article 82 to apply; but the cases indicate that this is not difficult to establish. Consider the following. Under UK law the decision to investigate a monopoly situation under the Fair Trading Act 1973, or anti-competitive practices under the Competition Act 1980, is a discretionary one and does not give rise to rights or remedies to individuals. Article 82 on the other hand is directly effective and gives rise to rights and remedies for individuals.

Mergers under EU law

A regulation known as the 'merger regulation' came into effect on 30 October 1990. It applies to 'concentrations' with a 'community dimension' that are:

- mergers;
- acquisitions (ie of shares); and
- joint ventures that create an autonomous economic entity (ie 'concentrative' joint ventures, not 'cooperative' joint ventures);
- between undertakings;
- with a combined worldwide turnover of more than 5,000 million euros;
- where at least two of the undertakings have a combined turnover of more than 250 million euros within the EU; but
- do not earn more than two-thirds of their turnover in a single member state (ie their combined turnover).

Concentrations falling within the threshold defined by the last three points above have a 'community dimension'. 'Concentrations' falling within the regulation must be notified to the Commission, which has exclusive jurisdiction. That is to say, national courts have no jurisdiction at all and cannot apply national or EU law. The Commission has taken exclusive jurisdiction in order to create a 'one-stop shop' that enhances 'certainty in commerce'.

Where the market share of the undertakings concerned does not exceed 25 per cent either in the common market or a substantial part of it, then undertakings can presume that the merger regulation is not infringed. This is a non-binding guideline of the merger regulation but notification is still required.

Concentrations falling outside the regulation will be subject to:

- national law on such activity;
- possibly Article 82 applied by the national courts of member states, where the 'concentration' affects trade between member states. Here national courts may refer a point of EU law with which it has difficulty to the Commission. Any decision of a national court on EU law can be appealed to the ECJ.

12
The law of agency

Definitions

An *agent* is a person employed by their *principal* to make contracts on the principal's behalf with *third parties*.

Agency is a *contract*, and can therefore be created in the same way as any other contract (orally, in writing, etc).

In the agency situation there are two contracts in force: one between the principal and the third party, negotiated by the agent on the principal's behalf, and one between the principal and the agent, called the 'contract of agency'.

The special methods of creating agency are:

By conduct
Where Party X does something on Party Y's behalf on a regular basis, they will be appointed Party Y's agent by law, although they were never actually told that that they were an agent by Party Y (eg a clerk going to the bank each week to collect the firm's wages is the firm's agent for that purpose).

By necessity
Where a person not appointed an agent takes urgent steps to protect someone else's property. For example, your neighbour's house is burgled and the back door smashed while he is on holiday. In arranging for the door to be replaced or repaired, you are his agent of necessity and can recover the cost of restoring security.

The Commercial Agents Regulations 1993

On 1 January 1994, The Commercial Agents Regulations 1993 came into effect in order to implement the EU Directive on Commercial Agents. For the purpose of these regulations, commercial agents are defined as agents engaged in transactions involving goods rather than services. A commercial agent can be an individual or a company.

Important provisions of the regulations

The regulations introduce a number of important provisions:

- A duty on the part of the agent to comply with the principal's reasonable instructions, and on the part of the principal to provide necessary documentation and information to the agent to enable the agent to carry out their work and to inform the agent when a transaction is not to be executed. These duties are in addition to any common law duties. The duties under the regulations cannot be excluded from any contract.

- An agent's entitlement to commission where a transaction is concluded either as a result of the agent's action or where the transaction is made with a previously acquired customer. This allows for commission payments on repeat orders, even if the agent does not undertake any work in securing the repeat order. The right to commission terminates if it is clear that the contract between the principal and the prospective customer will not proceed, provided that this is not due to the fault of the principal.

- Regulation of the conclusion and termination of agency contracts. The provisions for conclusion and termination are complex but may be summarized as follows:

  - Either the principal or the agent can request a signed written contract setting out the terms and conditions of the agency.

  - If fixed-term agency continues beyond the term, it is converted to an agreement of indefinite period.

  - The minimum period of notice of termination of an agency is one month for the first year, two months in the second year and three months for the third and all subsequent years. (Note that some agreements incorporate much longer notice periods.)

  - The agent has the right to claim damages as compensation if the agency agreement is terminated. The right arises where age, illness or infirmity makes it no longer reasonable for the agent to continue. A prudent principal is likely to stipulate that the agent, if an individual, must take out insurance against illness at their own expense and for the principal's benefit. It is not clear what the measure of compensation is likely to be on termination.

  - Compensation is not payable where the principal has terminated the agency agreement on grounds of breach by the agent.

Authority of the agent

The agent's power to make contracts depends on what type of agent they are. There are the following types of agent:

Special agent
A special agent has authority to do only one act. They can perform that act many times, but that act is the limit of their authority. If they exceed that authority in any way, the principal is not bound by the agent's action. For example, the clerk going to the bank weekly to draw out £500 for the firm's wages is a special agent only for that amount. If one week the clerk draws out £10,000 and disappears, the bank cannot take that amount from the firm's account.

General agent
A general agent (eg the manager of a business) has authority to do a whole range of acts for their principal. The principal is bound by any act the agent performs that is within the agent's *ostensible* authority, which is the authority that they appear to have to a reasonable third party. It must be emphasized that each case depends on the evidence as to what is the apparent authority of the agent.

Universal agent
A universal agent is a person who has power to do anything that the principal could have done. Such an agency is usually created by deed and is called a 'general power of attorney' – not to be confused with a general agent.

Confirming houses
Confirming houses find suppliers for foreign buyers and make contacts as an agent of the buyer. However, they do confirm or guarantee the sale to the seller so that if the buyer does not pay, then the confirming house in the UK will be liable for the price.

Del credere agents
Del credere agents guarantee that, in consideration of additional commission, they will pay to the principal any amounts not paid by the buyer within the agreed credit period. They differ from confirming houses in that they do not guarantee the sale itself. They are not liable if the buyer refuses to take delivery of the goods, only if they do take delivery but do not pay.

Freight forwarders and combined transport operators (CTOs)
A CTO may act as principal or agent depending on the contract agreed with the seller or buyer. When acting as legal carrier for the seller or buyer they will contract as principal, being legally responsible under the contract of carriage to the seller or buyer even though, as is usual, they will make contracts with the actual carriers performing the physical transport.

When acting as forwarding agents they will act as agents of the seller or buyer, making a contract of carriage and other related contracts on the seller's or buyer's behalf. When acting as principal they will have different duties and obligations than when acting as an agent.

Breach of warranty of authority

An agent who purports to act for a principal, knowing that they have no authority to do so, even if they believed that the principal would ratify their actions, is liable to the third party in deceit. The following rules apply in an action brought by the third party against the agent:

- If the third party knows or has reason to suspect that the agent is exceeding their authority, the implied promise that they had authority is overridden.
- If the agent misinterprets ambiguous instructions, they will not be liable for breach of warranty of authority.
- Even if the agent has the authority of one of two principals, that is not enough.
- The agent must pay damages to the value of the amount of loss sustained.

Effect of contracts made by agents

The general rule is that the contract is between the principal and the third party, and that the agent has neither rights nor duties under it. However, the agent is exceptionally liable in any of the following circumstances:

- if they sign a deed for their principal and their own appointment was not by deed;
- where they sign a bill of exchange if the words 'per pro' or 'for and on behalf of' are not used;
- where the agent contracts as the principal (see further below);
- where trade custom makes the agent liable (eg it is trade custom that an insurance broker will pay a marine insurance premium if the client does not do so).

Where the agent contracts for an unnamed but disclosed principal

In such cases the agent will not be liable provided that they make it clear that they are acting as agent.

Where the agent does not disclose the principal's existence

In this situation the principal can reveal themselves at any time. The third party also has a choice: if breach of contract occurs and they sue, they will discover the principal. They can elect to sue either the principal or the agent, but not both. Once they have made the election they cannot change their mind.

Rights and duties of principal and agent

The overriding duties of the agent are as follows:

- Not to disclose confidential information or information specially collected for the principal's use. Confidential information comprises information that no one else has, such as a secret industrial process.
- Any information that is specially collected by the agent for the principal's use must not be disclosed.
- Not to let their interest conflict with their duty.
- Not to serve more than one principal. This does not mean that an agent cannot have masses of clients – it merely means that they must not represent more than one side in the same case.
- Not to delegate their authority, except where:
  - the principal allows delegation;
  - delegation is obviously essential. For example, solicitors cannot do all the work personally, and are permitted to delegate it to clerks.

Sometimes an agent may be appointed, with exclusive rights to commission on sales in an overseas territory, simply by means of a verbal agreement. However, in most cases a written agency agreement is desirable.

Key clauses in an agency agreement

A typical agreement would need to include the following clauses:

1 Statement of parties to the agreement.
2 Definition of purposes of the agreement.
3 Description of goods (either the whole or a part of the principal's range).
4 Definition of territory (not always a whole country).
5 Duties of the principal (where not expressed elsewhere), eg promotional literature, samples, training visits, pre- and after-sales service levels, levels of commission and payment terms, etc.

6 Duties of the agent:
  - must not handle, sell or have any interest in competitive goods;
  - not to sell goods outside the territory;
  - sell under the principal's description only;
  - access for the principal to agent's books, offices, warehouse, etc;
  - maintain books/records;
  - provide periodic reports, etc.

7 Commission: methods of calculation and payment.

8 Exceptions, reservations or restrictions, eg house accounts, buying houses, etc.

9 Method of quoting by principal, method of purchase by agent (if applicable), consignment stock details, eg stock levels, records, warehouse costs, resale price levels, discounts, etc.

10 Allocation of costs, eg telephone/fax, administration, promotion, etc.

11 Limitation of powers: agent shall not, unless agreed:
  - sell goods under warranty;
  - pledge principal's credit;
  - commence legal proceedings;
  - release confidential information.

12 Force majeure.

13 Duration of agreement, termination, period of notice.

14 Reasons for breach of agreement.

15 Law governing agreement; method of arbitration.

16 Assignment: benefits and obligations cannot be passed on.

17 Del credere clause.

PART FOUR
The export order process

13
The export office

The fundamental functions of an export department may be broken down into just two areas:

- sales, ie order getting;
- shipping, ie order filling.

Add to these specific functions the need for overall management control and the whole department can revolve around those three.

It is perhaps easier to identify what particular things are done within each of these areas if we identify the duties of the individuals responsible for their operation. See Table 13.1

TABLE 13.1 Duties of export, sales and shipping managers

Export manager
Liaison with directors
Negotiation of budgets and targets
Market selection
Product development
Pricing policy
Promotional strategy
Channel management
Cost and credit control
Staff selection and development
Control of major accounts

Sales manager	Shipping manager
Order negotiation	Assist with price calculation
Price calculation	Check letters of credit
Quotation production	Transport negotiations
General sales correspondence	Document production
Order processing and progress	Payment collection
Maintenance of records	Maintenance of records

Table 13.1 defines a simple structure of a sales and a shipping manager directly responsible to an export manager. Of course, it is always possible that there could be an export director or that the export manager could report to a marketing director.

Also, it is not unusual that an export marketing manager should run the office and an export sales manager handle the field sales operations. There are no rules that can apply to every company because all will be different in terms of size, product range, type and number of markets, channels of distribution and even their stage of development.

In particular, the size of the export office will have a great effect on its organization. Some companies' export departments will consist of one person, perhaps with secretarial support, in which case any division of labour is somewhat irrelevant. At the other extreme is the company with major export business, that employs many hundreds of people within its export department. In such a case it is essential that the functions are defined down to very specialized levels of responsibility.

Whatever the size of the operation, there is a logical sequence of tasks that is necessary to develop an initial enquiry into a profitable payment, virtually all of which are examined in detail in the chapters that follow.

The export order process

This comprises:

- enquiry;
- quotation;
- order;
- order acknowledgement;
- order process and progress;
- packing and marking;
- space booking;
- documents prepared;
- transport;
- customs;
- insurance;
- payment;
- goods dispatched;
- payment received.

Companies will develop internal procedures to deal with this process, which will vary enormously from one to another depending on the nature and size of their business, number of shipments, number and expertise of staff.

There are a number of systems available to manage the process and the sequencing of functions, the simplest of which are based on tracking files or folders that can be completed manually, and the more complex of which are software packages that can produce all export documentation and be linked with internal production and inventory systems.

The computer-based packages are covered in Part 9 of this book. The examples shown in Figures 13.1 and 13.2 are typical manual folders.

FIGURE 13.1 The order action file, example A

Export order no......	Order approved	Customer	Delivery date......
Customer's order no......	Date..............	XYZ Imports New York,	Confirmed..........
Date.................	Signature...........	USA	
Product		A/C approved	
Price currency		Value	
Quantity		Credit insurance cover	
Incoterm		Agent................... Commission..............	
Terms of payment		Bank..................	
Sub: file to works/production/stores			
Works delivery date			
Assembly and packing Completion date		Documents to bank.................... Advice to customer................... Payment received.....................	
Transportation method		Invoices: Documentation requirements	
Dispatch to port/ICD, etc		Bill of lading/waybill	
Vessel closing date		Insurance documents	
Documentation closing date		Consular invoice	
L/C expiry date		Contents note Weight lists, etc	

FIGURE 13.2 The order action file, example B

Customer			Destination			Order number	Contract delivery date	L/C received..... Checked.....
Packing type							Mark--------------------	Goods description
Stores promise	Packing date	Closing date	Insurance date	Dispatch date	L/C shipping date	B/L/waybill required by		

The enquiry

It is pretty obvious that the beginning of the process is the enquiry from a potential overseas buyer. This may have been instigated from many sources, such as personal contact, advertising or recommendation, or it could simply be a regular buyer coming back for more. The enquiry will take almost as many forms as there are overseas buyers; it could even be a verbal request, but is often a simple piece of correspondence, either post or e-mail, detailing the requirements, or it could be a more formalized tender document.

Careful examination of the initial enquiry could be facilitated by the use of a checklist:

- Does the enquiry require translating?
- Is it a new or regular customer?
- Are there any restrictions by the UK authorities, eg export licensing?
- Are there any restrictions by the buyer's authorities, eg import licensing?
- Does the enquiry match our own product/service specifications? If not, what modifications are required?
- Can we produce the quantity required in the time required?
- What delivery terms are requested?
- What payment method and terms are requested?
- Has a status report been taken up on the buyer?
- Can the delivery period be met?
- What is the most suitable mode of transport?
- Are there any special packing and marking requirements for the market in question?
- Are there any special documentation requirements?
- What insurance is required?
- What ancillary (third-party costs) need to be built into the price, eg freight, insurance, packing, documentation?

14
The export quotation

The quotation in response to an export enquiry may be just as informal as an original verbal enquiry, or could be an extremely formalized completion of tender documents. Of course, it is advisable that all communications are in writing and recorded.

Many of the problems that exporters face could be avoided by an improved understanding of the nature of export quotations, the correct procedures for their production and the contractual consequences of the information they contain.

A variety of quotation formats exists in practice and will be examined in this chapter, but it may be useful to first identify the range of information that would need to be included in a simple export quotation. The essentials are listed in Table 14.1.

TABLE 14.1   Essential information in a typical quotation

Goods	Rubber hammers as per attached specification
Quantity	2,000
Price	€26.00 per unit FCA Zeebrugge Freight Terminal
Terms of sale	Except where otherwise specified, this quotation is governed by the current version of Incoterms
Packing	Each unit carton packed (in five extra-strong fibreboard containers, 20 per container)
Delivery (lead time)	12 weeks from receipt of an acceptable order
Terms of payment	Cash against documents by means of a sight bill of exchange presented through Chase Manhattan Bank, New York

Goods

As the description of the goods is directly relevant to the range of tariff and non-tariff barriers that they might attract at destination, we should carefully consider the wording even at this early stage of the process. If choices exist, it could be advantageous to be selective as to product descriptions. (More on this point later in this chapter.)

Price

This is perhaps the most important element of the quotation and one that many exporters actually get wrong.

First, the price makes no sense without a specific Incoterm, such as FCA, FOB, CIP or CIF, and the importance and meaning of these terms are not always understood.

Second, the actual process of calculating an accurate export price is one that causes problems for many exporters, the worst scenario being that the relevant costs are underestimated. Most exporters can get an Ex-works (EXW) price correct but additional costs are often closer to guesstimates.

Delivery

One of the most common mistakes made at this stage is the habit that exporters have of suddenly becoming super optimists as far as delivery times are concerned. While it is tempting to quote short lead times in order to make the quotation more attractive to the customer, the long-term consequences of subsequent late deliveries really make the exercise pointless. It is far better to promise 12 weeks and deliver in 10 than to quote 10 but deliver in 12. From a purely practical point of view the deadlines imposed by carrier's schedules and letters of credit mean that the consequences of late delivery can be far more severe than simply an unhappy customer.

Terms and method of payment

The exporter's estimate of the risks involved with certain customers and certain markets should lead to sensible choices regarding the method of payment and the credit terms granted. A brief point here: the credit risk in international trade is now perceived as being worse than it has ever been, and this does not just refer to developing countries. Many nations of the world are bankrupt in strict business terms, and as businesses would have been liquidated long ago.

This has been exacerbated by the banking crisis of 2009 and the continuing recessionary pressures that have a direct effect on global trade.

Credit risk management is essential to all exporters and starts at the beginning of the process, not at the end when attempting to collect money. (See Risk assessment below and Part 7, Risk management.)

Order acknowledgment (acceptance)

It is important to understand that a simple quotation made by an exporter is seen in most legal systems not as an offer but as an invitation to treat. That is, an invitation for the buyer to offer to buy. The order from the buyer is therefore an offer to buy that can be accepted or rejected by the acknowledgement or acceptance of the seller. This means that the terms and conditions of the contract can be defined in the order acceptance and are therefore the seller's term and conditions (see Part 3).

Forms of export quotation

Verbal

This speaks for itself: in many cases price and delivery information may be given during personal meetings or over the telephone. It is very important that such quotations are confirmed in writing as soon as possible so as to avoid any possible misunderstanding. Don't forget, a verbal contract isn't worth the paper it's not written on.

Standard letter/e-mail

This is the most common form of quotation that requires no specific format as long as it contains the relevant information mentioned above. Many companies use pre-printed letterheads or templates, and these may merely cover price lists and not state any quantities or specific requirements.

Tender documents

Particularly when dealing with overseas governments or state buying agencies, it is common for the enquiry to be received in the form of a tender document. These are also often related to large projects, but not exclusively to large companies, as smaller exporters may tender for parts of a large tender.

There are a number of problems related to tender documents:

- There is no standard format and the exporter is required to complete the tender document. This involves some quite time-consuming investigation of the tender itself in order to complete it correctly and to ensure that the stated terms are acceptable.

● The requirement for bonds or guarantees.

A tender bond must be provided by the seller along with the completed tender document. This will need to be issued by a bank and promises an amount of money (a percentage of the tender value) payable to the potential buyer in compensation should the tenderer withdraw the tender before expiry or refuse the order when placed. This compensates the buyer for the expenses involved in the complex process of examining all tenders. It may also be seen as a sign of good intent by the tenderer. A typical example of a tender bond is shown in Box 14.1.

Box 14.1 Example of a tender bond

Guarantee number:

We understand that (*applicant's name*) ('the Applicant') (*applicant's address*) are tendering for the (*description of goods*) under your invitation to tender (*tender/contract number, etc*) and that a bank guarantee is required for ......% of the amount of their tender.

We, (*name of applicant's bank*) hereby guarantee the payment to you on demand of up to (*amount in figures*), say, (*amount in words*) in the event of your awarding the relative contract to the Applicant and of its failing to sign the Contract in the terms of its tender, or in the event of the Applicant withdrawing its tender before expiry of this guarantee without your consent.

This guarantee shall come into force on (*commencement date*) being the closing date for tenders, and will expire at close of banking hours at this office on (*expiry date*) ('Expiry').

Our liability is limited to the sum of (*amount in figures*) and your claim hereunder must be received in writing at this office before Expiry, accompanied by your signed statement that the Applicant has been awarded the relevant contract and has failed to sign the contract awarded in the terms of its tender or has withdrawn its tender before Expiry without your consent, and such claim and statement shall be accepted as conclusive evidence that the amount claimed is due to you under this guarantee.

Claims and statements as aforesaid must bear the confirmation of your bankers that the signatories thereon are authorized so to sign.

Upon Expiry this guarantee shall become null and void, whether returned to us for cancellation or not and any claim or statement received after expiry shall be ineffective.

This guarantee is personal to yourselves and is not transferable or assignable.

When the order is placed and accepted it will then be necessary for the seller to produce a performance bond, which again guarantees an amount of monetary compensation should they not perform according to the contract conditions. See Box 14.2.

Box 14.2 Example of a performance bond

Guarantee number:

We understand that you have entered into a Contract (*tender/contract number, etc*) ('the Contract') with (*applicant's name and address*) ('the Applicant') for the (*description of goods*) and that under such Contract the Applicant must provide a bank performance guarantee for an amount of (*amount in figures*) being ......% of the value of the contract.

We (*name and address of applicant's bank*) hereby guarantee payment to you on demand of up to (*amount in figures*), say, (*amount in words*) in the event of the Applicant failing to fulfil the said Contract, provided that your claim hereunder is received in writing at this office accompanied by your signed statement that the Applicant has failed to fulfil the Contract. Such claim and statement shall be accepted as conclusive evidence that the amount claimed is due to you under this guarantee.

Claims and statements as aforesaid must bear the confirmation of your bankers that the signatories thereon are authorized so to sign.

This guarantee shall expire at close of banking hours at this office on (*expiry date*) ('Expiry') and any claim and statement hereunder must be received at this office before Expiry and after Expiry this guarantee shall become null and void whether returned to us for cancellation or not and any claim or statement received after Expiry shall be ineffective.

This guarantee is personal to yourselves and is not transferable or assignable.

This guarantee shall be governed by and construed in accordance with the laws of England.

The problems associated with these bonds relate to the fact that the banks make a charge for their issue, and regard any monies guaranteed as being unavailable to the exporter. That is to say, the seller's facility at the bank will be reduced. When one considers that performance bonds can be valid for the validity of a contract, then this can be quite restrictive.

Also, most overseas governments insist on unconditional, sometimes referred to as 'on demand', guarantees. This means that the buyer simply has to call on the bond and the bank will pay, there being no requirement for any explicit proof of the seller's breach. The only possible solution to this, assuming that conditional guarantees are not acceptable, is to arrange, through a credit insurance company, for unwarranted calls cover. The other solution is, of course, not to give them, but this almost certainly means that the tender would not be considered.

Pro-forma invoice

The primary function for this document is as a form of quotation and it is intended to demonstrate what the final invoice will look like should the order be placed. That is, it is an advance copy of the final invoice. In this case it is obvious that the quantity and type of goods required will have to be clearly specified. It is laid out in invoice format, and invariably contains a breakdown of the ancillary charges, such as freight and insurance premiums, commonly being prepared as a CIF or CIP quotation.

This type of quotation is extremely common when dealing with developing countries and is specifically related to their requirement for a specific import licence and/or to comply with exchange control regulations. The buyer will use the pro-forma to provide detailed information to the authorities before an order can be placed on the supplier. It is not, as is often thought, necessarily needed for the buyer to raise a letter of credit.

Import licensing controls are used by all countries but the developed countries tend to issue open general licences covering most goods, and use specific licensing very selectively. However, most developing countries use specific import licensing control regimes, which require the potential importer to obtain a licence for each consignment.

The information on the pro-forma invoice is essential to the buyer's licensing authorities and the licence will be issued for the exact amount. In some cases the importer will be granted an annual licence, for certain goods and a limited value, but the value of each consignment will be deducted from the floating balance of the licence. This means that the exporter will have to be very sure of the accuracy of the price quotation as any cost increases before delivery cannot be passed on.

The other major function of a pro-forma invoice is to obtain advance payment, sometimes referred to as cash with order or pro-forma payment. Some years ago advance payment was quite unusual, and only occurred where the buyer had little or no choice as to supplier. So, for example, a company like Unipart could insist on cash with order in risk markets, and Marlboro operated on the same basis in West Africa.

Most suppliers are not in such a strong position but nevertheless the incidence of advance payment has increased. The reason for this is that many exporters perceive the risk of non-payment, or delay in payment, as being so great in many markets that the only basis on which they will do business is cash in advance.

The buyer has no alternative but to deal on such a basis, and in many cases is not unhappy to do so. This is not uncommon when dealing with African, Near and Far East and sometimes Latin American markets. When the eventual shipment is made, the exporter must still produce a final invoice that should be identified as being for customs valuation purposes only and should, of course, be for the full amount paid.

Risk assessment

The comments above regarding the increased incidence of cash in advance in international trade introduces one other essential consideration for an exporter at the time a quotation is being prepared. In order to decide what is the most appropriate method (how) and term (when) of payment, we should carry out some informed risk assessment.

What choices do we have as to method of payment? Viewed from the point of view of risk to the seller we could produce a 'ladder' as illustrated in Figure 14.1.

FIGURE 14.1   The risk ladder

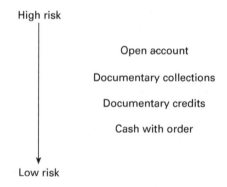

High risk

Open account

Documentary collections

Documentary credits

Cash with order

Low risk

The detailed operation of each of these methods is covered in Part 8. For now, we need to consider what sources of information are available to allow us to make some informed judgments about the credit risk inherent in a particular market and a particular buyer, ie country risk and buyer risk.

Country risk

Certain methods of payment are clearly more common in particular markets than are others; so the exporter invariably has a 'rule of thumb' as to the usual method for a particular market. In this context it is no surprise that for the high-risk markets, for example West Africa, cash in advance is not uncommon and letters of credit are very common. On the other hand, in a developed market like Germany, 'open account' contracts are the most common.

There are sources of information available that can help make an objective estimate of country risk and normal payment methods. Rating agencies like Standard & Poor's and Moody's produce medium- to long-term gradings of countries and large corporations, including banks, in a sort of league table descending from AAA (triple A) down. These gradings are of concern to organizations looking to make direct and long-term investments in overseas markets, but the typical exporter is concerned about short-term risk, up to a maximum of 180 days.

Such short-term country risk is assessed by organizations such as Dun & Bradstreet, who produce the *International Risk and Payment Review*. They grade countries on a scale:

1 DB1(a, b, c, d): highest creditworthiness
2 DB2: good
3 DB3: creditworthy
4 DB4: adequate
5 DB5: questionable
6 DB6: poor
7 DB7: ???

They also recommend a minimum method of payment for each.

Also, most export credit agencies/insurers, such as Atradius and Euler Trade Indemnity in the UK, Coface in France and Ex-Im Bank in the USA, will also offer short-term country ratings and payment recommendations.

Buyer risk

Irrespective of the traditional and accepted method of payment in a particular country, the seller's perception of the particular buyer risk, or lack of it, can override any rule of thumb.

The seller's perception may simply be based on a trading history with a buyer over a period of time, which has established an element of trust that allows for methods of payment such as open account in what may be regarded as letter of credit markets.

However, for newer buyers we need other sources of information:

- Trade references: from other UK companies with which they do business;
- Bank report: which will at least tell us that they exist;
- Credit report: from specialist agencies and more expensive but more detailed. Credit risk insurers; for the smaller exporter the use of a specialist export credit insurer not only provides a safety net for non-payments but also provides the ability to request written credit limits on new buyers.

Whatever decisions are made, they should be the result of the operation of a credit management system that takes a pragmatic approach to the calculation of country and buyer risk and establishes operative credit limits based on the methods of payment in use.

There is one other essential element of our export quotation and it is one that can be seen as the cornerstone of the contractual obligations that each party accepts. This is the matter of international delivery terms, which form the subject of our next chapter.

15
Incoterms

The major elements of the export quotation have been discussed earlier, but it is obvious that the prices quoted are central to its purpose.

It can also be seen that for an exporter to simply say to a potential overseas customer that a particular product is, for example, $25.00 per unit, does not really say much, in that the goods could cost the buyer $25.00 each in the seller's warehouse or $25.00 each delivered into their own warehouse, and there is obviously a big difference between the two.

So, for the export price to make any sense there must be some expression as to what is included, and not included, in that price, as in $25.00 per unit FOB (free on board). It is here where the use of what are referred to as *delivery terms* or *trade terms* is necessary, and this has been the case for centuries. The fact is that international traders have established, over many centuries of international trading, a range of standard expressions to cover most types of sales contracts.

But perhaps the most important development was in 1936 when the International Chamber of Commerce (ICC) produced the first version of Incoterms, which set out to produce standardized and globally accepted definitions of the seller's and buyer's obligations under a range of terms in common use.

This publication has been amended and updated on a number of occasions since then and the current version (in mid 2010) is Incoterms 2000 (ICC Publication No 560), available from your local Chamber of Commerce or direct from the ICC on **www.iccbooks.com**.

However, two years' work in examining Incoterms 2000 and its current applicability have led to the proposal to introduce an updated version of Incoterms. This is likely to launch in September 2010 and become operative at the beginning of 2011. The changes in the new version are, at the time of writing, going through final consultations with various national committees but are effectively finalized.

As 10 of the 13 terms in Incoterms 2000 will remain basically unchanged in the new version, the following account will deal with the continuing application of Incoterms 2000 and then deal with the changes envisaged from the 2000 to the 2010 version.

Incoterms 2000

What Incoterms 2000 does is provide definitive definitions of 13 trade terms in common use, in the form of a very detailed breakdown of the seller's and buyer's duties under each term. While exporters can invent any term they choose, it is clearly better to use terms for which standard definitions are available. It has to be said that it is also unlikely that terms could be invented that are superior to the ICC Committee's work, or that an Incoterm is not available to suit any requirement.

It should also be stressed that Incoterms have become the global norm for all international trade and the use of such standard terms will ensure that both parties in the contract of sale have a clear and shared understanding of their duties and obligations under the contract. To reinforce this, it is advisable that the seller include in their trading terms and conditions a reference to the fact that Incoterms are the applicable rules, eg 'Any reference to trade or delivery terms shall be deemed to refer to the current version of Incoterms as published by the International Chamber of Commerce.'

As the trade term specified on the quotation is such a vital factor in the conditions of the contract of sale between seller and buyer, and as it has such a direct relevance to the price calculation, it is extremely important that all exporters have a firm grasp of the meaning of the various terms. The current 13 terms in Incoterms 2000 can be grouped into four categories as shown in Table 15.1.

The listed terms all identify a very specific point, on the journey from the seller to the buyer, for the passing of *costs*, *delivery* and *risk*.

Costs

As we have already seen, the export price quoted makes very little sense without some reference to what is included in the price and what isn't. Each trade term acts as a statement as to what costs will be met by the seller, and are therefore already included in the quoted price, and what costs will have to be paid by the buyer, in addition to the purchase price.

Thus an EXW (Ex-works) price means that the buyer will have to pay all the costs of the physical distribution of the goods from the place of collection at the seller's premises, but a DDP (Delivered duty paid) price means that the seller has included all those costs in the quoted price.

Delivery

This defines the seller's and buyer's responsibilities for the transport and documentary arrangements for delivery of the goods to a specified location. In this context it is not enough for an exporter to quote, as in the previous example, $25.00 each FOB; it is also necessary to define a particular geographic location (as specified within brackets in Table 15.1).

TABLE 15.1   The categories of Incoterms 2000

Group E (departure)	
EXW	Ex-works (named place)

Group F (main carriage unpaid)	
FCA	Free carrier (named place)
FAS	Free alongside ship (named port of shipment)
FOB	Free on board (named port of shipment)

Group C (main carriage paid)	
CFR (C&F)	Cost and freight (named port of destination)
CIF	Cost, insurance and freight (named port of destination)
CPT	Carriage paid to (named place of destination)
CIP	Carriage and insurance paid (named place of destination)

Group D (arrival)	
DAF	Delivered at frontier (named place)
DES	Delivered ex-ship (named port of destination)
DEQ	Delivered ex-quay (named port of destination)
DDU	Delivered duty unpaid (named place of destination)
DDP	Delivered duty paid (named place of destination)

Thus the seller needs to be specific, as in $25.00 per unit FOB UK port, in which case the buyer can request shipment out of any UK port, or for the seller to be even more specific, as in $25.00 per kilo FOB Dover. The point of delivery, once identified, confers obligations on both parties for the transport arrangements and production of the relevant documentation.

An important question here would be, 'How would a seller actually prove that they had delivered goods FOB Dover?' The answer, of course, is not a photograph of the smiling driver watching his load being lifted onto the vessel with the white cliffs of Dover in the background. It is documents that will prove performance, and in this case the relevant document would be the receipt from the shipping line, ie a bill of lading. The fact that export documents evidence performance of contracts is vital to many of the topics covered in this book.

Risk

One of the most contentious issues in international trade is the relative responsibilities of the parties involved when the goods are damaged or lost during transit. It is important to establish first of all where the risk of loss or damage to the goods passes from the seller to the buyer, which is in fact defined by the trade term, and second to attempt to establish exactly where the loss or damage occurred during the transit.

In simple terms, if loss or damage occurs before the point specified by the trade term, then it is the seller's problem (they have not in fact delivered in accordance with the contract); but if loss or damage occurs after that point, then the seller has fulfilled a contractual obligation and it is the buyer's problem.

Each of the Incoterms defines the seller's and buyer's duties within a formalized structure, as illustrated in Table 15.2

TABLE 15.2   Seller's and buyer's obligations

The seller's obligations	The buyer's obligations
A1: Provision of goods in conformity with the contract	B1: Payment of the price
A2: Licences, authorizations and formalities	B2: Licences, authorizations and formalities
A3: Contracts of carriage and insurance	B3: Contracts of carriage and insurance
A4: Delivery	B4: Taking delivery
A5: Transfer of risks	B5: Transfer of risks
A6: Division of costs	B6: Division of costs
A7: Notice to the buyer	B7: Notice to the seller
A8: Proof of delivery, transport document or equivalent electronic message	B8: Proof of delivery, transport document or equivalent electronic message
A9: Checking, packaging, marking	B9: Inspection of goods
A10: Other obligations	B10: Other obligations

The definitive version of the seller's and buyer's duties under these terms is, of course, Incoterms 2000 itself. However the following is an overview of the main points of each term and Figure 15.1 shows the points in the journey where risk passes from the seller to the buyer as identified in the Incoterms.

FIGURE 15.1 Incoterms 2000

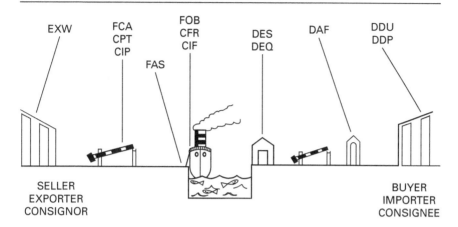

Ex-works (EXW)

The lazy exporter's term! This is the easiest term for the seller and it may be that it is perfectly acceptable to the buyer, particularly for inter-EU trade. However, to use EXW as a matter of policy is unacceptable when we are dealing with buyers who would have significant problems in arranging collection and shipment from a seller located in another country. We often have to do more for the buyer.

Under EXW, the seller must 'place the goods at the disposal of the buyer at the named place of delivery, not loaded'.

It is at this point that the seller fulfils their contractual obligations and the risk of loss or damage to the goods passes from the seller to the buyer. The 'named place of delivery' is invariably the seller's premises, before the loading of the vehicle. The buyer is responsible for arranging the collection, transport, all customs clearances and paying all costs from this point.

The seller actually has no responsibility for loading the goods, but in practice often does so, and therefore then has an implied contractual obligation to load the goods safely.

Even though the buyer is responsible for the movement of goods from the seller's premises, the Incoterm does impose an obligation on the seller to pack the goods for the journey 'to the extent that the circumstances related to the transport (for example modalities, destination) are made known' to them. In order to avoid any problems, the seller should be aware of where the goods are going and how they are being transported in order that they can pack them suitably for the transit.

So EXW is the easiest in terms of contractual obligations for the seller, and is unfortunately often used because of this. However, there are factors that make it perhaps less attractive than it might appear:

It gives the buyer control over when goods are collected from the seller's premises. Many exporters find that this can take more time than they would have hoped, with all the subsequent problems of storage space, security, etc.

It is the buyer who chooses the shipping agents in the seller's country and the carriers. There are many incidences of exporters being forced to deal with agents with whom they would rather not deal.

Related to the above, if the seller is producing an export invoice for this transaction, then that invoice will be free of tax, eg in the EU the export will be 'zero rated' for Value Added Tax (or equivalent). In order to do this, the seller is obliged to provide 'proof of export' to customs authorities where requested. An unfortunately common problem is that, as the shipping agents arranging the shipment are working for the buyer, they do not provide such proof of export to the seller.

Where the payment method is a documentary collection or letter of credit (see Part 8) there is an inbuilt contradiction in that the seller in an EXW contract does not have direct access to any of the shipping documentation.

Because of these factors it is far more logical for an exporter to avoid the use of EXW, which remains perfectly applicable to a domestic transaction, and use a term like FCA (Free carrier) as described below, which is more appropriate for an export contract.

Free on board (FOB)

FOB is a term in very common use worldwide and has in fact been used by international traders for centuries. The seller is responsible for the goods until they 'have passed the ship's rail at the named port of shipment'. It is at this point that the costs, risk and responsibility end for the seller and begin for the buyer.

A major consideration here is that traders today do not now exclusively use sea freight for their exports but a whole range of air, road, rail, express and courier services. Indeed, even when moving goods by sea the goods are invariably containerized and delivery is to a groupage depot for 'less than container load' (LCL) shipments or the shipping line will collect the goods at the seller's premises for a 'full container load' (FCL) movement.

Add to this the fact that container ships do not actually have a 'ship's rail', and this means that FOB, no matter how standard is its use, is inappropriate for most modern, multimodal forms of transport, including sea freight, where not only does the ship's rail not exist, it is also irrelevant to the place at which the seller hands goods over to the carrier.

In practice, the term FOB is really only appropriate for traditional, but increasingly rare, conventional sea-freight movements (ie non-containerized), where the goods may actually cross a ship's rail. The 2000 revision of Incoterms contained more appropriate terms for container sea freight, air, road, rail, express and courier services.

In fact, the preamble to FOB in the Incoterms 2000 publication states:

This term can only be used for sea (or inland waterway) transport. If the parties do not intend to deliver the goods across the ship's rail, the FCA terms should be used.

Free carrier (FCA)

FCA is one of the newer terms incorporated originally in the 1990 revision of Incoterms. Instead of specifying the ship's rail, the FCA term gives the seller the duty to deliver the goods to the 'carrier ... nominated by the buyer ... at the named place'. This place will invariably be the inland depot (container base, road depot, rail terminal or airport) *not unloaded* for LCL shipments, or the seller's premises when the goods are *loaded* on the buyer's collecting vehicle for FCL shipments.

This is particularly suited for the multimodal movements of goods from depot to depot, or door to door, which characterizes modern international transport.

Free alongside ship (FAS)

The seller must 'place the goods alongside the vessel nominated by the buyer ... at the named port of shipment'. This term is clearly applicable only to sea freight and, in fact, its main relevance now is where vessels may be berthed in deep water and lighters or barges are needed to move the goods alongside. It is therefore very unusual for it to be used in developed countries.

Cost and freight (CFR – often stated as CandF or C&F); Cost, insurance and freight (CIF)

CFR and CIF, as is the case with FOB, have been in use for centuries. They are appropriate only to conventional sea freight, where a ship's rail actually exists, and inappropriate for multimodal movements. For CFR the contract for the international carriage must be arranged and paid for by the seller and, for CIF, the seller will additionally arrange and pay for cargo insurance on behalf of the buyer.

Therefore the costs and responsibilities for the seller end when the goods effectively arrive at the port of destination. However, it is very important to note that the risk ends for the seller when the goods 'have passed the ship's rail at the port of shipment'.

It is at this point in the performance of the contract that the seller can produce a set of documents proving full performance of a CFR or CIF contract, eg bill of lading or waybill, invoice, certificate of origin, insurance certificate, etc. Therefore if the goods are subsequently damaged in transit before they arrive at the destination port, this is contractually the responsibility of the buyer. It is perfectly feasible for the overseas buyer to make a claim on insurance arranged by the seller.

CFR and CIF are therefore 'shipment contracts', not 'arrival contracts'.

Carriage paid to (CPT); Carriage and insurance paid to (CIP)

CPT and CIP can be seen as the multimodal versions of CFR and CIF respectively. As with FCA they have been introduced to address the irrelevance of the ship's rail to modern international movements. The only difference between CIP and CPT is again the cost of the insurance for the goods in transit.

Therefore the costs and arrangements for the seller end when the goods effectively arrive at the named place of destination, which is often an inland depot in the buyer's country.

However, the critical point where the risk ends for the seller is when the goods have been delivered to 'the first carrier at the named place', such place being a specified point in the seller's country. The expression 'first' carrier is used because it may be the case, particularly in road freight, that there is a 'subsequent' carrier who completes the delivery.

This means that, in a similar way to FCA and for the same reasons relating to the seller producing a full document set, the risk passes to the buyer when the seller has delivered the goods to the carrier at the named place. Damage in transit following this point is again the buyer's responsibility.

These are again 'shipment contracts', not 'arrival contracts'.

Delivered ex-ship (DES)

The seller arranges, and pays for, the carriage to the named port of destination and must 'place the goods at the disposal of the buyer on board the vessel at the unloading point'. This term tends to be used for bulk goods only.

Delivered ex-quay (DEQ)

The seller arranges, and pays for, carriage to the port of destination and must 'place the goods at the disposal of the buyer on the quay (wharf)' at that point. This term also tends to be used for bulk goods only.

Delivered at frontier (DAF)

The seller arranges, and pays for, the carriage to the named point of delivery at the frontier and must 'place the goods at the disposal of the buyer ... not unloaded' at that point. There is no obligation to arrange cargo insurance, and risk passes at the frontier.

Delivered duty unpaid/paid (DDU/DDP)

The opposite of EXW is DDP, the most onerous term for the seller in terms of costs, risks, and responsibilities. The seller must 'place the goods at the disposal of the buyer ... not unloaded ... at the named place of destination', which is usually the buyer's premises in the country of import.

Under a DDP the seller would have to arrange and pay the costs of customs formalities at import, ie import declarations, duty, tax, excise, etc, while under a DDU these would be the responsibility of the buyer. In either case there is no obligation for the seller to insure the goods as they are responsible for loss or damage until goods are delivered to the named place but do not have to insure that liability – however, most would. These are therefore 'arrival contracts'.

The final point to make about the selection of appropriate trade terms is relevant to the introduction of the relatively new terms of FCA, CPT and CIP. Their introduction reflects the changing nature of international movements, in that the traditional port-to-port transit of goods, where the ship's rail was an important point in the journey, has given way to the depot-to-depot, or door-to-door, movement of unitized (mostly containerized) loads.

What this leads to is the almost heretical statement that FOB, CFR and CIF are actually obsolete for the majority of exports and imports. The fact that they are still the most commonly used terms is somewhat unfortunate.

Incoterms 2010

As international trade practices change and develop over time, so Incoterms have also had to develop to remain appropriate to current international trade practices and procedures.

As we have already seen, the development of containerization has had a marked effect on the appropriateness of certain terms and in fact led to the introduction of new terms. Another example of this, which has impacted the more recent versions of Incoterms, is the amendment of references to specific documents being expanded to incorporate electronic versions of such documents. In the same way, other ICC publications such as the Uniform Customs and Practice for Documentary Credits (UCP 600) have also required updating.

The continual monitoring process of the relevant ICC and national committees has heightened over the last two years and has addressed a number of issues that would lead to amendments to the current version of Incoterms.

In effect, as of mid 2010, we are close to the finalization of the next version, ie Incoterms 2010, which is scheduled for publication in September 2010 and for operation at the beginning of 2011.

Problems with Incoterms 2000?

The detailed examination of Incoterms 2000 in practice has identified some issues with all the current terms, which a new version could correct or clarify:

- EXW: seen as being used too often. As stated above, there is a clear preference for the use of EXW by many exporters simply because it is the easiest term for them. The ICC also considers that EXW is increasingly inappropriate for international trade.
- FCA: not used enough and perceived (incorrectly) as being appropriate to road and air shipments only. It is, of course, appropriate to all forms of unitized transport. Also, the use of 'FCA seller's premises', which would be perfectly logical (see below), is very rare.
- FAS: seldom used, but when used is applied correctly. As detailed above, this term may be perfectly appropriate where vessels are berthed in deep water and there is lighter loading.
- FOB: used too often and inappropriately. Should not be used for containerized transport.
- CFR/CIF: used too often and inappropriately. Should not be used for containerized transport.
- CPT/CIP: not used enough and not sufficiently known.
- DAF: seldom used and often incorrectly.
- DES/DEQ: seldom used, but when used is applied correctly.
- DDU: frequently used.
- DDP: seldom used.

Changes to Incoterms

In brief:

- Revised classification; E, F, C and D classes replaced by 'Maritime only' and 'Any mode'.
- Eleven terms instead of 13.
- Omission of DES, DAF and DDU.
- Addition of new term: Delivered at place (DAP).
- A clearer distinction between domestic and international terms.

In more detail, the revised classification moves away from the concept of E, F, C and D terms to a simple distinction between:

- 'Any mode' (of transport) terms: EXW, FCA, CPT, CIP, DAP and DDP; and
- 'Maritime only' terms: FAS, FOB, CFR, CIF and DEQ.

'Any mode' terms

EXW (named place)

Remains unchanged. Appropriate to any mode of transport but should only be used for domestic transactions, ie home sales, in view of the facts that the seller has only to 'render the buyer ... every assistance in obtaining any documents' and has no obligation to load the goods. In addition, the buyer has limited obligations to provide the seller with proof of export.

FCA is more appropriate to international trade and the new terms will stress this.

FCA (named place)

To be highlighted as the most appropriate term for international sales with minimum obligations for the seller. Has the advantage, when compared with EXW, that the seller is responsible for any export licensing and customs export clearance, thus easing the problem of proof of export, and the seller must load the goods (which is generally the case in practice).

New focus on 'FCA seller's premises' as the appropriate term for international sales if the seller wants to limit their obligations to the loading of the goods and export clearance.

CPT/CIP (named place of destination)

Strong recommendation that the parties define the place of delivery (in the seller's country) as well as the place of destination (in the buyer's country) because of the fact that risk passes to the buyer at the named place of delivery.

DAP (named place of destination)

New term merging the former DAF, DES and DDU terms and appropriate to both domestic and international sales.

Seller delivers when 'the goods are placed at the disposal of the buyer ... ready for unloading by the buyer ... at the named place'. All import customs formalities and costs are the responsibility of the buyer.

DDP (named place of destination)

Remains unchanged.

'Maritime only' terms

FAS (named port of shipment)

New wording proposed. To be used only for sea (or inland waterway) transport. Where the goods are containerized, the FCA term should be used.

FOB (named port of shipment)

To be used only for sea (or inland waterway) transport. Where the goods are handed over to the carrier at a point other than the ship's rail, eg goods in containers, the FCA term should be used.

CFR/CIF (named port of destination)

To be used only for sea (or inland waterway) transport. Where the goods are handed over to the carrier at a point other than the ship's rail, eg goods in containers, the CPT or CIP term should be used.

DEQ (named port of destination)

Typically used for bulk shipments, sometimes referred to as commodity business, and where the parties identify a point, a quay or wharf, following the unloading of the goods, ie the seller must arrange and pay for unloading.

DAP would be inappropriate in these circumstances in that the seller has only to place the goods 'ready for unloading'.

Figure 15.2 shows an overview of the 11 terms incorporated into Incoterms 2010 (in contrast to Figure 15.1, Incoterms 2000).

FIGURE 15.2   Incoterms 2010

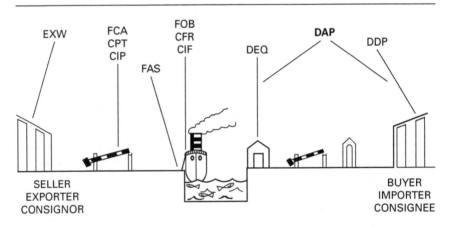

Price calculation

The calculation of accurate export selling prices is clearly dependent on the relevant trade term but does, at the risk of stating the obvious, depend on the starting point of an accurate EXW price.

The trade terms directly affect the component, and cumulative, elements of the price that are added on to an EXW base. On the assumption that most companies are able to calculate an EXW price, based on an accurate costing plus a profit margin, then the components of the final quoted price would be:

Production costs + profit
+
EXW export packing
+
FCA inland carriage & insurance to
FAS named place or port
FOB
+
CFR international freight
CPT to named destination
+
CIF cargo insurance premium
CIP
+
DEQ unloading costs
+
DAP on-carriage
+
DDP customs clearance

Plus:

- contribution to fixed costs (general overheads and expenses);
- export sales/promotion expenses;
- cost of credit/late payment;
- documentation – production and fees;
- other third-party fees, eg forwarding agents, banks;
- and any other penalties, eg warehousing, demurrage, customs fines!

Exactly how costs such as freight and insurance premiums are calculated is covered in detail in other chapters in this book.

A final point: there seems to be a perception within some companies, particularly in the sales departments, that export has 'hidden costs'.

Of course there are no such things as hidden costs, only those that we do not choose to find.

Conclusion

At the time of writing, the content of Incoterms 2010 is relatively clear but is not yet completely finalized.

There may still be some last minute rethinking before its launch and therefore it is important that any trader obtains a new version when available, from **www.iccbooks.com** (**www.iccbookshop.com** in the UK), and ascertains the exact changes. There is little doubt that there will also be a wide-ranging coverage and promotion of the new terms with extensive explanations as to the changes and new applicabilities.

Nor is there any doubt that Incoterms will remain the global cornerstone of all international trade contracts and that a familiarity with the current version is essential to all practising traders.

PART FIVE
International transport

16
Modes of international transport

The modern exporter is now faced not only with a range of modes of transport (sea, air, road or rail) but with a wide variety of specialized services within each mode. It is no longer enough to simply decide to send the goods by sea or air, but decisions need to be made regarding the use of unitized systems, FCL or LCL services, RO/RO or LO/LO, LASH or BACAT, and so on. An understanding of the wide range of modern freight services is essential to the exporter attempting to compete competitively in world markets.

Freight forwarders

Most exporters, and nearly all importers, use freight forwarders. Some use only one, others use dozens, but clearly the freight forwarder plays an essential part in most countries' international trading activities.

Their basic function is to act as intermediaries between shippers with goods to send, and carriers with space to be filled, as defined in Figure 16.1.

FIGURE 16.1 The freight forwarder as intermediary

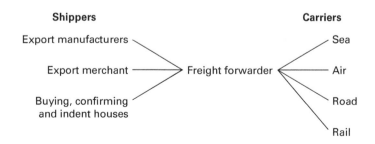

The traditional situation represents a clear-cut distinction between the range of organizations providing cargoes, either as pure manufacturers, merchants or as representatives of overseas buyers, and the freight forwarder acting as an agent between them and the various shipping lines and airlines, and road and rail carriers.

However, over the last few decades the distinction has become somewhat blurred. The exporter is now more likely to become involved in own-account operations; that is, they will carry their own goods. This is perfectly feasible for road-freight movements, although much more difficult for other modes of transport where the initial investment is significant.

Also the increase in containerized movements and the growth of inland clearance depots (ICDs) have made it easier for the carriers to move their operations inland and offer their own groupage and documentation services.

Finally, and most importantly in terms of future developments, all customs authorities are proceeding ever faster towards the collection of trade information through computerized systems that provide customs declarations in electronic form. While this has increased the importance of the forwarder's ability to make direct inputs, it has also meant that more customs declarations can be produced by traders themselves and submitted online rather than by agents.

All of these developments have caused the freight forwarder to do one of three things: go out of business; get bigger; or become more specialized. There are actually fewer forwarding agents than there used to be in most developed countries but the range of services that they offer has expanded into almost every area related to the movement of goods or people.

The services of the forwarder

Advice

As a service industry, the major function of all agents is to provide specialist advice. In the case of the forwarding agent this advice will be specific to the complex procedures of international trade. Good agents will have detailed knowledge of transport and customs procedures in particular, and can save the trader much time and money, both in terms of legal compliance with systems and the selection of optimum procedures.

Documentation

Much of the day-to-day work of the forwarder is concerned with the completion of a range of documents to do with international physical distribution. Some exporters produce nothing but an invoice and leave all other documents to their agent. Others subcontract the more specialized documentation, particularly customs documents, but complete the remainder in-house.

Customs clearance

In relation to the above, the role of the forwarder in arranging customs clearance of both export and import consignments is extremely important, and the majority of such declarations are completed by agents on behalf of traders. As will be mentioned later, this does not mean that the exporter or importer can abdicate responsibility for the accuracy of these declarations.

Transport booking

Exporters can approach carriers directly and book space on their own behalf, but many find it more convenient to use forwarders who can perhaps make more efficient arrangements for carriage. The agent will also be able to predict accurately the carriage charges for particular transits.

Groupage

The expression 'unitization' describes the movement of goods in standard size units, the most obvious example of which are the International Standards Organization (ISO) six-metre (20-foot) and 12-metre (40-foot) containers. Since many exporters are not able to produce 'full container loads' (FCL), to take advantage of containerization they deliver 'less than container loads' (LCL) to forwarders who group a number of different exporters' consignments into one full load. Containerization and groupage are covered in more detail later in this chapter.

In addition to the main services mentioned above, the larger forwarders will also be involved in many other functions, which could include any or all of the following:

- packing and marking;
- storage;
- personal and business travel;
- personal effects;
- exhibition goods;
- courier services.

As most traders make use of forwarding agents to a lesser or greater extent, then they are clearly seen to offer advantages to the trade.

Advantages of using freight forwarders

Expertise

As previously stated, the forwarder operates within a service industry that offers specialized knowledge in certain areas. All forwarders should have a good grasp of basic international trade procedures and be able to give advice in a wide variety of areas, not just on physical distribution. Some will also specialize in certain market areas (often having contacts and offices at destination), or specific types of transport (refrigerated, large indivisible, and so on) or types of goods (hazardous, foodstuffs, livestock and even antiques).

Contacts

The contacts forwarders have in the home market and overseas may be official ones with carriers, customs, receiving authorities, warehouse keepers and other agents, but just as important are the personal, and informal, contacts that individuals have with other individuals. These should not be underestimated in terms of avoiding problems and finding quick solutions when they occur.

Facilities

Most forwarders can offer or arrange a wide range of physical facilities for traders, including storage, packing and repacking, sorting and checking, as well as the actual movement of goods. Of increasing importance are the computer facilities of the forwarders, which take advantage of the growing 'direct trader input' of customs declarations.

Convenience

While convenience may not seem to be such a powerful advantage in the use of forwarders, it has to be said that for many traders it is the main reason why they use agents rather than do it themselves. The point is that many exporters and importers choose to do what they do well, which is to manufacture or procure goods and sell them overseas, and are very happy to subcontract the physical distribution problems to third parties.

Disadvantages of using freight forwarders

To be perfectly equitable, it has to be said that the use of forwarders may also involve some disadvantages.

Increased cost

Because a third party is involved, and which is attempting to be a profit-making organization, then it must cost more for traders to use intermediaries rather than do it themselves. It can be argued that the savings that agents can generate more than compensate for the fees that they charge, but there is still no doubt that a trader, doing the job properly, would reduce costs.

Loss of control

Some exporters find it difficult to accept that a third party should have such control of, and access to, their business, and endeavour to keep everything in-company. Increasingly, bottlenecks can sometimes happen, with the typical forwarder representing a very large number of traders.

A final point regarding the use of freight forwarders should be emphasized. The exporter or importer has a perfect right to delegate the business of physical distribution and documentation to an agent but it should never be forgotten that the forwarder is an agent, and the trader remains the principal in any dealings. This is particularly important in respect of the mandatory obligations to comply with customs requirements, which cannot be abdicated to an agent. Customs will always hold the trader liable for the accuracy of any declarations, even if they are made by an agent on the trader's behalf.

Alternative modes of international transport

Sea freight

The two basic forms of ocean cargo carriers are identified in Table 16.1.

TABLE 16.1   Alternative forms of ocean cargo carriers

Liners	Tramps
General cargo and passengers	Mostly bulk cargo
Regular sailing schedules	No schedule (react to demand)
Regular routes	No fixed routes
Firm freight rates	Rates subject to negotiation
Bill of lading	Charter party

The distinction between liners and tramps is based on the nature of the service and not the type of vessel. Tramp vessels are not so called because they are rather scruffy, but because they have no fixed abode. Perhaps the most appropriate analogy is that the liners are the buses of the shipping world, while the tramps are the taxis.

Liners offer regular schedules, between the same ports, based on an advertised sailing schedule, and carry the majority of international sea transits (certainly in terms of the number of consignments). Tramps will carry, generally, bulk cargoes from almost anywhere in the world to anywhere else, and negotiate a rate for the job.

Many liner services, operating on the same routes, voluntarily form together into *freight conferences*. They cooperate on both rates and schedules and are usually illegal, particularly for example in terms of European Union competition law and American anti-trust legislation. However, while the lines do not compete on rates, they do benefit the shipper in terms of their cooperation on schedules and the exporter is virtually guaranteed a regularity of service. Just like buses, when operating efficiently, there will be one vessel for a particular destination, receiving cargo every seven days, rather than three receiving all at once and then nothing for a month.

There may also be non-conference lines operating on some routes, in competition with the conferences, and this means that the exporter has basically three choices:

- conference line;
- non-conference line;
- tramp.

The cheapest freight rate per tonne of these three will invariably be the tramp, but very few exporters can produce cargoes of sufficient size to interest even small tramp steamers. The choice between conference and non-conference lines is influenced by the fact that the conferences offer immediate discounts, usually 9.5 per cent, off the freight invoice to shippers who contract to use conference vessels only. Alternatively, deferred rebates, usually 10 per cent, are given following periods of loyalty to the conference. It may also be the case that non-conference services are either not available on certain routes or are seen as being less reliable than the conference services.

The simple consequence is that the majority of exporters use conference lines for all of their sea-freight consignments.

The equivalent distinction in terms of air freight would be between schedule and charter; tramping is also an expression used to describe road-haulage operations across national frontiers.

Charter party

Before we examine the range of liner services available to the exporter, it is sensible to briefly look at the arrangements that could be made with a tramp operator, and which could be relevant to larger traders. There are basically three types of charter that can be arranged:

Voyage charter

The vessel is chartered for one specific voyage between specified ports. This may involve more than one port of call but is nevertheless just one voyage.

Time charter

The vessel is chartered for a period of time. During that period the charterers might have a degree of freedom regarding the use of the vessel, or it may only allow a number of repetitive voyages.

Bareboat (demise) charter

Both of the previous charters depend on the vessel owner operating and crewing the ship, and the vessel owner's own Master will be in control. A bareboat charter is almost self-explanatory in that the charterer takes over the vessel, often for periods of time as long as 15 years, and operates the vessel as if it were their own. This is not uncommon, for example, in the oil industry, where the tankers carrying oil companies' cargoes are crewed by oil company staff, but will revert back to the vessel owners at the end of the charter period.

In all these cases, the contract will be based on the charter party, and a charter party bill of lading will be issued. It should be noted that such bills are not acceptable to banks against letters of credit requiring shipping companies' bills, as the banks have no knowledge of the contract of carriage conditions (more on this in Chapter 26).

On the assumption that the average exporter will be using liner services for most, if not all, sea freight there are still alternatives from which to choose.

Types of sea-freight services

Conventional

The traditional, but now less common, service carrying break-bulk, that is non-unitized cargoes. The development of containerization over the last 40 years has severely reduced the number of conventional vessels in operation.

Containerized

By far the most common sea-freight service used by the average exporter. The principle was first developed in the mid 1950s and is based on the concept of moving goods in standard-sized units, ie unitized loads. The service is sometimes referred to as 'lift on/lift off' (LO/LO) in that the container is lifted from one mode of transport on to another.

The majority of containers are built to the ISO specification and a wide range of different designs is now in common use. These include:

- insulated and/or refrigerated (reefers);
- open topped;
- curtain sided;
- liquid and powder tanks;
- half height (donkey);
- hazardous cargo tank containers (tanktainers).

There are few cargoes that cannot be containerized, except for the very large indivisibles.

It is also important to note that the standard container is suitable for all surface freight, and not just sea, which yields major advantages.

Multimodal

The risk of loss or damage to the goods is much reduced because the goods are not handled as they transfer from one mode of transport to another, for example road trailer to vessel. This allows an exporter who can fill a container, that is supply full container loads (FCL), to actually arrange door-to-door deliveries during which the goods will not be handled at all.

Through documentation

Because containers move goods door to door, or depot to depot, the documentation covers more than just the sea-freight part of the journey. This also means that 'through freight rates' are used, which cover the greater part of the journey.

Vessel efficiency

There are a number of advantages to the vessel owner, notably the ease of segregation of cargoes that require separation from others; and the turn-round time of the vessel, that is the time spent in discharging and receiving cargo, is minimized because of the speed with which the container units can be handled.

Container security

The Container Security Initiative (CSI) was launched in 2002 by the US Bureau of Customs and Border Protection (CBP), an agency of the Department of Homeland Security. Its purpose was to increase security for container cargo shipped to the USA. As the CBP put it, the intent was to 'extend the zone of security outward so that American borders are the last line of defense, not the first'.

Rationale

Containerized shipping is a critical component of international trade. According to the CBP:

- About 90 per cent of the world's trade is transported in cargo containers.
- Almost half of incoming US trade (by value) arrives by containers on board ships.
- Nearly 7 million cargo containers arrive on ships and are offloaded at US seaports each year.

As terrorist organizations have increasingly turned to destroying economic infrastructure to make an impact on nations, the vulnerability of international shipping has come under scrutiny. Under the CSI programme, the screening of containers that pose a risk for terrorism is accomplished by teams of CBP officials deployed to work in concert with their host-nation counterparts.

The initial CSI programme has focused on implementation at the top 20 ports shipping approximately two-thirds of the container volume to the USA. Smaller ports, however, have been added to the programme at their instigation, and participation is open to any port meeting certain volume, equipment, procedural and information-sharing requirements. Future plans include expansion to additional ports based on volume, location, and strategic concerns. In the UK, Felixstowe, Liverpool, Thamesport, Tilbury and Southampton are CSI approved.

Global impact

The CSI programme offers its participant countries the reciprocal opportunity to enhance their own incoming shipment security. CSI partners can send their customs officers to major US ports to target ocean-going, containerized cargo to be exported from the USA to their countries. Likewise, CBP shares information on a bilateral basis with its CSI partners. Japan and Canada are currently taking advantage of this reciprocity.

In June 2002, the World Customs Organization (WCO) unanimously passed a resolution that will enable ports in all 171 (as at 2010) of the member nations to begin to develop programmes along the lines of the CSI model. In April 2004, the European Union and the US Department of Homeland Security signed an agreement that calls for the prompt expansion of CSI throughout the EU.

The US government sees the rules as a critical part of its ongoing efforts to improve the security of international supply chains and therefore worth the increased costs that will be borne by importers, retailers and ultimately consumers.

'10 plus 2' update

In late November 2008, US Customs and Border Protection issued its importer security filing rule (also known as '10 plus 2', in view of the fact that a first declaration containing 10 items of data is followed by a second declaration containing two elements), which had been in the works for nearly a year. Under this rule companies importing goods into the USA and the shipping lines carrying those products have to provide customs with a range of additional cargo and shipment information from January 2009.

To its credit, US Customs has watered the rule down somewhat from its original version in response to industry concerns. Full enforcement isn't slated to take effect until 2011, following a year of education, outreach and informed compliance efforts. There's additional flexibility as to when some information can be reported and how accurate it has to be when initially filed.

Even so, the new regulations could be a heavy burden on US importers, especially small and medium-sized enterprises that may have a hard time obtaining the required information. Liability for the accuracy and timeliness of the information rests solely on the importer, regardless of whether it uses a customs broker or other intermediary to file it. Violations can be met with penalties of up to $5,000 and instructions not to load the shipment on board the vessel.

Other transport modes

Specialist barge services

There is a growing use, particularly in mainland Europe and parts of the USA, of vessels that are designed to carry floating lighters or barges. These units are like floating containers but carry up to 600 tonnes of cargo, and their main advantage is that they make use of inland waterway systems, the cheapest means of inland transport. The barges are floated into the main deep sea ports and the ocean-going vessels load them for the deep-sea movement. The most common versions are 'lighter aboard ship' (LASH), 'barge aboard catamaran' (BACAT) and Sea Bees.

While this list does not exhaust the range of sea-freight services, others are more appropriate to road or rail modes and are covered below.

Road freight

The function of the international road hauliers has become increasingly important to international trade in that not only do they provide an efficient cross-border mode of transport for eg continental Europe, but they also provide the option of a road transit to overseas destinations.

These transits are dependent on 'roll on/roll off' (RO/RO) services for both short sea transits, eg North Sea and deep-sea movements such as trans-Atlantic to the USA. The load may be accompanied by the driver who continues the journey, or be unaccompanied and a subsequent carrier will collect the trailer and continue the transit to an inland destination.

Rail freight

Important as rail freight is in many parts of the world for internal domestic movements, it handles only a relatively small proportion of international transits. Those that are international often use the rail equivalent of RO/RO, that is a train ferry service. However, the environmental problems of increased road-freight usage mean that, in many developed countries, there is great potential for the growth of international rail freight.

European and US freight movers have, for many years, operated road–rail services, often referred to as 'piggyback', based on road trailers being carried on specially designed rail wagons. There is also a growing use of 'swapbodies', which are flatbed wagons, without wheels, carried on rail wagons.

Air freight

The traditional use of air for high-value, low-volume cargoes will always exist but there is now a clear trend towards the increased use of air transport for many other cargoes.

The benefits of speed and security, very competitive rates and the increased appreciation of the total distribution cost of a transit rather than just the freight cost (see later) have persuaded many exporters that air freight is a genuine and viable option.

Much of this cargo is carried on scheduled passenger aircraft rather than dedicated freight flights and there has also been an increase in combined services, which link either sea or road transits with air-freight legs, using combined transport documentation.

Just as many of the shipping lines form together into freight conferences, so some 80 per cent of scheduled air traffic is operated by members of the air-freight equivalent, which is the International Air Transport Association (IATA). The IATA traffic conferences operate in the same way in terms of cooperation on rates, but also attempt to promote safe, regular and economical air commerce. While IATA deals with the commercial aspects of airline operations, the International Civil Aviation Organization (ICAO), which is a branch of the United Nations, governs relationships between member countries.

Groupage

This applies to all modes of transport and describes the grouping of a number of distinct export consignments into one unitized load. The most typical unit is the ISO container, carrying 'less than container loads' (LCLs), but road trailers and rail wagons are also units that require certain quantities of cargo to fill.

In air freight the expression more commonly used is *consolidation* and the standard unit is referred to as a 'unit load device' (ULD), sometimes called an igloo because of its distinctive shape. These services may be offered by the carriers themselves or by specialized groupage operators, who are often general freight forwarders.

Express services

Express operations are an area of rapid development, specializing in relatively small consignments, generally up to 40 kilos, and use large networks of vehicles and aircraft to guarantee deliveries within specified time limits. They may also be linked with courier services that specialize in documents and very light items, again guaranteeing fast and personal delivery. It will be clear from the above that the international trader has a very wide choice as to the specific transport mode and nature of service for each consignment. What factors will need to be considered when making that choice?

Choosing a mode of transport

Destination

The final destination of the goods will clearly have a direct influence on the transport service used. Certain modes of transport become a logical rule of thumb for particular markets, unless there are reasons why other modes should be used.

It is not surprising that over 80 per cent of the UK's exports to Western Europe are by road, and that the most common transport mode for markets in developing countries is sea freight, although there is a growing use of air freight into those countries.

Availability

In relation to the above comments it is generally the case that the most available transport services, in terms of number, regularity and quality, will be those most commonly used for certain destinations.

Type of goods

There are many factors to do with the nature of the goods to be shipped that will affect the mode used. These include:

- Size: large indivisibles (which cannot be broken down) require very special treatment and routing. It may also be that very dense cargoes cannot be moved as full loads because they will exceed legal weights.
- Segregation: some goods are liable to taint others or be easily tainted themselves. That is, they impart on other goods, or pick up themselves, odours or flavours that are not desirable. This may preclude the use of a normal groupage service.
- Fragility: not only does this affect the nature of packing but it also leads to modes of transport that minimize handling and maximize speed of transit.
- Value: likewise, highly valuable goods will require minimum handling and maximum speed. It is also the case that certain services, for example express, can provide greater levels of security and personal care than others.
- Perishability: perishable goods need maximum speed of transit and often special stowage.
- Special requirements: apart from the above there are many other special needs that the transport method must accommodate. These include refrigeration, insulation, ventilation and even heating. Plus all the packing, marking and stowage requirements of hazardous goods.

Speed of transit

It is not only perishable or high-value goods that are appropriate to fast transit times, but also those for which there is an urgent demand. This would include items such as replacement components for broken-down equipment, or vehicles off the road. It should also be borne in mind that a faster transit invariably leads to earlier payment with calculable financial benefits. More on this later.

Cost

A factor that is always of concern whenever choices must be made in business. In the case of international transport it is pretty obviously the case that the freight rate charged will differ from one service to another, and that the fastest method, that is, air freight, will be the most expensive, and the slowest, usually sea freight, will be the cheapest. It is extremely important that the exporter is able to make accurate predictions of the freight costs, not only as an aid to choice of mode of transport, but also to ensure that the quoted prices adequately cover all costs.

Freight calculation

It is an unfortunate fact that many exporters' method of calculating a freight cost is to telephone a freight forwarder and ask them to do it. Some exporters have only a vague idea as to the true cost of international movements, and operate on rough and often outdated figures. It is not uncommon that a percentage of the value of the goods is used as an estimate of freight for various destinations. This could work, but not when the percentage has not been checked for the last few years. 'Guesstimates' of a cost per tonne, with no reference to current tariffs, represent another way of taking the easy way out, and another way of losing money.

There is no reason why every exporter cannot calculate the freight charge for each individual consignment, without the need to rely on a third party such as the freight forwarder, and get it right every time. All carriers operate on the basis of open and firm tariffs for the whole of their service, and the principle that governs the calculation is the same for all modes of transport.

Sea-freight calculation

An enquiry to a shipping line for a specific freight rate could elicit a response such as: 'US$285.00 per freight ton ... weight or measure.'

Quite what is meant by a 'freight ton' or 'weight or measure' we will look at soon, but first we should examine the criteria that affect the actual base freight rate quoted.

The rate quoted by carriers is based on:

Destination
  Logically enough, the carrier offering a range of services to different destinations will charge different rates depending on the final point of delivery. Typically lines will operate regular (scheduled) services to specified destinations, and will specialize in certain geographic areas.
  Clearly, the further away the destination, then the higher the freight rate is likely to be, but distance is not the only criterion affecting rates. The carrier must also consider other operating costs related to specific destinations such as routing costs (canal and inland waterway links), port or harbour dues, berthing fees, lighterage and/or handling charges, and any other costs specific to a particular route and destination.
  Many carriers will therefore operate on a tariff that contains a number of basic freight rates per freight ton for the specific points of delivery on their schedule.

Commodity

In addition to the differing destination rates, which is perfectly logical, carriers also charge a range of different rates dependent on the nature of the goods themselves, which might appear to be somewhat less logical. It is not unusual for shipping lines to have anything up to 22 different commodity rates for each destination.

The explanation is partly to do with the fact that higher-value goods do increase the carrier's liability for loss or damage but is mostly to do with the range of cargoes carried by sea. Imagine the situation if all goods attracted the same freight rate. Freight as a percentage of the value of the goods would differ enormously in that high-value goods would pay very low percentage freight, while low-value goods would be paying very high percentages of their value as freight.

A final consideration regarding commodity rates is the carrier's need to accommodate the *stowage factor* of goods. This refers to the weight of a commodity in relation to its volume, that is the density of the goods. Clearly the stowage factor would differ greatly from, say, stainless-steel sheet to foam rubber, and this affects the available capacity of the carrier.

As we shall see when we actually look at the calculation of a freight charge for a particular consignment, the method of calculation does directly relate to the weight and the measure (or volume) of goods, but some carriers use a tariff that ignores the nature of the commodity but contains perhaps eight classes based on the weight-to-measure ratio of the goods.

Box rates

Because of the predominance of containerized movements for modern ocean freight, it is not surprising that there is a move towards the calculation of freight based on the standard container load, as opposed to the weight or measure of its contents. The typical situation is that the carrier will apply a small number of broad commodity bands and calculate a 'lump sum' charge for the box. By definition this FCL 'box rate' can only apply to exporters able to supply full container loads as opposed to less than container loads, but it does also allow for large shippers to negotiate very favourable rates for sufficient FCL shipments.

It is also possible that so-called 'freight of all kinds' (FAK) rates can be obtained. This represents a situation in which a relatively large number of containers, composed of a wide range of different commodities, are shipped as one consignment. The carrier may be prepared to charge an 'averaged' rate rather than be involved in a complex breakdown of the individual commodities. While this is not a common method of charge, it can be seen that it has a clear relevance to grouped or consolidated consignments and could be negotiated by the groupage operators rather than the exporters.

Ad valorem

In rare cases the freight rate may be calculated as a percentage of the value of the goods. A quoted rate per freight ton may be followed by a comment such as 'or 3 per cent ad valorem', in which case if 3 per cent of the value of the goods is greater than any weight or measure charge, then that percentage is charged. It serves to reflect the increase in the liability of the carrier but is quite unusual in practice.

Whatever the basis of the freight rate, the carriers will also operate a *minimum rate* that will be charged should the calculated freight fall below the specified minimum. This clearly applies to relatively small consignments and can be avoided by the use of groupage (LCL) services.

Unfortunately, finding the appropriate freight rate for a particular commodity is not the end of the exporter's problems in that there are often adjustments to the basic rate that have to be taken into account.

Typical adjustments would include:

- Conference discounts or rebate. Either 9.5 per cent immediate discount (for contract signatories) or 10 per cent deferred rebate.
- Currency adjustment factor (CAF). As most shipping lines use the US$ as the basis for their tariffs, they make adjustments to allow for fluctuations in the value of the $ against the currency in which they earn their revenues. The actual £ or € rate used will be based on the agreed conversion rate on the sailing date.
- Bunker adjustment factor (BAF). Bunkerage is the expression used to describe the fuel used by the vessel and derives from the coal bunkers used on the original steam ships. The BAF therefore reflects any changes, generally increases, in the cost of fuel to the carrier.

Having considered all of the above we should now have a basic freight rate per freight ton which can be applied to an individual consignment to calculate the specific freight charge. As we saw earlier, this would often be expressed as US$285.00 per freight ton ... weight or measure.

The shipping line will charge either on the weight of the consignment or its volume, whichever gives them the greater return. This is still sometimes referred to as 'W/M ship's option'. This is perfectly reasonable as the carrier's capacity is limited both by the space available for cargo and the maximum weight (deadweight) that can legally be carried.

A vessel fully loaded with steel sheet will still have volume unused, and a vessel full of foam rubber would not use anywhere near its deadweight capacity. The process of freight calculation takes into account the different stowage factors of the wide range of commodities carried.

For sea freight the units used are: metric tonne (1,000 kg) or cubic metre (CBM or M^3).

The weight unit is 1,000 kg, commonly known as the metric ton or tonne, and the freight will be calculated on the gross weight of the consignment. That is to say that the weight of the packing (tare weight) will also be included for freight purposes.

As an example, a consignment of two cases each 4,000 kg would generate a total of 8 freight tons.

The volume, or measure, unit is the cubic metre and is calculated by a multiplication of length by breadth by height. Thus if our two cases were each 200 cms × 200 cms × 150 cms, then each would be 6 cubic metres (CBM), giving a total of 12 CBM.

This can be calculated by a multiplication of the cms to give cubic centimetres, and then a division by 1,000,000 (1 CBM = 1,000,000 cubic cms) or, more easily, by converting cms into metres by dividing by 100, and then multiplying. Thus, in our example our two cases are 2 m × 2 m × 1.5 m, that is 6 CBM per case.

Given that the freight rate for these two cases was, for example, $285.00, then the freight cost would be:

$$12 \text{ CBM} \times \$285.00 = \$3,420.00$$

And *not*:

$$8 \text{ tonnes} \times \$285.00 = \$2,280.00$$

The carrier is charging on volume, not weight.

Road/rail freight calculation

The other two modes of surface freight are based on exactly the same method of calculation, that is weight or measure, but there does tend to be a greater range of rates applied, particularly in the highly competitive area of road haulage.

Also, it is very common that the ratio of weight to measure changes, the most common being 1,000 kg or 3.3 CBM. Sometimes, because the average consignment size may be smaller than 1,000 kg, the carriers will quote rates based on smaller units of 100 kg or 0.33 CBM.

Air freight calculation

Just as with surface freight, the principle of weight/volume is applicable to air freight, but the structure of the carrier's tariff is different.

The typical airline will base its tariff on:

- General cargo rates (GC): these apply to non-unitized consignments of mixed commodities.
- Specific commodity rates (SC): shippers of large quantities of specific commodities between specific airports can apply for SC rates, which will be much lower than the GC rates.

In the case of both GC and SC rates, the lines will often offer quantity discounts once a certain level of business is achieved.

- Classification rates: certain categories of goods, for example live animals, cadavers and bullion, attract charges based on a discount or surcharge on the GC rate.
- Unit load device rate (ULD): ULDs are the air equivalent of the ISO container. The ULD rates ignore the nature of the goods and charge for a specific unit up to a specified maximum weight. They are the air equivalent of the 'box rates' that may be available for sea shipments.
- Freight of all kinds (FAK): there is a growing use of FAK rates as a means of simplifying the rate structure and avoiding SC rates. A rate per kilo is charged subject to a minimum weight requirement.

The actual calculation of air-freight charges is again based on a ratio of weight to volume that is somewhat different from sea freight. The most common ratio is 1,000 kg or 6 CBM.

It will be clear that volume does not become relevant to air consignments unless the cargo is extremely voluminous. So while the majority of sea shipments are charged by volume, it is more usual for air cargoes to be calculated on the basis of weight.

In practice the ratio of 1,000 kg or 6 CBM is somewhat too large for the average air consignment and it is therefore more usual for rates to be quoted per kilogram or per 6,000 cubic cms, that is the volume unit is one thousandth of 6 CBM. A 6,000 cubic cms unit is referred to as a 'volumetric unit' or a 'chargeable kilo'.

Take as an example a case of 50 kilos, 100 cms × 100 cms × 50 cms at a rate of £9.00 per chargeable kilo.

The freight charge will not be:

$$50 \text{ kilos} \times £9.00 = £450.00$$

but will be:

$$83.33 \text{ volume units} \times 5,9.00 = 5,750.00$$

(The volume units being the product of 100 cms × 100 cms × 50 cms = 500,000 cubic cms, divided by 6,000 cubic cms.)

In conclusion, each transport mode will generate its own basic tariff, based on factors such as destination, commodity, value and standards units, and will apply that basic rate to the weight or volume of the cargo in order to maximize revenues in relation to the carrier's limits on deadweight and space available. The ratio of weight to volume will differ from one mode of transport to another, but the principle of W/M (weight or measure) is one that applies to all modes.

Total distribution cost

Assuming that we are now in a position to calculate an accurate freight cost, we still must accept that the freight itself is not the only cost item that should be considered in comparing one mode of transport with another. The concept of total distribution cost, mentioned earlier in this chapter, is based on the fact that a number of other transport-related factors, in addition to freight cost, can be quantified, in order to make a more realistic choice as to transport mode and route.

A simple comparison of freight costs will always reveal air freight as being far more expensive than surface freight, but a consideration of other cost factors could change that perception.

Elements of the total distribution cost, other than the freight charge, would include:

- Packing: the need for protection is reduced where the transit time and level of handling are reduced.

- Documentation: a simplified documentary regime, which is offered by air freight, and to a lesser extent road and rail, can lead to savings in administrative costs.

- Inland carriage: it is often the case that there are major differences between the costs of transport into the port of departure, and from the port of destination, which will depend on the mode, and specific ports, involved.

- Insurance: it may be the case that the cargo insurance premiums will differ depending on the mode of transport, the most common distinction being between air and surface freight.

- Unpacking and refurbishing: with some goods, following surface movements, extensive renovation of the goods and packing is necessary. This can be minimized by fast transits such as air freight.

- Speed of transit: many of the points raised lead to a conclusion that air shipments provide a number of advantages as compared with surface freight, many of which are related to the reduction in handling time and the speed of transit. Perhaps the most obvious consequence of a faster transit time is the fact that, whatever the terms of payment, then payment will be received sooner. The higher the interest rates faced by exporters, then the greater are the savings from quicker payments.

Taking all these factors into consideration, it is possible to prepare a *total distribution cost analysis* that compares the transport options available to the exporter for a particular consignment.

Table 16.2 illustrates how a simple comparison of sea and air freight might look.

TABLE 16.2 Comparison of sea and air total distribution costs

	Air $	Sea $
Ex-works value	26,000	26,000
Freight	1,170	220
Packing	190	530
Inland transport: domestic	50	200
Inland transport: overseas	130	430
Insurance	60	70
Total	27,600	27,450

The additional saving from faster payment of the delivered price if we were to assume that the reduction in transit time between air and sea transits was 28 days (which would be perfectly reasonable for any dispatch to a developing country) and if interest rates were, for example, 5 per cent, is calculated in Table 16.3.

TABLE 16.3 Comparison of total distribution costs adjusted for interest

	Air $	Sea $
Delivered price	27,600	27,450
Interest saved	–106	
Total cost	27,494	27,450

While this example is not representative of all consignments, it does illustrate the point that a consideration of all the quantifiable factors of physical distribution may well lead to a more objective choice of transport modes that takes into consideration more than just the freight costs. The narrowing of the gap between air- and surface-freight cost is typical of a genuine and comprehensive comparison that all exporters should attempt.

The calculation of a true total distribution cost can provide great advantages to all exporters and could lead to a more professional approach to the whole area of physical distribution management. This would involve the consideration of all aspects of the physical movement of goods, from the receipt of raw materials through the whole process of internal handling and storage to the actual delivery to the end user.

It is not the purpose of this text to examine physical distribution management (PDM), often referred to as logistics, in any detail, but perhaps the example of Toyota's success in PDM could be instructive. Toyota (allegedly) have achieved the ultimate level of efficiency by making Just in Time (JIT) principles actually work. They claim to hold zero inventory, that is, no stock at all. Components arrive from suppliers JIT to be fitted, JIT to be tested, JIT to be packed, JIT to be dispatched, JIT to be shipped, JIT to arrive and JIT (it is hoped) to be sold.

Well, it is worth thinking about, and is certainly an improvement on the more common British version known as JTL (Just Too Late)!

17
Packing and marking for export

The vital importance of correct packing and marking of export consignments is often not appreciated by many companies, even though they may take great pains with other elements of the export process. This is particularly short-sighted when one realizes that in virtually all export sales it is the seller who will be responsible for adequate export packing and correct marking.

Not only can this represent a significant cost element in terms of price calculation but also if the goods get to the customer smashed to pieces, or with half of them missing, or they arrive in perfect condition in the wrong place, this can be extremely expensive in terms of direct financial loss, time taken in corrective action and loss of customer goodwill.

What must be accepted is that packing and marking for export are a highly specialized function, and what is considered adequate for domestic dispatches is invariably inadequate for overseas dispatches.

There are a number of reasons why export consignments face greater risks of theft, pilferage and damage than do domestic consignments.

Distance and handling

On a purely statistical basis there is more likelihood of loss or damage, the longer the transit. Most loss and damage occurs to goods during handling. Not only do goods tend to be handled more often when exported but also the quality of handling may leave something to be desired.

Environmental conditions

Overseas consignments are often subject to far more arduous conditions than are domestic transits.

As a final point, the exporter should be aware that goods need to be prepared for the whole of the journey, not just the easiest part. Even containerized goods are broken down and carried on towards the end of their journey in conditions that may be much inferior to those prevailing at the beginning. It is a sensible exporter who prepares goods for the worst possible element of the transit, not the best possible.

So what do we expect from our packing? It must:

- protect;
- contain;
- identify.

The packing protects against damage and pilferage, contains the goods so that they can be handled, even when protection may be less relevant, and bears the marks that enable the goods to be identified.

While there is little problem in identifying what export packing is required to do, the actual choice as to how goods will be packed is far more difficult. An increasing problem is the huge choice of methods that exporters now have.

Packing methods

Cartons

The carton is now the most widely used type of outer packing, and available in a range of materials, in particular double- or triple-walled cardboard. In most cases this combines adequate protection with low cost and lightness.

Cases or crates

Traditionally made of wood, but less common now because of the ever-increasing cost of timber, the case is a solid box, while the crate is composed of a skeleton, or slatted, structure. Apart from the material cost and the added weight (which increases the freight cost) it may also be necessary for the wood to be treated with pesticides and be certified as such for certain markets.

Bales

Used regularly in certain trades where goods can be compressed and then wrapped, often with hessian, and banded, the bale is sometimes referred to as a 'truss', particularly when not banded.

Drums

Drums are produced in a very wide range of materials apart from the traditional steel variety. They are suitable for many liquid and powder goods.

Sacks

Again available in a range of materials from paper to plastic, sacks are often used when containment is more important than protection.

In addition to the above, there is also a range of highly specialized forms of export packing suitable for specific goods, such as carboys, which are glass containers for corrosive liquids, steel cases for highly pilferable items, shrink wrap for goods that could be damaged by moisture, and so on.

For advice on the range of packing materials available the exporter can, of course, consult the manufacturers, but must accept that they may be biased. A good forwarder or carrier can also be very helpful. An element of the British Standards Institution known as Technical Help to Exporters, and the Paper and Board Printing and Packaging Industries Research Association (PIRA) can also offer specialized advice.

Factors affecting choice of packing

Given a fair knowledge of the choices available to the exporter, what factors actually impact on the method eventually chosen?

Nature of goods

The special requirements of the goods must be considered. They may be bulky, fragile or valuable, or may require specific packing, handling and stowage, perhaps to avoid sweating or tainting. The very special requirements of dangerous goods are examined in Chapter 18.

Destination

This relates to the distance to be travelled, the quality of handling and the range of climatic conditions experienced by the goods. Also there may be specific regulations in the country of destination regarding the type of packing. Typically, this would be an insistence on the treatment of organic packing with insecticides, or even a total ban. Such regulations would affect not only wooden cases or crates but also wool and straw.

Mode of transport

The need for protection, and the particular packing regulations, will differ from one mode of transport to another. As a broad example, it is often the case that packing for air freight needs to be less robust than for sea freight, on the grounds that the transit is shorter and handling more sophisticated.

Customer's requirements

In some cases the type of packing the exporter would normally use is replaced by a type requested by the customer. Assuming the buyer is prepared to pay any extra costs that this may involve, then the exporter would normally comply. Care should be taken if the buyer requests inferior packing in an attempt to save money, if only to ensure that the seller has no contractual obligations for damage in transit.

Cost

If cost was not a factor in the selection of packing methods, then the great majority of goods would be packed in solid wooden cases. Because this is a very expensive method, cheaper but adequate alternatives must be found, such as cartons. We should also remember that the freight charge is based on the gross weight of the shipment, which includes the weight of the packing, known as the 'tare' weight. Heavy packing is therefore not only a cost factor in its own right but also increases the freight charge.

The use of second-hand packing as a means of reducing cost may be possible but the exporter should take great care to ensure that the packing is still adequate, and that any previous marks are completely removed. There is a potential risk that the carriers may issue claused receipts if they consider packing to be inadequate (see Chapter 18).

Marking for export

Once the goods are packed, the exporter must make certain that they are marked sufficiently well to ensure that they get to the intended final destination. In this context, the only rules that apply are those concerning the marking of dangerous goods, and these are addressed later.

So far as non-hazardous goods are concerned, the only recommendations are available from Simpler Trade Procedures (SITPRO) and the International Cargo Handling Co-ordination Association (ICHCA).

For air, road and rail movements it is not uncommon that the goods simply carry the full address of the consignee, in which case they would be labelled as opposed to marked. The parties involved should seriously consider whether the naming of the consignee poses any security problems in terms of the possible identification of the nature of the goods.

Where sea-freight shipments are concerned, it is far more common for the goods to carry identification that is basically a coded shipping mark. This has the great merit of being simple and does not clutter the packing with large amounts of possibly irrelevant information. SITPRO suggests that the marks should be 'sufficient and necessary for goods in transit'.

A typical mark is shown in Figure 17.1.

FIGURE 17.1 Sample coded shipping mark

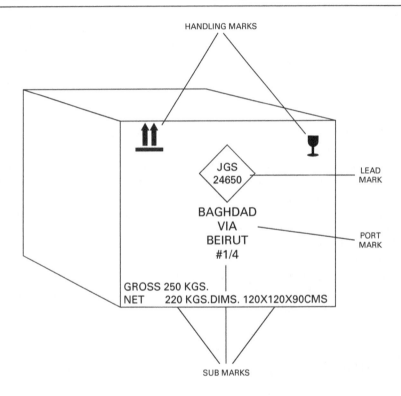

Lead mark

Identifies the consignee and, maybe, the consignment or order reference number.

Port marks

It is important that the mark not only contains the final destination but also that the port of discharge is clearly displayed.

Sub marks

These, for example, include gross and net weights in kilograms, dimensions in centimetres, and running numbers that identify the unit number; for example, 4 of 8 or 4/8 would identify case number 4 of a total of 8 cases.

Handling

A range of standardized pictorial handling marks has been established by the International Standards Organization (ISO) and gives clear instructions regarding the handling of goods. These marks are recognized throughout the world.

The more common pictorial handling marks are illustrated in Figure 17.2.

FIGURE 17.2 Some pictorial handling marks

Sling here	Fragile	Use no hooks
This way up	Keep away from heat	Keep dry
Center of gravity		

Exporters should also consider:

- Legibility: lead marks and port marks should be at least 7.5 cms high and sub marks at least 3.5 cms high. Care should also be taken that any banding does not mask the marks.

- Indelibility: obviously the mark needs to be permanent in all conditions. One that washes off in the rain is not particularly effective.
- Position: it is important that the marks are always visible and this therefore requires at least two, and sometimes three, marks on different sides of the goods.

18
Transport documentation

One of the biggest problems for many companies involved in international trade is the number of 'bits of paper' that are essential to the performance of their export contracts. That is to say that the documentation involved in the administration of their overseas business is perceived as being abundant in quantity, complex in character and designed to hinder rather than help their export effort.

While there is an element of truth in this perception, it has to be said that many companies suffer from the consequences of this complexity because they make very little effort to understand the purposes and functions of the range of documents with which they deal. There is often an element of negligence in their own management, in particular in terms of staff training, which translates itself into a continuous saga of documentary errors and their sometimes disastrous consequences.

The fact that something like 70 per cent of document sets presented to banks against letters of credit are rejected on first presentation due to documentary discrepancies does serve to prove this point.

It is an unfortunate fact that many personnel involved in export documentation have only received what is sometimes referred to as 'standing next to Nellie' training. The administrative procedures are passed on to new operatives by the more experienced ones, so that it is often clear what is to be done, but very rarely is it so clear why it needs to done.

Not only is this an extremely boring way to perform office functions for the personnel involved, it is also an error-prone process, simply because there is no real understanding of the consequences of procedures, and documents are simply completed or produced by rote. Also, the systems become very inflexible and unable to accommodate anything out of the ordinary. Moreover, just because something works does not make it right, and it can often be the case that company systems incorporate mistakes that become almost 'carved in stone' because they work, despite being incorrect practice.

It could be said, with some validity, that because of the use of forwarding agents and of computerized systems, such an understanding is of less value in modern offices, but agents have to be instructed, monitored and, most importantly, paid; and computer systems have to be set up on the basis of a clear understanding of procedural requirements, all of which work much better with a knowledgeable principal.

This chapter looks at the 'why' of documentary procedures rather than just the 'what', and shows how logical the procedures are (yes, even customs procedures) once it is clear exactly what they do.

An overview of export documentation

As has already been mentioned, the range of documents encountered by exporters is often seen as intimidating and confusing, and those involved directly in the procedural elements can find it difficult to take a step back and, as it were, see the wood for the trees.

This is aggravated by the perhaps obvious fact that it takes more than one piece of paper to move an international consignment. A set of documents is required that may be relatively simple and involve only three or four or may be extremely complex and include a number of specialized documents. Also, the set will differ from one consignment to another depending on the specific collection of variables including the type of goods, method of transport, destination, method of payment and the buyer's requirements.

It is possible to take what is a veritable 'mountain' of documents and rationalize them into four smaller 'hills' in that we can categorize any document used in international trade into one of four types depending on its origin or application.

The four categories are:

1 Transport.
2 Customs.
3 Insurance.
4 Payment.

With a little flexibility all international trade documents can be listed under these headings and the list below shows the documents that will be described in the chapters that follow:

Transport:
- Bill of lading (B/L);
- Air waybill (AWB);
- Road waybill (CMR note);
- Rail waybill (CIM note).

Customs:
- Intrastat;
- Single administrative document (SAD);

- Export invoice;
- Certificate of origin;
- Status documents;
- ATA carnet.

Insurance:
- Policy;
- Certificate;
- Declarations.

Payment:
- Letters of instruction;
- Bill of exchange;
- Letter of credit.

If any of the titles or abbreviations are not clear or familiar, rest assured that they will be explained in full in the following chapters.

Thus an international consignment will require a set of documents that can be selected from those listed. As an example, a simple document set could be composed of a bill of lading, an export invoice, a certificate of origin, a cargo insurance certificate and a single administrative document.

This could also be supplemented by a wide range of more specialized documents, depending on each consignment's specific requirements.

The transport conventions

There is a fundamental problem associated with international trade that is so obvious that it is often missed. It is the fact that there are always at least two nationalities involved in the export transaction. This is most obvious when one considers the contract of sale in which the buyer and seller are of two different nationalities and where the law governing the contract must be established.

These problems are compounded by the fact that the international carrier is often of a third nationality.

The problems that this could cause to the exporter can be divided into two areas: the contract of carriage and the transport document.

The fundamental question is whether the carriers impose their conditions of carriage (dependent on nationality) on the shipper, in which case the exporter will potentially be involved in many different contracts of carriage; or whether the shippers impose their conditions on the carrier, in which case the carrier, working for a range of different nationalities of shipper, has the same problem.

The same complexities could apply to the transport document, in that many different bills of lading and waybills could exist depending on the nationality of the shipper or the carrier.

The situation in practice is that a range of international conventions addresses and solves the problem of the mix of nationalities involved in the contract of carriage. Each mode of international transport operates within the scope of a convention that standardizes the documentation and the contract of carriage and which, in practice, means that the exporter can generally ignore the nationality of the carrier.

The International Transport Conventions are (briefly):

- Sea: Hague-Visby or Hamburg rules.
- Air: Montreal (previously Warsaw).
- Road: CMR.
- Rail: CIM.

These are the titles of the major international transport conventions that have been ratified in many countries, including the United Kingdom's Carriage of Goods Acts, and which standardize the conditions of carriage and the documentation. In practice, they mean that an exporter can deal with a variety of nationalities of carrier and still operate with standard documentation. (See Clause paramount below.)

The bill of lading

Procedure

The exporter, or their agent, completes an export cargo shipping instruction (ECSI), from which the bills will be produced by the shipping line's computers.

The goods are delivered into the port or depot with a shipping note.

Goods are recorded, compared with the stowage plan and booking references, and entered on to the ship's manifest.

Once the goods are in the possession of the carrier, the bills of lading are produced on behalf of the ship's Master and returned to the exporter/agent. Computer-produced bills may carry facsimile signatures, but are still issued on behalf of the ship's Master.

While the layout of bills differs from one carrier to another, the majority are now produced with very similar A4-size layouts and contain broadly the same information. This would include:

1 the parties involved (shipper, consignee and notify party);
2 ports/depots of loading and discharge;
3 vessel name/s and voyage number;

4 number of original bills;

5 marks and numbers;

6 description of goods;

7 type of packages;

8 gross weight (kg) and measurement (M^3);

9 received and/or shipped dates;

10 reference to payment of freight, that is prepaid or forward.

And, of course, there will also be the important signature on the original bills on behalf of the ship's Master. All bills will contain most of these items and all operate in the same way.

Functions

The bill of lading has three major functions:

- a receipt for the goods;
- evidence of the contract of carriage;
- a document of title.

Receipt for goods

A bill of lading will contain the words 'apparent good order and condition', thus obliging the carrier to deliver the goods in the same condition. Such a bill is known as a 'clean bill' and acts as a clean receipt for the goods.

However, there may be situations in which the shipping line does not think that the goods are in good order and condition and will say so on the face of the bill. Such a reference is known as a clause on the bill that overrides the 'good order and condition' reference. These claused bills are sometimes referred to as 'dirty' or 'foul' bills of lading and cause great problems to exporters.

The clauses can be stamped or handwritten and typical examples might be: 'inadequate packing', 'second-hand packing', 'one case short'; 'five cases short shipped', and even 'five cases thought to be short shipped ... if on board will deliver', or 'three drums leaking'.

This reflects the justified attitude of the shipping lines that they will honour their part of the contract of carriage, if at all possible, and earn their freight, but protect themselves from the misconduct of the shipper.

The problem for the shipper is that a claused bill of lading clearly provides no evidence of contract performance to the buyer, in fact quite the opposite, and will not be acceptable to a bank against a letter of credit.

However, the incidence of claused bills has been much reduced over the last few decades because of the widespread use of unitized, ie containerized, transport. In fact, the shipping lines very often do not see the goods at all but simply receive the containers that have been loaded in a groupage depot or even the shipper's own premises.

The slight downside to this is that the lines will often issue a bill that states 'said to contain...', sometimes referred to as an STC bill, ie a receipt for a container which it is claimed contains a particular quantity of specified goods. While this still generates clean bills it can make it more difficult to take action against the shipping line for partial loss within containers.

Evidence of the contract of carriage

The first point to be made is that the bill of lading is not the contract of carriage itself, but merely evidence of it. The actual contract is a verbal one made at the time the space is booked and the bill is produced part way through the performance of the contract. In practice it is rare that the conditions expressed on the bill do not represent the contract of carriage conditions.

As the contract is a verbal one made at the time the space is booked, this also means that the carrier is able to charge freight for space booked even if it is not used by the shipper. This is known as dead freight and is reduced should the carrier obtain alternative cargo to take up that space.

The second point is that the bill evidences the conditions of the contract and will often contain, on its back, a wide range of contract clauses. As has already been mentioned, the majority of contracts for the carriage of goods by sea are carried out by shipping lines whose national legislation has ratified the appropriate convention (either the Hague-Visby or the Hamburg Rules) and the clause that specifies this is known as the clause paramount or paramount clause. Thus the carrier is committed to the standard rules, which will take precedence over the rest of the carrier's conditions should there be a conflict. The fact that these rules are ratified in legislation also means that carriers cannot contract out of such obligations.

A typical clause paramount is shown in Box 18.1.

Box 18.1 Typical clause paramount

The Hague rules contained in the International Convention for the unification of certain rules relating to bills of lading, dated Brussels 25 August 1924, or in those countries where they are already in force the Hague-Visby rules contained in the Protocol of Brussels dated 23 February 1868, as en-acted in the country of shipment, shall apply to all carriage of goods by sea and, where no mandatory international or national law applies, to the carriage of goods by inland waterways also, and such provisions shall apply to all goods whether carried on deck or under deck.

The Hague-Visby rules are currently in force in most countries that have merchant fleets and are ratified in their legislation. The Hamburg rules as an alternative are not well accepted and are rarely applicable. In an attempt to rationalize the situation, the United Nations has produced, towards the end of 2009, the UN Convention on Contracts for the International Carriage of Goods wholly or partly by Sea, known as the Rotterdam rules, designed to update previous conventions, particularly in relation to multimodal containerized movements.

However, the intended new rules have met with much criticism and, in fact, active rejection by organizations such as FIATA, the Fédération Internationale des Associations de Transitaires et Assimilés (International Federation of Freight Forwarders Association). The most common criticism is their unnecessary complexity. Such arguments continue into 2010 and it will be some time, if ever, before the Rotterdam rules are ratified by the majority of trading nations.

Document of title

This is the most relevant, and unique, feature of the bill of lading and one that has important implications in terms of its functions and applications in practice.

The first point to make is that bills are issued in sets containing two or three originals and any number of copies. The originals are signed on behalf of the ship's Master and are referred to as 'negotiable', as they contain, and are able to transfer, property in the goods.

The copies are unsigned and non-negotiable, and merely convey information. The availability of at least two original bills means that they can be dispatched to the destination port separately to ensure that at least one is available.

The reason why this is so important, and an explanation of the practical importance of the bill of lading's status, is the fact that one signed original negotiable bill must be presented back to the shipping line at destination for them to release the goods.

The bills may be sent direct, or through the banks, and once one is accomplished (by presentation to the line) the others are void. Facsimile or photocopy versions are not acceptable.

The relevance of this to the exporter should not be underestimated in that it is possible to restrict the buyer's access to the goods at destination, by withholding the bills of lading. Thus payment terms can be arranged that require buyers to pay not for goods but for documents, and this does create some security for the seller.

The relationship between documents and methods of payment is examined in detail in Part 8.

The negotiability of the bill is affected by the manner of its completion, in that the title may be addressed to a specific consignee, in which case it is not freely negotiable. The consignee may then endorse the back of the bill, which can then transfer title.

More commonly, the bill is made out 'to order' rather than to a named consignee, endorsed by the exporter (signed on the back), and naming a notify party that the carriers will advise of the arrival of the goods. In this case the bill is drawn up as a 'negotiable instrument' as in Box 18.2.

Box 18.2 Bill of lading completion

	Either	Or
Shipper	Exporter (or agent)	Exporter (or agent)
Consignee	Importer	'Order' or 'To order'
Notify party	....	Importer or agent or bank, etc
	Title addressed to a specific party	Title open to bearer
	No endorsement	Endorsement needed
	Named consignee may endorse and transfer	

It is clearly important for an exporter to be careful in the handling of bills of lading, as a 'to order blank endorsed bill of lading' confers title in the goods to the bearer.

The face of the bill will always show how many signed originals there are and the banks will invariably require the full set of bills, which may be expressed as 2/2 (that is, two of two) or 3/3.

From a purely practical point of view it is obviously necessary to ensure that bills are available at destination in order to clear the goods on arrival. Should the goods have arrived but not the bills, they are then known as stale bills of lading, and this will inevitably lead to delays in clearance.

In some cases extra charges for such a delay may be imposed; these are known as demurrage and can be expensive, particularly in congested ports and depots.

Banks dealing with letters of credit will describe a bill as being stale when it is presented outside the days allowed for presentation of documents against the credit. This will often be 7 or 15 days, and if no time period is specified, the bank will assume 21 days.

A bill of lading glossary

Received

Confirms that the goods are in the possession of the carrier, but not that they have been loaded. The increase in containerized, depot-to-depot movements has led to the increased use of received bills, which are issued as the goods arrive at the inland container base.

Once the goods are loaded, the received bill can be stamped with a 'shipped on board' notation and date and therefore become a shipped bill of lading.

Combined transport

This refers to the fact that the typical containerized sea-freight consignment will move from one inland depot of departure to another at destination. The whole transit will be organized under one contract of carriage evidenced by the bill of lading, and therefore covers, for example, a road–sea–road transit. Most bills issued by container lines are 'received combined transport bills of lading'. A bill showing an inland destination may also be referred to as a 'through bill of lading'.

Transhipment

In the case where the goods are not shipped direct to the port of discharge, but via a third port, using two vessels, it is possible to obtain a bill covering both vessels. These may be referred to as the feeder vessel and the ocean vessel, and the transhipment port will be shown as well as the ports of shipment and destination.

Letters of credit may not allow transhipment but as long as there is one single transport document the banks will not regard it as a transhipment.

Groupage

It is common that exporters who cannot provide full loads, for either containers and/or road trailers, will make use of groupage operators. The groupage operator will group or consolidate a number of exporter's consignments into one shipment that will be covered by a set of groupage bills of lading issued by the shipping line.

The groupage operator may issue a certificate of shipment, which simply acts as a freight forwarder's receipt or a 'house bill of lading', which is often referred to as a 'non-vessel-owning common carriers bill' (NVOCC) and is inferior in status to a shipping company's bill of lading.

FIATA

Issued on behalf of the Fédération Internationale des Associations de Transitaires et Assimilés (International Federation of Freight Forwarders Association) and acceptable as an ocean bill of lading against a letter of credit. It is perceived as being issued by an agent of the shipping line.

Common

Sponsored by SITPRO (Simpler Trade Procedures), the common bill of lading is intended to replace the range of individual bills produced by the lines. The carrier's name is not pre-printed on the bill but a space is left for the name to be added. Unfortunately, the common bill of lading is not in common use.

Short form

The detailed clauses on the reverse of many bills are omitted and instead the carrier's 'standard conditions of carriage' are referred to along with the clause paramount on the face of the bill.

Both common and short-form bills are acceptable against letters of credit, unless the credit says that they are not.

Lost or destroyed bills of lading

In this case delays are inevitable but can be reduced by the use of a letter of indemnity. This will allow release of the goods at destination without presentation of a valid bill. The original, or replacement, set will be produced at a later date. The indemnity is invariably required to be countersigned by a bank and should not be accepted at destination without the approval of the shipper.

Waybills

Waybills, used for air, road and rail transits, have a number of characteristics in common with the ocean bill of lading but have one very important difference, as shown in Table 18.1.

TABLE 18.1 Comparison of ocean bill of lading and waybill

Bill of lading	Waybill
Receipt for the goods	Receipt for the goods
Evidence of the contract of carriage	Evidence of the contract of carriage
Document of title	Not a document of title
Goods released in exchange for an original bill	Goods released to named consignee

Where waybills are issued, the carriers will release the goods at destination. It is not necessary to produce a transport document to obtain possession of the goods. The advantage of this is one of convenience in that the availability of a document at destination is not related to the release of goods.

However, it should be realized that a waybill is not a document of title and cannot be used to transfer property in the goods as part of the payment procedures. The most obvious problem area is associated with air freight into high-risk markets.

Air waybill procedure

The exporter or agent completes a letter of instruction to the airline. In the great majority of cases air freight is arranged through agents rather than direct with the airline. Because of this it is not uncommon that house air waybills, ie issued by a forwarding house as agent, are issued as opposed to the carrier's air waybill. However, as long as the carrier countersigns the house air waybill, it will be accepted as a carrier's receipt against a letter of credit.

The air waybills are issued in sets of anything up to 12 copies but will contain at least three originals:

1 retained by airline;

2 forwarded to consignee;

3 returned to exporter.

There will also be any number of copies for internal control and information. The air waybill does not protect ownership of the goods but it may be possible to arrange cash on delivery (COD) in certain markets.

In cases where the exporter perceives a risk and is looking for some security, it is possible for a party other than the buyer to be named as consignee. If you do not entirely trust the buyer, then do not name the buyer as the consignee; name a party that you do trust, such as a bank. It is not uncommon that banks are named as consignees for air, road and rail shipments, and subject to specific instructions will collect payment against release of the goods as opposed to release of documents.

Air-freight and passenger movements are covered by the Montreal Convention (which replaced the Warsaw Convention in 2009).

Road waybill

Covered by the CMR Convention (Convention des Marchandises par Route), the road waybill provides a standard, non-negotiable, consignment note used by most nationalities of international road haulier.

Rail waybill

Covered by the CIM Convention (Convention Internationale Concernant le Transport des Marchandises par Chemin de Fer), the rail waybill again acts as a standard consignment note for international rail carriers.

Both the road waybill and the rail waybill act as receipts and evidence of the contract of carriage but not as a document of title.

They all contain their equivalents of the clause paramount in terms of the references to the Montreal Convention (Air), CMR (Road) and CIM (Rail).

Sea waybill

As we have seen, the bill of lading is specifically a sea-freight document and is unique in that it operates as a document of title. This confers great advantages in terms of the security afforded to the exporter in controlling physical access to the goods, but can be very inconvenient where the bills become stale due to late arrival at destination.

This is a particular problem where short sea transits are concerned, in which case it is very difficult to get bills to destination before the goods arrive. In these cases it is not unusual for a sea or liner waybill to be issued by the shipping line. This document serves as a receipt for the goods and evidence of the contract of carriage but not as a document of title.

Such waybills are now being used for deep-sea transits to low-risk customers and markets such as the USA, Australia and South Africa, and are sometimes referred to as express bills in that the goods are subject to express release without the presentation of a bill of lading.

Carrier's liability

It is not the intention of this book to examine the complex articles of the transport conventions but it is important to highlight a potential problem regarding the liability of the carrier for loss or damage to the goods while in their charge.

The conventions basically define liability as 'the value of the goods at place and time of collection', but it should be noted that this is subject to a maximum that protects the carrier. The ceiling will differ from one convention to another but the current versions all use a unit of account known as a 'special drawing right' (SDR), the value of which is published in the national financial press.

Very approximately, the maximum carrier's liability for the current conventions (the SDR being on a par with pound sterling in 2010) is:

- Sea: (Hague-Visby): £660 per package or £2,000 per tonne; (Hamburg): £840 per package or £2,500 per tonne.

- Air: (Montreal): £17,000 per tonne.
- Rail: (CIM): £17,000 per tonne.
- Road: (CMR): £8,330 per tonne.

It should be noted that these figures represent the maximum liability of the carrier, but exporters of high-value goods may well find it worthwhile to negotiate higher limits with the carrier.

Dangerous goods

The exporter of dangerous goods is responsible for the actions identified in Figure 18.1.

FIGURE 18.1 Actions for dangerous goods

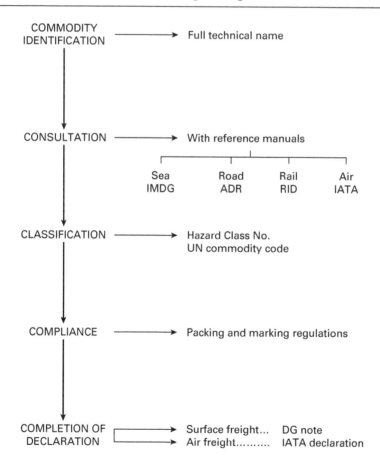

International regulations

The United Nations Committee of Experts on the Transport of Dangerous Goods produce revised 'recommendations' every two years in a publication known as the 'Orange Book'. This is then incorporated, with adaptations, in the published regulations of each of the authorities involved with the major modes of international transport. These separate authorities and their sets of rules are:

- Sea: International Maritime Organization (IMO); International Maritime Dangerous Goods code (IMDG code).
- Road: Economic Commission for Europe (ECE); Accord Dangereux Routier (ADR).
- Rail: Central Office for International Rail Transport (OCTI); Règlement International Dangereux (RID).
- Air: International Civil Aviation Organization (ICAO).

Technical instructions

Fundamental requirements for all dangerous goods procedures are:

- identification of goods;
- packing and marking requirements;
- documentary declarations.

Identification of goods

The correct technical name of the product or substance must be used and not brand or proprietary names. Thus 2,000 litres of 'Gramoxone' would be unacceptable because that is a brand name; these goods should be described as '2,000 litres of paraquet dichloride in solution'.

However, word descriptions of goods are not specific enough for the detailed identification necessary, and more precise classification systems are needed. The broadest classification is the United Nations Commodity Classification system, which covers all goods, including dangerous ones. The UN four-digit code must be included in the written declarations. In addition, hazardous goods are classified into nine hazard classes. This is the basis of the IMDG code and other modal classifications (with amendments for air freight) and also leads to a standardized hazard warning labelling system.

The classes are:

1 Explosives;
2 Gases:
    2.1 Flammable (same meaning as inflammable);
    2.2 Non-flammable;
    2.3 Toxic;

3 Flammable liquids:

    3.1 Flashpoint below 18°C;

    3.2 Flashpoint 18° to 23°C;

    3.3 Flashpoint 23° to 61°C;

4 **4.1** Flammable solids;

    4.2 Liable to spontaneous combustion;

    4.3 Emit flammable gas in contact with water;

5 **5.1** Oxidizing substances:

    5.2 Organic peroxides;

6 **6.1** Toxic substances;

    6.2 Infectious substances;

7 Radioactive materials;

8 Corrosives;

9 Miscellaneous substances (not covered by other classes).

Each of these has a globally standard graphic hazard warning diamond sign.

Packing and marking requirements

There is a simple UN classification of packing groups that is based on the broad level of hazard. It is:

Packing group I: High hazard.

Packing group II: Medium hazard.

Packing group III: Low hazard.

For international road and rail freight the group numbers become (a), (b) and (c).

Each transport mode also specifies more detailed packing types for each class. Most packing also needs to be approved by the Paper and Board, Printing and Packaging Research Association (PIRA).

Documentary declarations

It is essential that any exporter shipping hazardous goods makes a written declaration certifying that the goods are properly classified, packed, marked and suitable for carriage. The document used for surface-freight movements is the Dangerous Goods note (DGN). The DG note not only identifies the exact nature of the goods but also replaces the shipping note, which is not appropriate to dangerous goods, and should act as a written application for shipping space rather than the usual informal verbal booking.

For air-freight consignments the declaration is not the DG note but the shipper's declaration of the International Air Transport Association (IATA). The above are requirements that broadly apply to all modes of transport but each individual means of international transport has adapted and extended these procedures.

Dangerous goods by sea

The IMDG Code has been ratified in most trading nations – in the UK by the Merchant Shipping (Dangerous Goods and Marine Pollutants) Regulations. In addition to the four-volume code there is a supplement that contains emergency procedures, medical first aid guide, reporting procedures and guidelines for packing cargo in freight containers.

This means that the information needed from the exporter also includes the EmS number (Emergency Schedule) and MFAG number (Medical First Aid Guide). Finally, exporters should never attempt to identify goods with the IMDG page number. The IMO publications exist in various languages and therefore page numbers may differ and amendments may alter the page running order.

Dangerous goods by road

The Accord Dangereux Routier (ADR) is again ratified in most countries. It provides provisions that govern the goods and the vehicle. Annexe 1 covers goods classification, packing and marking; Annexe 2 covers vehicle type, loading, stowing, safety equipment and driver training.

The nine IMDG classes broadly apply but ADR does make a distinction between 'restrictive' goods that cannot be moved without special arrangements with the transport authorities of the countries of transit and 'non-restrictive' goods that can be moved, so long as they meet ADR provisions. Within the classifications ADR groups goods under item numbers that are expressed as 1°, 2°, 3° and so on; for example, Benzene is '3.3° (b) ADR'.

The standard hazard warning diamonds are acceptable under ADR but, in addition, the vehicle must be placarded with rectangular orange plates (sometimes referred to as Kemler plates), which not only identify the hazard but also carry a telephone number for specialist advice. A final and very important requirement under ADR within the European Union is the need for transport emergency cards (Tremcards) to accompany the goods in the languages of the countries of transit.

Dangerous goods by rail

The Règlement International Dangereux (RID) is the rail-freight equivalent of ADR. The requirements are very similar to the ADR because of the deliberate cooperation between the two regimes. In most countries RID has force of law through the ratification of the 'Convention concerning the International Carriage by Rail' (COTIF).

Dangerous goods by air

The 'Technical Instructions for the Safe Transport of Dangerous Goods by Air' are published by the International Civil Aviation Organization (ICAO), which is the air version of the International Maritime Organization (IMO) and ratifies in many countries.

However, in practice, the operational manual is the International Air Transport Association's (IATA) Dangerous Goods Regulations, which are published annually and which can be more restrictive than the ICAO in some areas. The written declaration is not the Dangerous Goods note, which is specific to surface freight, but the IATA 'Shipper's Declaration for Dangerous Goods' which *must* be signed by the shipper and not the agent.

The nine hazard classes also apply to air freight, with special additions such as magnetized material, and a distinction between cargoes that can be carried on passenger aircraft and those that are only permitted on pure freight flights. Specific packing and marking conditions are also specified in the regulations, particularly a restriction on the size of packing units.

An element of the ICAO legislation is that regular shippers of dangerous goods by air must be trained on an official CAA-approved IATA course. This is a three-day course involving a course examination to qualify. The delegate must also attend a refresher every two years to validate the certificate.

Air freight poses unique problems, particularly with regard to possible changes in temperature and pressure that the goods may experience. This means that goods that are non-hazard or low hazard for surface freight may be declarable, and potentially high hazard, for air freight. Examples of this would include barometers, manometers and other electrical equipment that contains mercury, solid carbon dioxide (dry ice) and even toys if they are made from cellulose-based material.

The one other problem relating to air freight is that of security. Following the Lockerbie disaster, the problem of cargo checking was addressed in the UK by the Aviation and Maritime Security Act 1990. Not only did this tighten up the definitions of 'known' and 'unknown' shippers, but it also required certifications as to the security of shipments. In addition, the Aviation Security (Air Cargo Agents) Regulations 1992 make it possible for agents and regular shippers, to be 'listed', based on the quality of their security systems, and thus avoid the more stringent checks, and related delays, experienced by other cargo providers.

Other ongoing events, particularly since the attack on the Twin Towers on 11 September 2001, have also impacting increasingly on cargo security in all modes of transport and these security issues are covered in Part 6.

PART SIX
Customs controls

19
Export procedures and documents

All exporters and importers must comply with customs regulations and cannot abdicate that responsibility to a third party. That is not to say that agents cannot be used, and in fact the great majority of customs declarations are made by agents on behalf of traders; but the exporter and importer always bear the ultimate responsibility for the accuracy of the information provided. It is this, coupled with the need to instruct and pay agents, that should persuade traders generally to at least attempt a basic understanding of customs requirements.

It is vital to understand that compliance with customs requirements is mandatory and the consequences of non-compliance can be very expensive, in terms of time as well as money. Link this to the fact that ignorance is *never* an excuse and it is obvious that all traders should be concerned with understanding those procedures that apply to them.

It may seem hard to believe, but there is a logic to customs controls. There is no document or procedure that is there simply to make your life more difficult. They all exist for good reasons and, in many cases, they actually simplify rather than complicate. In fact, it is probable that an improved understanding of customs procedures will actually present great opportunities to reduce the time spent and the costs of compliance. The customs authorities even give money back on occasions.

An overview of customs controls

Just as it is possible to rationalize the range of export documents into four basic categories (see Chapter 18), so it is possible to take the wide and complex range of customs procedures and rationalize them into three categories, or, more accurately, sources. These are:

- export (departure);
- transit;
- import (destination).

A little simplistic, perhaps, but it does allow some logical rationalization of the 'mountain' of customs procedures into three smaller 'hills'. It also makes an important, although perhaps obvious, point that goods moving internationally must move through customs controls for the whole of the journey. The same, of course, applies to people.

Goods depart from their country of export from a customs post of departure (where some form of export declaration will be required), through customs posts of transit (if applicable) and into a customs post of destination (where an import declaration will be needed). For some international movements only the departure and destination posts will be relevant, such as a sea- or air-freight movement between two ports or airports. However, for road and rail movements it is perfectly possible that the goods will cross a number of countries of transit, in between the departure and destination countries, and therefore move through posts of transit into and out of these countries.

So what sort of controls result from these movements?

Export

All countries are interested in goods leaving their territory, but invariably it is only because they wish to count them. All developed countries operate highly sophisticated systems designed to collect trade statistics, such information being considered, quite rightly, as vital to economic planning. While less sophisticated levels of collection may operate in the developing parts of the world, all countries still count and analyse their exports. In fact, the great majority of exports are only of statistical interest and are described by customs as 'non-controlled' goods (even sometimes as 'innocent' goods).

However, certain types of goods are subject to export controls as well as being of statistical interest. Thus, you cannot send your Typhoon fighter jets to Iran without encountering some controls: in such a case, export licensing control. The range of customs regimes that could apply controls to exports are examined later in this chapter.

Import

Just as logically, customs authorities throughout the world are interested in goods entering their territories. In fact, they are invariably a lot more interested in their imports than their exports. This is due to the fact that, while most exports do not attract controls, there is no such thing as a 'non-controlled' import. Imports are of statistical interest in the same way as exports but many other controls may also apply. These can be broken down into:

Tariff barriers: duty, tax, excise, levy, licensing, quotas.

Non-tariff barriers: standards: technical, medical, health and safety, etc.

There is also a wide range of specialized control duties affecting specific goods such as dangerous drugs, live animals (veterinary) and plants (phytosanitary). These will be examined in greater detail later, but it should be quite clear that all imports will be affected by a number of these control regimes. Even if goods are entering duty free they are probably subject to VAT within the EU or equivalent taxes in other countries.

We should also remember that when the first teams of excise men in the world were formed, in the 16th century in the UK, to collect revenue on behalf of the queen (Elizabeth the First) on alcohol and tobacco, the UK coastline was divided up into 'collections'. The job of excise employees is to *collect* and, in the UK, they collect almost 65 per cent of central government revenues through duty, tax, excise and levy on imports. Most countries throughout the world have modelled their basic customs procedures on this historical model.

There is a clear and logical progression of the UK excise *collecting* revenue eventually merging with customs who *control* movements of goods and people to become HM Customs and Excise, and more recently merging with the Inland Revenue, who *collect* direct taxes, and becoming HM Revenue & Customs.

Transit

As mentioned earlier, it is not unusual for goods to actually move through other customs territories between their departure and destination points. This is, in fact, quite common for international road and rail movements. In such a case, it would be nice for the road trailer driver to say to the first customs post en route that they were only passing through their country and did not intend to stop, and for the customs to take their word for it and allow the goods to enter. It would be nice, but you can guess that it doesn't happen. We have to remember that those goods, if they remain in that country, are potentially subject to all of the import controls mentioned above. The countries of transit need some way to ensure that goods allowed in actually leave, or that they collect whatever revenues are due if they stay.

Also, consider the fact that the vehicle is quite a valuable commodity in its own right, irrespective of the goods. A driver allowed in simply on the promise that they would leave, could sell the goods, sell the vehicle, even sell the diesel in the tanks, and there is a lot of revenue at stake, in the form of duty, tax and excise. It may even be that the goods are subject to other controls in addition to these fiscal ones. The result of all this is that transit procedures have been established to protect the countries of transit, and these are examined later in this chapter.

The European Union (EU)

Before we can actually look at these procedures there is one other broad overview necessary to put them into context. The UK is a member of not just a free trade area but a customs union. The distinction is of great significance.

A simple free trade area such as the North American Free Trade Area (NAFTA, comprising the USA, Canada and Mexico) is based on an agreement between its members that they will give duty-free entry to each other's goods. Thus, Canadian-origin goods will be allowed in duty free into the USA, but UK-origin goods will attract tariff controls. However, the controls that UK goods attract in the USA will not necessarily be the same as those applicable if the same goods were to enter Canada or Mexico. These countries do not cooperate on the treatment on non-member country's goods, only on each other's.

The distinction is that the EU not only has free trade between its members but also operates a common customs tariff against non-members. This means that there is a clear distinction between *internal* and *external* frontiers. The borders between member states are internal and those with non-members are external, and goods entering the EU from outside, ie from non-members, cross a common customs frontier – which means that they attract the same tariff controls whichever member state they enter; in particular, the duty rates will be identical in every member state.

The changes that occurred on 1 January 1993 in creating a single European market are clearly based on this distinction and the situation now is that the internal frontiers have been removed, allowing the 'four freedoms': free movement of goods, people, services and capital.

What happens in the future regarding the common external tariff is very much dependent on the ongoing negotiations within the World Trade Organization (WTO), which will generate a further lowering of duty rates worldwide. The scenario of a 'Fortress Europe' in which the EU raises barriers against non-member goods has almost certainly been consigned to history.

Which country?

In terms of basic EU customs procedures it is clearly vital for the EU trader to distinguish between EU and non-EU customers and suppliers.

The current member states of the EU (in the date order in which they joined) are:

- France;
- Germany;
- Italy;
- Belgium;
- Luxemburg;
- Netherlands.

- United Kingdom;
- Ireland;
- Denmark.

- Greece.

- Spain;
- Portugal.

- Austria;
- Sweden;
- Finland;
- Czech Republic;
- Cyprus;
- Estonia;
- Hungary;
- Latvia;
- Lithuania;
- Malta;
- Poland;
- Slovakia;
- Slovenia.

- Bulgaria;
- Romania.

In terms of potential new members, Iceland has always resisted joining the EU, mainly because it was never willing to risk opening its traditional fishing grounds to vessels from the member states. However, the economic crisis leading up to 2010 seems to have changed its mind, as its banks have been harder hit than most and as the protection offered by accession to the union has begun to look like an increasingly good idea. In the middle of 2009 its parliament voted in favour of presenting an application for EU membership.

Iceland has already spent 15 years as a member of the European Economic Area (EEA), the organization that allows it, together with Liechtenstein and Norway, to enjoy the benefits of freedom of movement of goods, workers and capital in exchange for applying the Union's single market legislation.

The above three countries, plus Switzerland, are also members of the European Free Trade Association (EFTA) and are all eligible for membership of the EU.

In addition, the European Parliament is continuing to monitor the progress of other candidate countries Croatia, Turkey, the Former Yugoslav Republic of Macedonia (FYROM) and potential candidate countries of Albania, Bosnia and Herzegovina, Serbia, Montenegro and Kosovo.

The consequences of EU expansion are examined in more detail in Chapter 29.

The complex picture of EU preferential trade agreements with non-member states is examined in more detail later, but for now we can make an important distinction between three categories of trading partners:

- EU member states: eg Germany, Belgium;
- EEA/EFTA member states: eg Norway, Iceland;
- Non-members: eg Japan, USA.

Table 19.1 shows the procedures that would apply to each element of control (export, transit and import) for each category of overseas country.

TABLE 19.1   Controls applying to category of trading partner

	Export	Transit	Import
UK→EU	Intrastat		Intrastat
UK→EFTA	SAD	SAD	SAD
UK→Rest of world	SAD	TIR or TIF	?

The terms used in the table will all be explained as we proceed to examine these EU procedures – beginning, quite logically, with the export of an international consignment.

Export procedures

The first point that should be made is that, since 1 January 1993, trade between the UK and other member states of the EU should not be referred to as export or import. In terms of trade statistics we are dealing with *dispatches* and *arrivals*, and in terms of VAT, *supplies* and *acquisitions*.

For the sake of simplicity we will continue to use the words export and import when describing general procedures, and the technically correct descriptions when referring to specific VAT or trade statistics applications for EU trade.

Perhaps the best way to examine current EU customs procedures for export clearance is to engage in a brief history lesson. Since the early 1980s there has been a continuous development of customs procedures, all of which have genuinely served to simplify the administrative burdens on traders (honestly).

Let us take, as an example, a consignment of washing machines from the UK to, say, Italy, by road, in the mid 1980s. The exporter, or their agent, would have had to complete and present a full export declaration to UK customs, primarily for statistical purposes. This would have probably been a C273 form or, if the goods were subject to specific export controls, then one of a range of 'shipping bills' such as a C63A, C1334, C1172 or GW60. In addition a transit document, such as a T1 or T2, would be needed to move the goods through the countries of transit, ie France, and in addition to that an Italian import declaration would have been lodged by the importer, or their agent, at the post of destination.

There were three distinct and separate customs declarations, all containing basically the same information, and all operating in what was, supposedly, a common market. If the goods were moving the other way, the situation would have been the same; an Italian export declaration plus a T form, plus a UK import declaration (C10, C11 or C1).

The next major development was the totally logical introduction of a single document that combined the three distinct areas of customs controls, export, transit and import.

Known as the 'single administrative document' (SAD), this was introduced on 1 January 1988 and is known as the C88 in the UK. The important point is that the SAD was not just introduced in the UK but in a total of 18 European countries (the then 12 member states of the EU plus six ex-EFTA countries). It actually replaced something like 150 separate customs documents throughout Europe, including every one mentioned for our Italian job.

The final and most recent development was on 1 January 1993 when, among a number of other single market initiatives, the Intrastat procedures were introduced, which replaced the use of the SAD for intra-EU trade but did not affect its use for EU trade with the EFTA countries. Therefore the SAD is now no longer relevant to trade within the EU.

We now have a situation, as shown in Table 19.1, in which the Intrastat procedure operates alongside the SAD, their use being dependent on the country of destination.

Intrastat

The collection of trade statistics on intra-EU trade is now accomplished via three levels of declaration by exporters, depending on their level of business:

1 All VAT-registered traders must complete normal VAT returns which, on the current VAT 100 form, require information on total sales to EU customers and acquisitions from EU suppliers, in boxes 8 (Ex-works out) and 9 (Delivered in).

2 Those organizations that are conducting EU business of less than a specified annual threshold (in 2010, £600,000 for arrivals and/or £250,000 for dispatches) need only supply an EC sales listing (ESL), usually on a quarterly basis (or annually for very small traders),

on form VAT 101, listing their EU business and specifying individual VAT numbers for customers and/or suppliers.

3 All traders above these threshold levels must, in addition to the ESLs, also supply supplementary statistical declarations (SSD) on a monthly basis within 10 working days of the end of the month.

It is not necessary to declare:

- temporary exports;
- packing;
- samples;
- exhibition goods.

While these might appear to be very complex arrangements, the fact is that for smaller traders (some 150,000 of them) the requirements are actually easier than they were, in that they no longer have to make individual SAD declarations for each consignment. For the larger companies (approximately 30,000) the situation is no worse; it is simply a different form of statistical declaration.

Submission of declarations

The introduction of Intrastat has not changed the option that the trader has to use an agent to make declarations on their behalf, and many have continued to do so. One of the potential problems is that, because the information is presented in an aggregated format, the use of a number of different agents can make the compilation of information more difficult. Perhaps it means that the use of a single agent/forwarder does have advantages.

There is, however, no reason why traders cannot make the ESLs and SSDs on their own behalf.

The second point to make is that customs are keen to encourage traders and agents to provide information in other than paper format. Intrastat forms can be submitted:

- via the internet: where data is submitted on an online form or CSV file;
- via electronic data interchange (EDI): data in the EDIFACT standard is transmitted by various methods.

There is also an online facility for amending previously submitted data. This facility is available to all Intrastat users, agents submitting on behalf of Intrastat traders and larger branches of companies submitting data independently of their head office.

The system is accessed by username and password – username provided when registered – via the customs website. There are two methods of completion: an online electronic form for typing the data and an offline option using a 'comma separated variable' (CSV) file format.

VAT and the single market

It will be clear from the above that the collection of intra-EU trade statistics is now closely linked to the VAT regime that operates throughout the EU. The current situation is that UK sales to member states are still covered by a zero-rated invoice and subject to proof of export if required. In addition, the buyer's VAT number must appear on the invoice.

Thus, what is known as the 'destination principle' still applies, in that EU VAT will be collected at the time of the acquisition import in the buyer's country. For UK acquisitions from EU suppliers, we have the postponed accounting system, which allows importers to account for VAT on the 'tax due' side of their VAT returns. There is, however, a requirement to pay or defer VAT on non-EU supplies.

The single administrative document (SAD)

As we have seen, the SAD (C88) was introduced on 1 January 1988 and replaced almost 150 customs documents within both the EU and EFTA countries, combining the requirement for export, transit and import declarations into one document used by 18 Western European nations.

Since 1 January 1993 and the introduction of the Intrastat procedures, the SAD has become irrelevant to EU trade, but it is still extremely important for trade with non-EU members. These can be divided into the EFTA countries and the rest, because the EFTA adopted the SAD on 1 January 1988 and have continued its use despite the EU moving over to Intrastat on 1 January 1993. Thus the SAD still operates as a full eight-page document for trade between the EU and Switzerland, Norway, Iceland and Liechtenstein. As we will see later, for trade outside these countries, only elements of the SAD will be relevant.

The combination of functions within the SAD can be simply expressed as:

- pages 2 and 3: export;
- pages 1, 4, 5 and 7: transit;
- pages 6 and 8: import.

As an example, a consignment from the UK to Norway could be export declared, pass through posts of transit and be import declared at destination by just one completed SAD. By the same token an import from, say, Iceland, could complete all customs controls with one SAD.

In practice, the so-called 'split use option' is more commonly used. This allows the distinct elements of the SAD to be separated so that the export declarations can be made separately from the transit documents and the import declarations. The separation of the import declaration from export and transit is very common, as the importer often lodges the import entry prior to the arrival of the goods.

National export system (NES)

Formerly the new export system, NES was launched at the port of Dover in March 2002 and implemented at all UK maritime ports on 28 October 2002, with airports going 'live' between then and mid 2003. It governs all non-EU exports and imports.

NES replaced the current export system and, although C88 paper declarations will still be accepted for full pre-entries, these documents will have to be keyed into CHIEF (see below) by customs' own staff before the goods can be permitted to progress for shipment.

NES is available to all exporters and freight forwarders, irrespective of their volumes and throughputs, and customs has encouraged them to take full advantage of the new system.

The CHIEF system

CHIEF (Customs Handling of Import and Export Freight) was originally responsible for controlling and recording all of the UK's international trade import movements, whether by land, sea or air. It links customs offices around the country to ports, airports, inland facilities and several thousand businesses. It now handles all export declarations as well.

Under the NES, declarations can be made via a number of electronic routes including:

- community system providers (CSPs);
- internet e-mail with EDIFACT attachments;
- X400 e-mail and EDIFACT attachments;
- completion of a web form online.

Export licensing control

The UK Export Control Act 2004 contains an updated and lengthy list of goods that require an export licence for certain destinations before they will be allowed out of the UK. Controls on the export out of the UK of tangible products have always existed. The new Act introduced controls that also apply to the movement of goods between third countries organized from the UK (sometimes called 'brokering') and controls on 'intangibles', ie information. All controls apply to UK citizens even when abroad:

1 Anything designed or adapted for military use and/or that appears in the government's 'military list', eg military, security and paramilitary goods, arms, ammunition, weapons of mass destruction, etc.

2 Physical exports of technical information, eg mail, on laptops, CDs.

3 Electronic transfers of military technology, eg telephone, email or fax.

It is very important to note that, even if the proposed end use of the goods does not fit into the above categories, if they have a 'dual use' that comes within the regulations they may still require a licence.

Application must be made to the Export Control Organisation of the Department for Business, Industry and Skills (BIS – formerly the DTI, then BERR) through SPIRE, the new fully electronic system for processing licence applications, which went live on 3 September 2007 and replaces all the methods to apply for any of the licences processed by the Export Control Organisation within BIS.

Agricultural produce will also attract similar controls enforced by DEFRA.

Exports from bonded warehouses

All imports into the EU enter into bond. This describes premises that are operated under a bond, or guarantee, to customs. Should the warehouse keepers allow goods to be cleared from the bond without the approval of customs, given via an 'out of charge' message, then the guarantee safeguards customs revenues. However, it is unusual for goods to be exported out of bond. Those that are taken out of bond are subject to excise duty if they are consumed domestically.

Excise, or revenue duty, is payable on certain imports, and has been for more than 400 years. The goods that are subject to this very specific charge in most countries in the world include:

- alcohol: spirits, beer, wine and even toiletries;
- tobacco: cigarettes, cigars, smoking tobacco;
- mineral oils: petrol, diesel, lubricants.

These goods attract excise on import into the UK and home-produced goods are subject to excise charges if consumed domestically; but if exported, they are excise free. Thus Scotch whisky, for example, is excisable if consumed in the UK but free from excise if exported.

While on this subject we should note that since 1993 the movement of excisable goods between bonded warehouses within the EU has been supplemented by the addition of a new type of approved trader known as registered excise dealers and shippers (REDS), who will be approved to receive excisable goods from other member states of the EU. A freight forwarder, acting for a number of importers, may be a REDS.

Processing relief

Inward processing relief (IPR)

If goods are imported from outside the EU and subsequently re-exported, then it is possible to obtain relief from the duty payable at import. The duty may be avoided by suspension at the time of import, in which case all the goods must be re-exported, usually within six months. Alternatively, the duty is paid and a drawback of duty is claimed for whichever goods are subsequently re-exported. It should be emphasized that the term 're-export' applies only to goods that are destined for a non-EU country; that is, they must leave the EU. This procedure applies where the re-export is simply a repacked version of the import or, more importantly, where the re-export is the result of processing of the import. Complex manufacturing processes can be approved for relief as long as it can be proved that the imported commodities are genuinely re-exported. As an example, the import of printed textiles from the Far East and subsequent re-export of garments to the USA could qualify for relief.

Outward processing relief (OPR)

This describes the equivalent procedure where goods are exported out of the EU for processing and subsequent re-import. Again subject to prior approval, customs will allow relief on the value of the goods before the process, and charge only for the 'added value' of the processing. Therefore this procedure also applies to repair or replacement situations where no duty at all is payable, if the work done is free of charge to the importer.

There is a further procedure known as returned goods relief, where duty and VAT may be avoided for goods returned in the same state as at export, which often applies to defective goods.

Finally it is perfectly feasible to combine these two procedures. For example, goods could be imported and processed under IPR and re-exported and re-imported under OPR. Discussions with your local customs collection are essential to investigate the possibilities.

Outside the EU

The detailed export procedures described above apply to all members of the EU. Countries outside the EU will have very similar procedures but the documentation would, of course, differ from country to country.

For example, the US Census Bureau requires mandatory filing of export information through the automated export system (AES) or through AESDirect, both of which are managed by the US Customs and Border Protection agency (CBP) and requires mandatory, pre-departure, electronic filing of export information through the AES.

The US CBP is also responsible for ensuring that all goods entering and exiting the USA do so in accordance with all applicable US laws and regulations. Although CBP enforces these export regulations for various other government agencies, specific questions pertaining to commodity licensing requirements can be directed to that lead agency.

Basic commodities that may require export licences can be identified by viewing lead agencies such as the US Department of Commerce, Bureau of Industry and Security, Department of State, Directorate of Defense Trade Controls, Bureau of Alcohol, Tobacco, Firearms and Explosives, Drug Enforcement Administration, Nuclear Regulatory Commission, Office of Foreign Assets Control or the Census Bureau websites. These sites include information from numerous other agencies with export control responsibilities.

USA: International Traffic in Arms Regulations (ITAR)

This is a set of US government regulations that control the export and import of defence-related articles and services on the United States Munitions List (USML). These regulations implement the provisions of the Arms Export Control Act, and the Department of State interprets and enforces ITAR. Its goal is to safeguard US national security and further US foreign policy objectives.

For practical purposes, ITAR regulations dictate that information and material pertaining to defence and military-related technologies (for items listed on the US Munitions List) may only be shared with US persons unless authorization from the Department of State is received or a special exemption is used. US persons (including organizations) can face heavy fines if they have, without authorization or the use of an exemption, provided foreign (non-US) persons with access to ITAR-protected defence articles, services or technical data.

A specific point about US-origin goods that attract this form of export control is that it is important to understand that such controls remain in place on all such goods, including any subsequent re-export. All re-transfers or re-exports must be authorized through the US State Department.

Such authorization would apply to any importer incorporating US-origin components, which are subject to US export controls, in their exports even if such exports qualify as, for example, UK origin after sufficient transformation.

Also, any information transfer about such goods to a foreign person inside or outside the USA is treated as an export. This therefore prohibits, without prior approval, transfers within the UK to individuals of non-UK nationality, including US and dual nationals. This is not the case with UK-controlled goods.

The penalties in the USA are also more draconian than in the UK, eg an e-mail forwarded to five people is five separate violations ($1m fine per violation).

Transit systems

Having covered the procedural requirements related to exports, it is logical for us now to proceed to the next stage of the international movement, which may involve the goods passing through customs posts of transit on the way to their final destination. The words 'may involve' are used advisedly as not all international consignments will pass through posts of transit.

In the case of a sea or air movement, the goods will not actually transit any customs territory during the journey. The goods on the vessel or aircraft will export clear out of a port of departure and import clear into a port of destination. They may call at other ports en route but they will not enter a country at one point and pass through to leave at another point, which is the essence of a true transit.

It is perfectly feasible for goods to be transferred from one ship or aircraft to another at a port part way through the journey, but this is actually a *transhipment*, not a transit. This transhipment will be done under customs control, invariably through bonded warehouses, and the goods will not be imported and re-exported as long as they stay within the bonded premises. The ultimate example of this type of transhipment is the use of free ports, in which case the goods could even be processed before reloading.

Therefore true transit, in which the goods enter a country at one point and leave at another, applies only to international road and rail transits.

Another look at Table 19.1 above will reveal that the distinction between EU, EFTA and non-EU/EFTA trade, which makes such a difference to the methods of export clearance used, is just as important when we consider transit procedures. The portion of the table that is relevant to us now can be seen in more detail in Table 19.2.

TABLE 19.2   Transit procedures by destination

UK→EU	no transit controls
UK→EFTA	SAD transit
UK→ Non-EU/EEA	TIR (road) or TIF (rail)

Why transit controls?

First, a brief reprise on why transit systems should exist in the first place. The example we used earlier was a road consignment travelling from the UK to Italy and crossing France en route. The historical problem that the French customs would have had is that they are allowing goods into their territory that may be subject to duty, tax, excise and levy, as well as other restrictions such as quota or licensing controls. The promise of the driver that the goods are not stopping in France is hardly likely to give the French customs the security they need in order to allow the goods in free from such controls.

To add to the problem, they would also consider the vehicle, and even the fuel in the tanks, to be of value, sometimes more than the goods. The solution for the customs authorities – all of them, not just France – was to insist on duty deposits being lodged to cover the potential customs revenues. Such deposits were refundable as long as the haulier could prove that the goods subsequently left the country.

The second major problem was the fact that, in order to assess the level of deposit necessary, customs would invariably examine the goods in order to determine their tariff classification and therefore the level of charges and controls appropriate. This would clearly be very time consuming on a journey involving a number of posts of transit, and greatly increased the possibility of damage, and even pilferage, during the journey.

The growth in international road freight since World War II served to highlight the need for a solution to the dual problems of duty deposits and examination. The solution was TIR.

Transports Internationaux Routiers (TIR)

The familiar white and blue plates that can be seen on many heavy goods vehicles represent the title of an international convention, established by the Economic Commission for Europe, which has been ratified by a very large number of customs authorities throughout the world. It was ratified in the UK in 1959 and includes the USA, Japan, and most of the Middle East and Eastern Europe. So how does TIR solve the problems?

Duty deposits

A TIR carnet must be issued by an approved authority and accompany the goods throughout the journey. First a brief word about these documents called 'carnets'. There are a number of different forms of carnet used in international trade, including ATA carnets and *carnet de passage en douane* (both covered in the next chapter) The word simply describes a booklet of tickets or vouchers (or *volets*). In the case of TIR, the carnet is issued in the UK by either the Freight Transport Association (FTA) or the Road Haulage Association (RHA) and in other countries by the agencies of the International Road Transport Union.

Duty deposits are avoided by the provision of a guarantee by the carrier to the issuing authority, usually countersigned by a bank or insurance company. The carrier must undertake to abide by all TIR regulations. In simple terms this guarantee acts as a duty deposit, lodged in the country of departure, and replaces the need for such deposits at each post of transit. The customs authorities in transit accept volets from the carnet, on entry into and exit from their customs territories, rather than a duty deposit. Carnets are available as 14- or 20-page documents, dependent on the number of transit posts involved.

Vehicle examination

The regular, and very time consuming, examination of vehicles and goods at posts of transit is avoided by the requirement for TIR vehicles to be approved. The approval, in the UK, is given, following inspection of the vehicle, by the Department of Transport (Vehicle Inspectorate) who act on behalf of customs. This takes the form of an approval certificate and is issued on the basis that:

- the vehicle can be sealed so that it is not possible to add or remove goods without breaking the seal(s);
- there are no concealed areas.

The purpose of the approval is to enable customs, at the point of departure, to seal the goods in the vehicle with one or more seals. The customs of transit then need to examine the seal(s) only and, as long as they are intact, will waive their right to examine the goods.

Approved vehicles carrying a TIR carnet are able to pass through any number of customs posts of transit without the need for examination or the payment of duty deposits.

While TIR is still very important to EU exporters, it is important to note that it has no relevance to EU trade, for which no transit controls exist.

EU transit

From 1973 to the end of 1992, goods were moved within the EU with either a T1 or a T2 transit form. However, as we have seen earlier, 1 January 1988 saw the introduction of the single administrative document (SAD). Not only did the SAD become the basic export declaration for all of those countries, but it also replaced the T forms. In fact, pages 1, 4, 5 and 7 of the SAD became the new transit form, retaining the concept of T1 and T2 status, but with a clearly different format.

The new computerized transit system (NCTS)

January 2003 saw the introduction of a Europe-wide system, based upon electronic declaration and processing, designed to provide better management and control of community and common transit. It involves all EU member states and a number of EEA and accession countries (31 countries in all in 2010).

The national administration of each country has developed its own NCTS structure, according to centrally defined architecture, which is connected through a central domain in Brussels to all the other countries. The NCTS links some 3,000 European customs offices and replaced the previous paper-based system.

Summary

It will be obvious that the development of the 'four freedoms' within a single market, the absence of transit controls within the EU, the simplification of procedures and the ongoing use of electronic declarations have all led to a severely reduced role for customs in the day-to-day control of movements.

The closing of many internal customs posts within the EU actually led to the European Commission sponsoring the St Matthew project, which is designed to retrain redundant customs officers.

Why St Matthew? Well, he is the patron saint of revenue collectors.

More seriously, for many of the changes to work, there has had to be a major change in the attitude of customs towards goods entering their territories. Traditionally there has always been an assumption that goods, and people, are *not* in free circulation unless they can prove differently. The mandatory check on documents such as T forms, and passports, has been necessary to provide the proof that the goods and people are not subject to specific controls.

One might, quite properly, regard this as an assumption of guilt until innocence is proved. The very important change in the philosophy of customs is that they now work on entirely the opposite assumption, that goods are 'regarded as community goods in the absence of anything to the contrary'.

While estimates vary, there is no doubt that major savings are already being made in avoiding the frontier delays that affected the majority of freight movements throughout the EU. We should not forget, however, that none of these developments has reduced the power of customs authorities to stop and examine people and goods, but only changed the regular and mandatory checks that previously affected all movements.

Customs would also say, with much evidence, that they are now using the resources they have in a much more efficient manner. By targeting deliberate evasions of controls, based on intelligence and internal system audits, they are becoming far more effective in the control of, for example, illegal drugs, while not interfering with the vast majority of legal movements of goods and people.

We also now have another major issue for customs authorities all over the world – that of security.

Security issues

Because of a developing focus on the security implications of international movements, both the EU and the USA have launched systems that audit a company's compliance capacity and, if approved, certificates such traders so that their consignments are less likely to be physically controlled by customs and more likely to be fast tracked through security control systems.

In the EU this is known as 'authorised economic operator'.

Authorised economic operator

The European go-live date of 1 January 2008 saw the beginning of the EU authorised economic operator system.

The basic criteria for considering applications are set out in Article 5(a)(2) of Council Regulation 648/2005 and include:

- an appropriate record of compliance;
- a satisfactory system of managing commercial and, where appropriate, transport records, that allows customs controls;
- proven financial solvency;
- appropriate security and safety standards (for a security and safety certificate).

HMRC is stressing the need for applicants to self-assess their likelihood of being able to meet the criteria before submitting an application, especially since the consequence of failing to meet the standard will mean that a business will not be able to apply again for three years.

Further information on the application process can be found in HMRC's explanatory notes and guidance (Notices C117 and C118), available on the HMRC website.

The US equivalent is the customs–trade partnership against terrorism.

Customs–trade partnership against terrorism (C–TPAT)

C–TPAT is a US government–business initiative that was introduced in 2001. It is designed to strengthen overall supply chain and border security by working in close cooperation with the key members of the supply chain: importers, carriers, brokers, warehouse operators and manufacturers.

Businesses must apply to participate in C–TPAT, which can be done via the US customs website. Shipments from participants in C–TPAT will be able to move across US borders more quickly than non-member shipments, because customs will offer potential benefits to C–TPAT members, most notably a reduced number of inspections (reduced border times).

Participants will sign an agreement that commits them to the following actions:

- to conduct a comprehensive self-assessment of supply chain security, using the C–TPAT security guidelines. These guidelines, which are available for review on the customs website, encompass the following areas:

- procedural security;
- physical security;
- personnel security;
- education and training;
- access controls;
- manifest procedures;
- conveyance security;

- to submit a supply chain security profile questionnaire to customs;
- to develop and implement a programme to enhance security throughout the supply chain in accordance with C–TPAT guidelines;
- to communicate C–TPAT guidelines to other companies in the supply chain and work toward building the guidelines into relationships with these companies.

Full details of C–TPAT requirements are available on the US customs website, which includes the following statement:

> The Authorised Economic Operator certificate was introduced in Europe from 1 January 2008. The standards and procedures required to obtain an AEO certificate are similar to those in C–TPAT, as are the benefits (simplified customs processes and shorter delays).
>
> How does AEO certification affect users of security seals?
> Applicants and holders of the AEO certificate should use seals that conform to the ISO/PAS17712 standard (the same standard required by C–TPAT).

The point being that an AEO in the EU will automatically be approved under C–TPAT and that this is not just an EU and US initiative. Many other countries, eg Canada, Australia, China, are already introducing their own schemes.

20
Import procedures and documents

This second chapter in our coverage of customs controls examines the final area of specific controls, that of import procedures. What we should always remember is that one company's export is another company's import, and all exporters should have a good knowledge of the controls that goods could attract at destination. We are therefore approaching the issue of customs import procedures from the point of view of the exporter rather than the importer. In reality the distinction is almost irrelevant to the modern international trader.

What we will also try to do is to identify the opportunities that may be available to exporters to minimize the costs and effects of customs controls by prudent management of information and procedures. There are many opportunities missed by exporters because of the short-sighted perception that import clearance is the buyer's problem.

However, it is worth just a few words regarding EU import procedures, if only to complete the picture we have built up in looking at export and transit procedures.

EU imports

Goods that enter the UK from another member state actually require no immediate import declaration. Just as Intrastat procedures collect export statistics using the VAT returns, EC sales listing (ESL) and supplementary statistical declaration (SSD), the import statistics, ie arrivals, are collected in exactly the same way. In addition, the VAT that is due on such imports is subject to the postponed accounting system (PAS), which actually operated in the early 1980s, which means it is simply accounted for on the 'tax due' side of the trader's VAT return.

For imports from non-EU members, the import element of the SAD (pages 6 and 8) serves as the import declaration for all EU members. Such entries may be made by the importing company, periodically for large traders, but the great majority are made by clearing agents on behalf of the importers. In such cases it is probable that the declaration is made using direct trader input (DTI) procedures. This describes the process that allows declarations to be made direct from the agent's computer to customs' computer. In these cases the requirement for payment of VAT on import has not changed, although it is very likely that such payment is deferred until the 15th of the following month.

While it is difficult, or even impossible, to cover every country's import procedures outside the EU, what we can do is to identify and explain the type and nature of import controls generally practised throughout the world. Outside the EU there is very little, if any, standardization of import declarations, but whichever particular document is required it will always fulfil the same basic purpose and apply the same range of controls.

Import controls

It is possible to break all import controls into two broad categories; they are either tariff or non-tariff barriers. 'Tariff' describes the product classification system that is the beginning of all countries' import controls and which is examined later in this chapter. These controls would include:

- Tariff controls: duty, tax, excise, levy, licensing, quota; and often: technical standards, health and safety standards (where imposed by customs authorities).

- Non-tariff controls: other standards requirements, cultural barriers, national buying habits, etc.

Duty

Duties are used as a specific fiscal control and applied selectively at a variety of levels by different countries. We already know that intra-EU trade is duty free and, as we will see later in this chapter, there are many situations where the origin of the goods may mean that they are not subject to duty.

Such duties are usually ad valorem, that is they are charged as a percentage of the (usually CIF) value of the goods. One of the great successes of the WTO negotiations over the years is that the average worldwide duty rate, which was 24 per cent in the 1950s, is now under 4 per cent in the new millennium. However, this does not preclude countries applying much higher rates on certain commodities, particularly when attempting to protect local manufacturers.

Tax

Within the EU it is Value Added Tax (VAT), or its equivalent in each member state, that is the standard fiscal charge on all transactions where there is a change of ownership, unless the goods are exempt. Rates within the EU currently range from 15 per cent (ignoring the exempt/zero rate) to 38 per cent for certain luxury items. Other countries may impose similar charges on imports in the form of purchase tax or turnover tax.

Excise

Sometimes referred to as revenue duty, which accurately describes its purpose in that, rather than acting as a pure control, excise is designed to collect government revenue. Chapter 19 examined the export controls relevant to excisable goods, chiefly alcohol, tobacco and mineral fuels, which are designed to ensure that excise is collected on such goods that are consumed domestically. Clearly such excise will be applied to imports of these goods and, of course, on entry into most overseas countries.

These charges can be very high – they certainly are in the UK – and are often specific duties in that they are expressed as a charge for a particular quantity or volume rather than as an ad-valorem charge. For example, the excise on spirits imported into the UK is expressed as euros per hectolitre (100 litres). As these charges represent some 25 per cent of total UK government revenues, it will be clear that customs prioritize their collection.

In markets like the USA, each state sets its own level of excise so that, for example, the excise tax on cigarette ranges from 7 cents per pack in South Carolina to $3.46 per pack in Rhode Island. The excise tax typically doubles or even triples the retail cost of cigarettes in some states.

Levy

Levies are a specialized charge that generally affects only agricultural products and items processed from them. Thus basic commodities like sugar and starch will attract levies, as may some foodstuffs. While the EU has levies, this is not necessarily a charge that would be encountered in all overseas markets.

Licensing

In previous sections of this book we have looked at both export and import licensing. Many overseas countries, particularly developing and underdeveloped countries, use specific import licensing to control every consignment. The existence of the required licence must be certain before any shipments are made, as the goods will not be import cleared without the appropriate licence.

Quota

This describes quantitative restrictions that may be imposed on certain goods, usually to protect local manufacturers. The quota may be a quantity that is allowed in free from duty, subsequent imports being allowed but at the full rate of duty, or it may be that licences are issued only for that quantity and, once used, no further imports will be allowed over the specified time period (usually 12 months).

Standards

Exporters will inevitably encounter an enormous range of different technical requirements across the world. The reason why these may act as a barrier is that the exporter may actually not be able to comply with the standard or the certification requirements for that standard. Secondly, the cost of compliance, in terms of product modification, testing and certification, may make the cost of the product uncompetitive in the overseas market.

The above represent the range of common import controls that the exporter may come across. We could also legitimately include the use of exchange control as more indirect import control, and we have to accept that in some overseas countries there have developed what might be termed 'unofficial' controls, which can introduce significant compliance costs. It is an unfortunate fact that in some countries, paying the right person can still be the only import procedure that matters.

In order to decide which controls are to be applied to each consignment, and at what level, there are three vital pieces of information that customs authorities need:

- description;
- origin;
- value.

While particular requirements differ from one country to another, there is invariably an import declaration accompanied by supporting documents. One of the most important supporting documents is one that is always prepared by the exporter, namely the export invoice. This may be accompanied by other statements, especially as to origin and value, all designed to provide the above elements of information to customs.

The export invoice

The exporter is faced with producing a wide variety of different invoices, involving a range of third-party procedures, dependent on the country of destination. Because the export invoice is of such importance to overseas customs authorities, it is they who insist on a particular format. The exporter could bill the buyer with almost any document from a standard commercial invoice to the back of an envelope, so the more technical invoice requirements are purely the result of import customs requirements.

Export invoices fall into five distinct types:

- commercial invoice;
- commercial invoice with a declaration;
- commercial invoice requiring third-party verification:
  - certified;
  - legalized;
- consular invoice;
- specific customs invoice.

Commercial invoice

The simplest situation is one where the importing country has no special requirements at all and the exporter uses the company's standard commercial invoice, just as for a home sale. The only difference will be the fact that the invoice is zero-rated for VAT.

Commercial invoice with declaration

It is quite common for countries to require a specific declaration to be included on the invoice. The wording differs from country to country, and is often in the language of the importing country, but invariably declares the origin of the goods and that the prices are correct export prices.

As we shall see later, the import customs are concerned that the origin and prices are legitimate. The exact wording of such declarations is available from a variety of reference sources.

Certified invoices

The above declarations sometimes require a third party to validate them, and the most common requirement is for a Chamber of Commerce in the exporter's country to certify a set of invoices. They will stamp the documents with their own certification stamp, an example of which is reproduced in Figure 20.1. In theory they are certifying that the invoice and declaration are correct, but in practice they certify that the signatory of the invoice is one authorized by the company to make such declarations on behalf of the company. Exporting companies lodge the signatures of approved signatories with the chambers for this purpose.

FIGURE 20.1   Typical Chamber of Commerce certification stamp

Legalized invoices

In some cases, in particular the Middle East, there is a requirement for a further stage of third-party verification. The certified invoices are required to be *legalized* by the commercial section of the embassy of the importing country in the exporter's country. Again it is often a rubber stamp or sometimes a more complex verification. The procedure is that the exporter arranges certification at the Chamber of Commerce and then presents the document set to the appropriate embassy for legalization. In the case of the 20-plus Arab League countries, all of which require legalization, a streamlined procedure exists in the UK in which the local certifying chamber sends the documents to the Arab British Chamber of Commerce (ABCC), who make the presentations to the individual embassies. This reduces the time taken for the operation to an average of five to seven days.

It is not only the time delay that exporters must consider but also that charges are made for certification and legalization. As an example, a set of documents certified and legalized through the ABCC will cost between £40 and £60.

In the case of Arab documents, it may also be necessary to append a further declaration to the invoice certifying that the goods are not of Israeli origin or contain any Israeli materials.

Consular invoices

Consular invoices are particularly common in Central and Latin American countries. They require their own unique consular invoice form to be completed and returned to the consulate for *consularization*. The format of such invoices varies enormously and they are often in the language of the country of destination. The consulates, which are actually commercial sections of the embassies situated in regional centres, will check the whole set of documents before what might be a very elaborate consularizing process. Quite apart from the time delay, it is possible that the consular fees could be quite high, sometimes even a percentage of the invoice value, so it is important that exporters have a good idea of the costs right from the quotation stage.

It is perfectly acceptable, and in fact might be seen as best practice, to show consular fees as a separate item on the original pro-forma invoice quotation, along with the freight and insurance charges.

The requirements detailed above for certified, legalized or consularized invoices can be seen as an attempt by the importing country to impose some controls in the exporter's country. The logic being that if documents are not appropriately verified, then the import should not take place. Coincidently, they also raise revenue for the overseas country's commercial sections in the UK.

Specific customs invoice

These invoice forms are particularly related to ex-Commonwealth countries and are hangovers from the obsolete commonwealth preference system which, as we will see later, has been replaced by broader EU agreements. There are a lot less of these invoices in existence than at one time, many countries having gone over to a commercial invoice with a declaration. Where they still apply, the exporter must complete the appropriate invoice form for the country of destination; these forms are available from specialist printers. They are often in the form of certificates of value and origin (CV/O) and may bear reference to current domestic values (CDV) to control dumping of goods. It is not uncommon that the exporter also produces a commercial invoice as a bill to the buyer.

Whatever the form of export invoice required, they will all contain basically the same range of information:

- seller and purchaser (not always be the same as the exporter and importer);
- goods description, quantity and value;
- trade terms (eg FCA, FOB, CIP, CIF, etc);
- terms and methods of payment;
- ancillary costs (eg freight and insurance);
- shipment details (points of departure and destination);
- packing specification: number and kind of packages, individual contents, sizes (in cms), weights (net and gross in kgs), marks and numbers.

This last piece of information may be included on the face of the invoice but it is just as likely that it is attached to the invoice as a separate packing specification. Sometimes referred to as a packing list or packing note, the packing specification is basically treated as an extension of the invoice.

We have now established that the country of destination will directly affect the type and format of export invoice used and that it represents an essential element of the buyer's import clearance declaration. As we noted earlier, the three vital pieces of information that the customs authorities at destination need in order to apply import controls are description, origin and value.

Description

This is the starting point for all customs controls, as the goods must first of all be very specifically identified in order to decide what particular controls apply to them. Customs authorities throughout the world are also wary about using words to identify commodities, as there is clearly a language problem and also words can be vague and misleading. Therefore the means used by customs to identify goods depends on the use of number classification systems, or *nomenclatures*, which translate vague words into the hard data of numbers that mean the same throughout the world. It should also be noted that exporters have a duty to declare their exports for statistical purposes based on accurate tariff numbers.

Such classification systems form the basis of customs tariffs and it would not be beyond the bounds of possibility that every nation state in the world might develop its own unique nomenclature. Thankfully this is not the case and in fact there is a marked degree of harmonization of classification systems across the globe. A potted history of the development of standardized classifications would start with the Brussels tariff nomenclature (BTN).

As the result of widespread discussions following World War II, progress was made on the development of a standard product classification system. Not only was this seen as valuable in removing ambiguities in identification of goods from one country to another but it also greatly facilitated the collection of meaningful international trade statistics. The classification was produced by the Customs Cooperation Council (CCC), in 1957, as a four-digit nomenclature that was promoted as a standard throughout the world. In fact, almost 150 countries used the BTN as the basis of their tariff. For developing countries the BTN gave a sufficient level of identification but for the developed nations it was quite common for the four-digit code to be extended to give a higher level of sophistication to the classification. As we will see later, the longer the number, the greater the specificity of the identification.

The BTN was partially redrafted in 1965 and renamed the Customs Cooperation Council nomenclature (CCCN) but remained a four-digit code until the introduction of the harmonized commodity description and coding system (HS).

The HS represented a wholesale update of the CCCN by the World Customs Organization (WCO, formerly the CCC) and is a six-digit classification developed in the 1980s, which has again been adopted by more than 200 trading nations and covers something like 98 per cent of world trade.

The reason for the update was the fact that the BTN had been drawn up in the 1950s and it had become quite clear that it was no longer relevant to the needs of customs in the 1980s. If one considers the range of goods that were traded in the 1980s onwards, which actually did not exist in the 1950s, it is quite clear that the original classification was inadequate.

As an example, a company dealing in highly sophisticated optical fibres for computer applications was forced to classify the goods as 'Chapter 70 glass ... others'. In the updated tariff such commodities are far more accurately identified in Chapter 90 as optical fibres. The predominance of 'others' as a safety-net classification for goods not specifically described in the old tariff, has been much reduced in the HS-based tariffs. Also, some trading nations, notably the USA, who have operated unique tariffs in the past, have now incorporated the HS and therefore facilitated the further harmonization of tariff classifications.

The current situation, as far as the EU is concerned, is that we operate the EC combined nomenclature, which is based on the HS and came into force on 1 January 1988 as the EU integrated tariff (TARIC) and provides for eight-digit harmonization within the EU and EFTA.

The typical structure of a tariff number for goods is shown in Figure 20.2.

The six-digit HS base is likely to be the same in most countries in the world and is extended by a further two digits common to all EU members. The seventh digit identifies the rate of duty applicable, which should be standard throughout the EU, and the eighth is the level of statistical collection of intra-EU trade (Intrastat); for imports from non-EU members a minimum 11-digit classification is necessary to identify the appropriate import controls on such goods. In specialized cases, such as agricultural produce, wine and where anti-dumping duties are concerned, it may be necessary to add a further four digits.

FIGURE 20.2 Typical structure of a tariff number for goods

1	2	3	4	5	6	7	8	9	10	11	12	13	14	15

A   B   C

A: six digits: Harmonized commodity coding system (HS)
B: eight digits: Intrastat
C: up to 15 digits: community TARIC for third-country imports

Finding a tariff number

We have established that the international trader has a duty to identify goods with the correct tariff number to customs for statistical purposes for both exports and imports. Also, the information supplied, for example on export invoices, could usefully identify the correct tariff number for import customs. In fact, many overseas buyers may request that a particular description and tariff classification are included on the invoice.

It would be quite time consuming to start with the first line of the appropriate tariff and work through over 2,000 pages until you reach one that seems right, and of course there is a more logical way. It may be that there is an alphabetical index that can immediately indicate the relevant part of the tariff. If not, then the logical process starts with finding the appropriate chapter. The HS is made up of 97 chapters listed from the most basic of commodities and gradually working through categories of products that become more and more sophisticated in terms of the amount of processing and technical enhancements.

Thus a very broad breakdown would look like:

- Chapter 1: Live animals;
- Chapters 2–25: Agricultural produce;
- Chapters 26–38: Chemicals;
- Chapters 39–49: Articles of plastic, leather, wood, paper, etc;
- Chapters 50–63: Textiles;
- Chapters 64–84: Articles of clothing, ceramics, glass, iron, copper, etc;
- Chapters 85–97: Machinery, locomotives, aircraft, ships, furniture, etc.

Once the correct chapter has been found, it is then a matter of finding the appropriate first four digits (referred to as the *heading*), then the next two digits (referred to as the *subheading*), which identify the goods more specifically, and then the correct sub-subheading. As the classification number gets longer, the identification of the goods becomes more and more exact.

To give some examples:

Riding horse

- 01: Live animals;
- 0101: Horses, asses, mules and hinnies (male horse/female ass, before you ask);
- 010119: Horses (not for breeding), (HS level);
- 01011990: Horses (not for slaughter).

Thus 01011990 would describe a horse not for breeding and not for slaughter. Admittedly not a 'horse for riding' but there isn't much else you could do with a horse, is there?

X-ray tubes

- 90: Medical and surgical;
- 9022: Apparatus based on the use of X-rays;
- 90223000: X-ray tubes.

It will be clear that the exporter would need detailed advice from the overseas buyer to assess the most appropriate tariff classification.

What is meant by 'most appropriate'? The fact is that not only are tariff classifications highly complex, but also it may be that an exporter could legitimately describe goods in a variety of ways. Should this be the case, it is potentially beneficial to consider carefully the description and tariff number quoted to importing customs. However, it must be made very clear that it is vital that the correct and most accurate tariff number is declared, as misdeclaration is an extremely serious offence and the penalties can prove very expensive to all parties.

Thus it may be perfectly acceptable to describe parts for the diesel engines of tractors as either 'agricultural equipment and parts thereof' or 'diesel engines and parts thereof'. Even if the overseas customs reject the latter description in favour of the former, it is unlikely that penalties would be imposed for misdeclaration (although there are never any guarantees). As an example of a clear misdeclaration, describing children's buckets and spades for the beach as 'agricultural equipment' is not a description that could very easily be justified.

It is also advisable that brand names or proprietary names of products are avoided, as they will not be used as part of a tariff description. Likewise it is possible to describe goods on the basis of the materials of which they are made, but it is the application to which the products are put that is often more important. Describing computer hardware as 'plastic components' would clearly be unacceptable.

So exporters should take advice from their buyers and at least consider if there is scope for a legitimate choice of product descriptions used for particular overseas markets. It should be said, however, that customs would adopt the view that the tariff allows only one valid classification for any commodity.

Origin

Once overseas customs have accepted the tariff classification, or reclassified the goods themselves, then the tariff will indicate the range of controls, such as duty, tax, licence and quota, that apply to each particular commodity. In the case of the EU tariff, the controls are actually integrated into the body of the classification (known as the schedule). Such controls may be selectively applicable depending on the origin of the goods. This is because the EU has agreed a wide range of free and preferential trade agreements with other trading nations.

These can be broken down into:

- Free trade: Switzerland (plus Liechtenstein), Norway, Iceland, Albania, Bosnia-Herzegovina, Chile, Croatia, Egypt, Faroe Islands, Israel, Kosovo, Macedonia, Mexico, Montenegro, Northern Cyprus, Palestinian Authority, Serbia, South Africa, West Bank and Gaza, Algeria, Morocco and Tunisia, Egypt, Jordan, Lebanon and Syria.
- Preferential trade (reduced or zero): Economic Partnership Agreement (EPA) (formerly Africa, Caribbean and Pacific: ACP), overseas countries and territories (OCT), generalized system of preferences (GSP).
- EU association: Turkey (ATR).

The free trade agreements above are all bilateral, that is they give EU goods free entry into the overseas market as well as vice versa. The preferential agreements, which allow for free or reduced duty, are sometimes applicable to EU imports only and not necessarily to EU exports to those countries.

Thus it may well be that the duty, and perhaps other controls, that commodities attract can be avoided by their originating in particular countries of supply. All such trade agreements are based on very precise *rules of origin*.

If goods are genuinely wholly produced in a particular country, then proof of origin is not normally a problem. However, where goods are processed in some way, it can become more difficult. The principle used by most customs authorities is that of *sufficient transformation*. In simple terms, the customs will require a breakdown of the component elements of a product and require a sufficient proportion of the value (in the EU a minimum of 60 per cent) of the finished product to originate, that is be wholly produced, in that country.

Rules of origin are invariably very complex because customs are attempting to control what is known as *deflection of trade*. This describes the shipping of goods via a third country to establish an erroneous origin: for example Japanese DVD players, shipped into Malta, where they are relabelled and repacked and shipped into the EU as Maltese origin and therefore duty free. Clearly, repacking is never 'sufficient transformation' and such a process would be a serious offence.

Certificates of origin (CofO)

We have already established that the export invoice is sometimes accompanied by other supporting documents. In the cases where a declaration of origin on the invoice is insufficient, then a variety of other documents may be appropriate, depending on the country of destination and, in some cases, the goods. These are:

1 European EU CofO: issued by Chambers of Commerce, they can be certified by the chamber, along with the invoices, or may be self-certified by the exporter.

2 Arab British Chamber of Commerce CofO: as above but specific to Arab league trade and certified and legalized along with the invoices.

3 Certificates of value and origin: described earlier in this chapter as a form of export invoice. The origin declaration is incorporated in the invoice. May apply to ACP, OCT or GSP countries.

4 Status and movement certificates: in the previous chapter we identified the function of the transit element of the SAD in terms of moving through customs posts of transit. You may recall that since 1993 this has applied only to goods destined for ex-EFTA countries. In such cases the T2 status of goods is also certified by the transit document.

In addition, for all those free trade countries mentioned above, a specialized so-called movement certificate is appropriate. This is the EUR1, which is a four-page document requiring authentication by the exporters customs or (in the UK) local chamber. Such authentication may require the provision of proof of origin to the customs or chamber. For consignments below €6,000 (typically) in value, the EUR1 is replaced by an invoice declaration.

Trade with Turkey is quite a specialized area as Turkey is an associate member of the EU going through a transition period to full membership. Exports to Turkey are covered by a particular form of movement certificate, the ATR.

While the major consequence of origin is the potential avoidance of customs duties, it should also be noted that origin will also be relevant to the application of other controls such as quotas and to the collection of accurate trade statistics. It may even be the case that financial aid has been linked with purchases from particular countries.

Value

Once customs have decided on the description and the correct origin of the goods, then it may be the case that ad-valorem charges are applicable. In such a case the invoice value, often referred to as the *transaction value*, serves as the base for the calculation of charges. In the cases where the charge is specific to a particular quantity it is still the invoice that supplies the relevant information. In a number of countries, a statement of value is required, in addition to the invoice, for anything but low-value consignments.

Just as with description and origin, customs procedures are designed to avoid any manipulation of the value of consignments that could cause anything but an 'equitable market value' to be quoted. The potential manipulation is, of course, an undervaluation of the goods in order to minimize the duties and taxes payable on such value. The importer may, for example, have already paid in advance or be arranging transfer of funds for the elements of value not invoiced. Invoice valuations may be rejected by customs, in which case they have other methods of arriving at a value that is acceptable to them. Within the EU there are in fact five other methods of valuation if the invoice value is not acceptable.

It may seem rather silly but there can also be cases where values on invoices are actually overestimated. The offence here is usually an infringement of that country's exchange control regulations, that is, the buyer is moving hard currency out of the country. This may be held illegally in bank accounts outside the country.

The information given throughout this chapter leads us to the inevitable conclusion that sensible exporters should take a direct interest in the controls that their goods attract at destination, and how the document set prepared here affects the application of such controls. The three vital pieces of information – description, origin and value – are probably the pieces of information most manipulated in international trade. The reputable exporter should be wary of the consequences of cooperation in obvious misdeclarations; while direct action may only be taken against the importer, the long-term consequences to the exporter's trade in that market may be unacceptable. It may also be the case that this leads to export misdeclarations for which the chances of being the target of more direct action are obviously greater.

Customs management

Having examined the whole range of customs controls from export, through transit to import, the first point to bear in mind is that compliance with customs requirements is mandatory and, even if for no other reason than that non-compliance can be expensive, it is important that exporters are aware of those procedures that affect their exports.

Remember, ignorance is never an excuse. However, if we start from the premise that compliance is essential, this does not preclude opportunities for good management to reduce the impact of customs controls on a company's international trade.

An analogy, which may not appear at first to be directly relevant, is that of a case that was heard at the European Court of Justice some years ago. The company concerned had been fined a very large amount of money for unlawful claims of agricultural subsidies and its appeal was being heard. The peculiarities of the court's procedure require that all the legal arguments are prepared in writing prior to the brief verbal hearings. In this case the company's argument was in three parts:

1 We committed no offence and should not be fined at all.

2 We did commit the offences but the fine should be reduced.

3 Can we have time to pay (please)?

The fact that all three arguments were presented in one go seemed totally logical to the advocates concerned.

So how is this relevant to the way exporters approach customs procedures? It is simply that the same logic applies. You should:

- avoid controls and charges completely;
- minimize the costs and consequences of those that cannot be avoided;
- take as long as possible to comply or pay.

Avoidance

First, a very important distinction. Evasion of customs controls is illegal; avoidance is good management. There is a growing number of 'tax avoidance' consultants, but no 'tax evasion' consultants. Of the procedures we have examined in the last three chapters, several do provide opportunities:

Description: a selective and informed choice of product description could reduce charges and avoid quota restrictions.

Origin: correct statements of origin, properly documented, can again avoid all charges.

Inward processing relief: if imported goods are re-exported, relief or drawback of duty can be arranged.

Returned goods: goods exported and subsequently returned within three years, in basically the same state, can avoid duty and tax.

Temporary exports: certain types of goods that are temporarily exported can avoid all customs controls and charges by the use of an ATA carnet. We have seen that a carnet is simply a book of vouchers. In the case of the ATA carnet ('temporary admission; *admission temporaire*'), which is issued by Chambers of Commerce, three categories of goods are covered:

- exhibition goods;
- samples;
- professional equipment.

All of these can enter one or more countries only to leave at a later date. As long as all the goods that enter actually leave, the vouchers of the ATA carnet replace all other customs procedures.

It should be emphasized that this does preclude the sale of exhibition goods or samples in the overseas market. Also, if samples are genuinely of no commercial value, then they are not subject to customs controls anyway and the ATA would be irrelevant.

Remember, it is customs who decide what is of commercial value and what is not. Professional equipment can be a very wide definition including tools, measuring equipment, props, costumes, sound and lighting systems, instruments, display and demonstration equipment, etc.

Up to the end of 1992 the EU used an equivalent document called the EU carnet, but since the removal of internal frontiers on 1 January 1993 this document has become obsolete. By definition the ATA is also of no relevance to EU movements.

Free zones

A number of ports and depots throughout the world have been designated, by their government authorities, as free zones. They are areas in which goods are exempt from customs controls. In the UK they are:

- Sheerness;
- Southampton;
- Prestwick Airport;
- Liverpool;
- Tilbury.

There are many more throughout the world. They typically receive goods as imports and allow a wide range of handling, and selective processing, without any customs interference until the goods leave the free-zone area. If goods are re-exported, they actually attract no customs controls whatsoever.

Minimize

If we cannot actually avoid controls and charges, then we should look to at least reduce them to a minimum.

Valuation

It is important that the genuine transaction value is evidenced by the invoice, but it may also be the case that certain monetary amounts can legitimately be excluded. This does differ from one country to another but it may be that items such as on carriage (the transport costs from port of entry to final destination), turnover taxes, commissions, royalties and documentation fees can, and should be, excluded from the valuation.

Outward processing relief

Where goods are exported and re-imported following processing, the re-imports attract relief of part of the duty. The procedure must be agreed prior to the original export.

Take time

Whatever charges and controls are unavoidable, it makes sense to take as much time as is allowed before compliance or payment.

Warehousing

Many countries, including the whole of the EU, allow imported goods to remain in a customs warehouse, in which case they do not become subject to customs controls. In the EU, goods can be left up to two years in the warehouse, but the handling allowed is severely limited in that the goods can be checked and repacked but no real processing will be allowed. The goods do not have to comply with controls or pay duties and tax until they leave the warehouse.

Deferment

Both duty and tax can be deferred in many countries so that they are paid some time after the time of import. In the UK, approved traders and agents can supply guarantees that defer the payment of duty until the 15th of the following month. Tax, such as VAT, can be deferred in the same way, or, for EU imports, can be accounted for on the VAT returns.

PART SEVEN
Risk management

21
Cargo (marine) insurance

The exporter faces a great many risks in conducting business internationally, quite apart from the fact that the buyers may not be particularly keen to buy their goods. Even assuming that we have an established market for our products and services, there still exist many potential practical problems in ensuring that such business actually leads to the receipt of sufficient revenues. We can identify three major risks that must be addressed by the typical exporter.

Physical risk

Goods moving internationally face a very real risk of physical loss or damage. This may simply be damage caused to the goods in handling and transit, possibly due to inadequate packing or bad handling, or loss due to accidental diversion or deliberate pilferage or theft. It Is clear that the risks are generally far greater for export consignments than for domestic movements due to the length of international journeys, the range of transport modes involved, the increased handling and the great variety of conditions encountered.

A typical breakdown of the causes of loss or damage on an international journey would look something like this:

- Poor handling and stowage: 44%.
- Physical damage on/in conveyance: 33%.
- Theft and pilferage: 22%.
- General average: 1% (see later).

It is possible for the exporter to arrange insurance cover for all of these risks.

Credit risk

Even if the goods arrive complete and undamaged, the problems do not stop there, because there is the risk that the buyer will not actually pay for the goods. This may be perfectly legitimate in that there is a contractual dispute between buyer and seller; after all, the exporter may have shipped total rubbish to the importer. However, we must accept that non-payment may be the result of a dishonourable intention of the buyer. This takes many forms, from non-acceptance of the goods, through taking over the goods and deliberately delaying payment, to simply not paying for the goods.

It is possible for the exporter to arrange insurance cover for such risks.

Exchange risk

Even if we are able to deliver goods in good condition to the buyer and the satisfied buyer pays us on time, it is still possible for the unwary exporter to lose money. In the event that the exporter is invoicing in a foreign currency it is possible that the pounds sterling funds eventually received, following exchange of the foreign currency revenues, are less than was anticipated because of fluctuations in the relevant exchange rates.

It is *not* possible for the exporter to arrange insurance cover for such risks. It is, however, possible to manage the contingency for such risks.

Cargo (marine) insurance

Many forms of insurance cover exist throughout the world but there is little doubt that marine insurance is perhaps the oldest form. In the UK, the first rationalization of the marine insurance market was devised by an Elizabethan Act of Parliament in 1601, to be followed by the development of the Corporation of Lloyd's, which allowed, and still allows, underwriters to offer insurance cover. Until quite recently the language of marine insurance continued to use the flowery phrases of Elizabethan English, but modernization in the 1980s has supplied us with more efficient, but some might say much less interesting, policies.

The principle of 'averaging' is at the heart of marine insurance and is perfectly described by a phrase taken from the original Elizabethan Act:

> ... so that ... it cometh to pass that ... the loss lighteth rather easily upon many than heavily upon few, and rather upon them that adventure not than those that do adventure.

Wonderful stuff, and a very precise description of the fact that if only one or two people carried all the risks of, for example, a sea voyage, then they might be less inclined to adventure. In fact, as the Act goes on to say, it was an encouragement to trade internationally because the risks were shared by a large number of people:

> ... whereby all merchants, especially the younger sort, are allured to venture more willingly and more freely.

The underwriters of such risks were actually so called because they signed their name under the risk, stated on 'the slip', along with other underwriters who also took part of the risk. To this day Lloyd's underwriters accept risks on behalf of their 'syndicates' and company underwriters accept risks on behalf of their companies.

It should be noted that modern international trade now involves modes of transport other than sea freight and it is probably more appropriate to use the expression 'cargo insurance', which covers road, rail and air-freight movements, as well as the common combinations of transport modes now used.

General average

This is one of the oldest principles of cargo insurance and still has relevance today. It covers the situation where:

> ... there is extraordinary sacrifice or expenditure, intentionally and reasonably incurred, for the purpose of preserving the imperilled property involved in the common maritime adventure.

This will include situations where goods are jettisoned to save the ship, or are damaged by water used to extinguish a fire, or the vessel is diverted to a port of refuge, and many other situations where loss of certain goods preserves the rest of the cargo and the conveyance. The basic principle is that all the parties involved, including the vessel owners, contribute to the loss. General average is declared and an average adjuster will, eventually, calculate the amount of the claim. It is often necessary for the cargo owners to sign a general average bond and for the insurers to provide a general average guarantee in order to obtain possession of the goods from the carrier. As all standard policies cover general average claims, the cost of the claim will be met by the insurers.

To insure or not to insure

An exporter can choose not to insure the goods against loss or damage in transit and simply carry the risk. However, this poses a number of problems:

- The terms of sale agreed between seller and buyer may impose a requirement on the seller to arrange for cargo insurance. This would apply to terms such as CIF and CIP. In such cases the seller must arrange adequate insurance and prove it with documentation.

- In the event of loss or damage it may be that action is possible against the carriers in charge of the goods at the time. The carriers have limitations on their liability and it requires some expertise to sustain successful claims. One of the advantages of a cargo insurance policy is that the exporter does not have to carry out actions against liable carriers.

The situation in practice is that the vast majority of exporters arrange for insurance cover against the physical risk of loss or damage to the goods in transit. So how do they arrange this?

Specific (voyage) policy

It is perfectly feasible for an exporter with an international consignment for shipment to approach an insurance company, invariably through an insurance broker, and request that an insurance policy be drawn up for that particular consignment.

This is often referred to as a voyage policy as it covers only that specific shipment. Purely out of historical interest, the traditional Lloyd's voyage policy is reproduced in Figure 21.1. It should be noted that the Lloyd's policy, the SG (ship or goods) form in use from 1779, became obsolete in 1983 with the introduction of the modern-language marine all-risks policy (MAR), of which Figure 21.2 is the standard form.

It may be difficult to make out the fine print of the SG form but an examination would reveal that the cover offered is somewhat antiquated, as in 'men of war, fire, enemies, pirates, rovers, thieves, jettisons, letters of mart and countermart, surprisals, takings at sea, arrests, restraints, and detainments of all kings, princes and people…'.

While pirates do still attack cargo vessels, it will be clear that modern trade requires cover that is a little more sophisticated. Incidentally a letter of mart permits piracy on certain foreign vessels, and was granted, for example, to Francis Drake by Elizabeth I, the letter of countermart saying, 'You have to stop now.'

For many years this basic Lloyd's policy was extended by the addition of clauses produced by the Institute of London Underwriters, known as the Institute cargo clauses, which were basically 'all risks', 'with average (WA)', covering specified partial loss, and 'free from particular average (FPA)', excluding part losses. War clauses and strikes, riots and civil commotions clauses (SRCC) were often added as well as a number of quite specialized clauses covering particular situations or types of goods.

The update in 1983 saw the SG form replaced by a very simple MAR (see Figure 21.2) policy, the cover being expressed in the new clauses that are now (A), (B) or (C), plus war clauses and strikes clauses. In simple terms, cargo clauses (A) are the equivalent of 'all risks', (B) covers less than (A) and (C) covers less than (B), with a corresponding decrease in the insurance premiums. There is also an Institute cargo clauses (air), which is the equivalent

FIGURE 21.1   An example of the Lloyd's voyage policy

Be it known that   Reckitt and Watson Ltd.

as well in   *their*   own name as for and in the name and names of all and every other person or persons to whom the same doth, may, or shall appertain, in part or in all, doth make assurance and cause   *themselves* and them, and every of them, to be insured, lost or not lost, at and from

Warehouse Hackney via London to Warehouse Belo Horizonte via Rio de Janeiro

Upon any kind of goods and merchandises, and also upon the body, tackle, apparel, ordnance, munition, artillery, boat, and other furniture, of and in the good ship or vessel called the **Rail and/or Conveyance and S.S. Ionian sailing 1st May, 19xx.**

whereof is master under God, for this present voyage, or whosoever else shall go for master in the said ship, or by whatsoever other name or names the same ship, or the master thereof, is or shall be named or called ; beginning the adventure upon the said goods and merchandises from the loading thereof aboard the said ship, *as above* upon the said ship, &c., *as above* and so shall continue and endure, during her abode there, upon the said ship, &c. And further, until the said ship, with all her ordnance, tackle, apparel, &c., and goods and merchandises whatsoever shall be arrived at *as above* upon the said ship, &c., until she hath moored at anchor twenty-four hours in good safety ; and upon the goods and merchandises, until the same be there discharged and safely landed. And it shall be lawful for the said ship, &c., in this voyage, to proceed and sail to and touch and stay at any ports or places whatsoever *and whersoever for all purposes* without prejudice to this insurance. The said ship, &c., goods and merchandises, &c., for so much as concerns the assured by agreement between the assured and assurers in this policy, are and shall be valued at

£559.00 on 5 cases electric drills.
With average in accordance with the terms and conditions of the Institute Cargo Clauses (W.A.) including Warehouse to Warehouse.

Touching the adventures and perils which we the assurers are contented to bear and do take upon us in this voyage : they are of the seas, men of war, fire, enemies, pirates, rovers, thieves, jettisons, letters of mart and countermart, surprisals, takings at sea, arrests, restraints, and detainments of all kings, princes, and people, of what nation, condition, or quality soever, barratry of the master and mariners, and of all other perils, losses, and misfortunes, that have or shall come to the hurt, detriment, or damage of the said goods and merchandises, and ship, &c., or any part thereof. And in case of any loss or misfortune it shall be lawful to the assured, their factors, servants and assigns, to sue, labour, and travel for, in and about the defence, safeguard, and recovery of the said goods and merchandises, and ship, &c., or any part thereof, without prejudice to this insurance ; to the charges whereof we, the assurers, will contribute each one according to the rate and quantity of his sum herein assured. And it is especially declared and agreed that no acts of the insurer or insured in recovering, saving, or preserving the property insured shall be considered as a waiver, or acceptance of abandonment. And it is agreed by us, the insurers, that this writing or policy of assurance shall be of as much force and effect as the surest writing or policy of assurance heretofore made in Lombard Street, or in the Royal Exchange, or elsewhere in London.

1. Warranted free of capture, seizure, arrest, restraint or detainment, and the consequences thereof or of any attempt thereat ; also from the consequences of hostilities or warlike operations, whether there be a declaration of war or not ; but this warranty shall not exclude collision, contact with any fixed or floating object (other than a mine or torpedo), stranding, heavy weather or fire unless caused directly (and independently of the nature of the voyage or service which the vessel concerned or, in the case of a collision, any other vessel involved therein, is performing) by a hostile act by or against a belligerent power, and for the purpose of this warranty "power" includes any authority maintaining naval, military or air forces in association with a power.
   Further warranted free from the consequences of civil war, revolution, rebellion, insurrection, or civil strife arising therefrom, or piracy.
2. Warranted free of loss or damage
   (a) caused by strikers, locked-out workmen, or persons taking part in labour disturbances, riots or civil commotions ;
   (b) resulting from strikes, lock-outs, labour disturbances, riots or civil commotions.
3. (a) Should the risks excluded by Clause 1 (F.C.-& S. Clause) be reinstated in this Policy by deletion of the said clause, or should the risks or any of them mentioned in that clause or the risks of mines, torpedoes, bombs or other engines of war be insured under this Policy, Clause (b) below shall become operative and anything contained in this contract which is inconsistent with Clause (b) or which affords more extensive protection against the aforesaid risks than that afforded by the Institute War Clauses relevant to the particular form of transit covered by this Insurance is null and void.
   (b) This Policy is warranted free of any claim based upon loss of, or frustration of, the insured voyage or adventure caused by arrests restraints or detainments of Kings Princes Peoples Usurpers or persons attempting to usurp power.

And so we, the assurers, are contented, and do hereby promise and bind ourselves, each one for his own part, our heirs, executors, and goods to the assured, their executors, administrators, and assigns, for the true performance of the premises, confessing ourselves paid the consideration due unto us for this assurance by the assured, at and after the rate of

25p %

IN WITNESS whereof we, the assurers, have subscribed our names and sums assured in *LONDON, as hereinafter appears.*

N.B.—Corn, fish, salt, fruit, flour, and seed are warranted free from average, unless general, or the ship be stranded ; sugar, tobacco, hemp, flax, hides and skins are warranted free from average under five pounds per cent., and all other goods, also the ship and freight, are warranted free from average under three pounds per cent. unless general, or the ship be stranded.

Row know De that We, the Assurers, members of the Syndicate(s) whose definitive Number(s) in the attached list are set out in the Table overleaf, or attached overleaf, hereby bind Ourselves, each for his own part and not one for another, and in respect of his due proportion only, to pay or make good to the Assured all such Loss and/or Damage which he or they may sustain by any one or more of the aforesaid perils, and so that the due proportion for which each of Us the Assurers' is liable shall be ascertained by reference to his proportion as ascertained according to the said list of the Amount, Percentage or Proportion of the total Sum assured which is in the said Table set opposite the definitive Number of the Syndicate of which such Assurer is a member.

IN WITNESS whereof the Manager of Lloyd's Policy Signing Office has subscribed his Name on behalf of each of Us.

LLOYD'S POLICY SIGNING OFFICE.

MANAGER.

Dated in London, the   2nd April, 19xx.

(In the event of loss or damage which may result in a claim under this Insurance, immediate notice should be given to the Lloyd's Agent at the port or place where the loss or damage is discovered in order that he may examine the goods and issue a survey report.)

L.P.O. 80

(No.   )

Any person not an Underwriting Member of Lloyd's subscribing this Policy, or any person signing the same if so subscribed, will be liable to be proceeded against under Lloyd's Acts.

S.G.

£ 559.00

Printed at Lloyds, London, England.

INSTITUTE DANGEROUS DRUGS CLAUSE.

"It is understood and agreed that no claim under this Policy will be paid in respect of drugs to which the various International Conventions relating to Opium and other dangerous drugs apply unless
(i) the drugs shall be expressly declared as such in the Policy and the name of the country from which, and the name of the country to which they are consigned shall be specifically stated in the Policy
   and
(ii) the proof of the transmission (either by a licence, certificate or authorisation issued by the department of the country to which the drugs are consigned showing the importation of the consignment has been approved or by permission that consent has been approved for that Government, or, alternatively, by a licence, certificate or authorisation issued by the Government of the country from which the drugs are consigned showing that the export of the consignment to the destination stated has been approved) of that Government.
   and
(iii) the route by which the drugs were conveyed was usual and customary."

FIGURE 21.2 Marine all-risks policy

Lloyd's Marine Policy

We, The Underwriters, hereby agree, in consideration of the payment to us by or on behalf of the Assured of the premium specified in the Schedule, to insure against loss damage liability or expense in the proportions and manner hereinafter provided. Each Underwriting Member of a Syndicate whose definitive number and proportion is set out in the following Table shall be liable only for his own share of his respective Syndicate's proportion.

In Witness whereof the General Manager of Lloyd's Policy Signing Office has subscribed his Name on behalf of each of Us.

LLOYD'S POLICY SIGNING OFFICE
General Manager

FOR EMBOSSMENT BY • LLOYD'S POLICY SIGNING OFFICE •

This insurance is subject to English jurisdiction.

MAR
LPO 62A (1.1.82) Printed by The Carlton Berry Co. Ltd.

SCHEDULE

POLICY NUMBER

NAME OF ASSURED

VESSEL

VOYAGE OR PERIOD OF INSURANCE

SUBJECT-MATTER INSURED

AGREED VALUE
(if any)

AMOUNT INSURED HEREUNDER

PREMIUM

CLAUSES, ENDORSEMENTS, SPECIAL CONDITIONS AND WARRANTIES

THE ATTACHED CLAUSES AND ENDORSEMENTS FORM PART OF THIS POLICY of the (A) clauses but obviously for air movements. A detailed examination of the clauses provided by the insurance underwriters or brokers would clearly be of use to the exporter, but a brief comparison of the clauses is shown in Table 21.1.

TABLE 21.1 Comparison of (A), (B) and (C) clauses

	(A)	(B)	(C)
Loss or damage reasonably attributable to:			
Accidental damage, theft, malicious damage	✔	✔	✘
Fire or explosion	✔	✔	✔
Vessel stranded, grounded, sunk or capsized	✔	✔	✔
Collision with any external object except water	✔	✔	✔
Discharge of cargo at a port of distress	✔	✔	✔
Earthquake, volcanic eruption or lightning	✔	✔	✘
Theft	✔	✘	✘
Loss or damage caused by:			
General average sacrifice	✔	✔	✔
Jettison	✔	✔	✔
Washing overboard	✔	✔	✘
Entry of sea water	✔	✔	✘
Total loss of any package overboard or dropped while loading or unloading	✔	✔	✘

Later in this chapter we will look at what might be seen as more important: the risks that are excluded from these policies.

Today therefore, an exporter approaching a Lloyd's broker for a voyage policy would now receive a Lloyd's MAR policy with attached clauses and pay the appropriate premiums. Equivalent voyage policies would be issued by other insurance companies.

This is a perfectly feasible operation for the exporter making, perhaps, one or two consignments a month but it would clearly be very time consuming to approach an insurer for potentially hundreds, or even thousands, of shipments that the average exporter will be making. There has to be a better way, and, of course, there is.

Open policy

The most common situation is that exporters, in fact international traders generally, use a broker to approach insurance companies and agree the raising of a policy that is drawn up to cover many shipments and not just one. This may be a 'floating policy' that is raised for a particular value and which is gradually reduced by the value of each shipment until it is used up and requires renewal.

This type of policy is less common than it used to be, particularly because the insured is often required to make a payment of an averaged premium in advance. By far the most common form of policy is properly referred to as the 'permanently open policy', so called because it will be drawn up for a period of time, subject to renewal, and will allow any number of shipments over that period. The expression often used is that the policy is 'always open irrespective of declarations'. The wording of such a policy, designed to cover every shipment by that particular trader, imports as well as exports, might be:

Per: Any conveyances or held covered at a premium to be arranged for air and/or parcel post.

Voyage: World/World via any route and including transhipment.

On: Electrical materials and/or other materials.

Such a policy could hardly be more open, covering the shipment of any materials, from anywhere to anywhere, by any route, and by any means of transport. It may contain a schedule of premium rates, which will depend on the country of destination, or define a single premium for all shipments, and the level of cover, with the Institute cargo clauses detailing the actual cover. These open policies are sometimes referred to as 'declaration policies' because the trader is making shipments that the insurers know nothing about until they are declared to them, which they are periodically. But first, the exporter has a problem with the document set.

Under the contracts we mentioned earlier in which the exporter is responsible for arranging, and paying for, cargo insurance, there is a clear need to include, in the set of documents, some documentary proof that the contractual obligation to arrange insurance cover has been performed. The problem is that the exporter only has one open policy and it is not practical to send that to buyers as part of the document set. A hard copy may be buried in the company secretary's safe, but more likely it actually exists as a virtual document within the insurer's website.

The solution is that the exporter will produce an 'insurance certificate' **for** each individual shipment. Such certificates will be completed by the exporter on electronic templates supplied by the insurers, which have been pre-signed by the underwriter.

An example is reproduced in Figure 21.3 and it will be clear that they contain only very basic information regarding the shipment. Thus the production of documentary evidence of the cargo insurance is accomplished by the relatively simple completion of an insurance certificate, and this is invariably acceptable.

FIGURE 21.3 Certificate of insurance

CERTIFICATE OF INSURANCE

Exporter	CERTIFICATE NO. ZINT	
	Exporter's reference	
	Forwarder's reference	

Consignee	CONDITIONS OF INSURANCE

☐ Institute Cargo Clauses (A)

☐ Institute Cargo Clauses (B)

☐ Institute Cargo Clauses (C)

☐ Institute Cargo Clauses (Air) (Excluding sendings by Post)

Selling agent	

Further subject to Institute War Clauses and Institute Strikes Clauses (Cargo) (Air Cargo)

Institute Classification Clause

Institute Radioactive Contamination Exclusion Clause

Other Special Conditions (see reverse)

Other UK transport details		
Vessel	Port of loading	
Port of discharge	Final destination	Insured value	Premium

Shipping marks, container numbers	Number and kind of packages, description of goods	Gross Weight	Cube (m³)

PROCEDURE IN EVENT OF CLAIM

1 It is the duty of the Assured and their agents to take such measures as may be reasonable for the purpose of averting or minimising a loss and to ensure that all rights against Carriers Bailees or other third parties are properly preserved and exercised

2 Follow the procedures stated overleaf.

3 Apply immediately for survey of damaged goods to the Agent stated below or if none stated to the nearest Institute of London Underwriters or Lloyds Agent or to Zurich International Head Office as shown on reverse

Claims Payable at.

By

For Zurich International (UK) Limited

Dennis W White, Managing Director

This is to certify that Zurich International has insured the above mentioned goods for the voyage and value stated on behalf of

Under Policy No

This Certificate is not valid unless counter-signed
This Certificate requires endorsement by the Assured

Signatory's company
Name of signatory
Dated
Signed

ZURICH INTERNATIONAL UK

Principles of insurance

It is important that exporters have a basic understanding of some of the underpinning principles of insurance generally, and particularly their practical implications to cargo insurance.

Insurable interest

This expression refers to one of the functions of trade terms such as FCA, CIP, etc, described in Chapter 15, that identify a point in the journey where the risk of loss or damage to the goods transfers from the seller to the buyer. Technically there is an actual transfer of the 'insurable interest' in the goods.

The principle of insurable interest is a vital one to all forms of insurance. In order to take out a policy, the policyholder must have an insurable interest in the insured matter. In the case of cargo insurance this means that they must 'benefit from the safe arrival of the goods or be prejudiced by their loss'.

Without such a principle it would be possible for any individual to take out an insurance policy on any eventuality they could think of. For example, a policy could be raised that paid out if a football player broke a leg during a game. If this policy were taken out by the player's employers, they would clearly have an insurable interest, but if it were possible for any individual to take out such a policy, then it would simply be another form of gambling, that is a bet of premiums that pays out if a player actually does break a leg. Insurance is not intended to be a form of gambling and therefore the policyholder has to prove this 'vested interest'.

It is also necessary to prove insurable interest in order to make a claim against a policy, and this can pose a problem if the claim is actually made by a non-policyholder. This situation can arise in contracts subject to CIP or CIF conditions. As explained in Chapter 15, these terms mean that the seller is responsible for arranging the insurance and, as we have seen above, this will invariably done under an open policy in the seller's name. However the 'insurable interest' transfers either when the first carrier takes over the goods under CIP contracts or at ship's rail, port of shipment for CIF contracts.

Thus, the responsibility for loss or damage to the goods transfers to the buyer at the port or depot in the UK, even though the seller has insured right through to the final destination.

It is possible for the buyer to make a claim on the seller's open policy because of two clauses:

1 Claims payable abroad (CPA)
   The insurers will accept a claim either at the overseas destination, usually through the nearest Lloyd's or company's agent, or where the policy was issued. All they require is that the claim is properly documented and, as the original documents can only be in one place, there is no possibility of dual claims. Thus it is perfectly possible for

the buyer to pay the seller the full CIP or CIF value and use the documents to make the insurance claim for the insured value.

Just what claims documents are required we will examine later but we still have the problem of the buyer establishing an insurable interest in order to make the claim. This is solved by the next clause.

2 Policy proof of interest (PPI)

In simple terms, this means that possession of the policy is sufficient to prove insurable interest. In reality it is the insurance certificate and supporting claims documents that provide such proof. Such certificates would be endorsed on the reverse side to make such a transfer possible, in the same way that a bill of lading may be endorsed to transfer title in the goods.

Indemnity

Most insurance is based on the fact that the insurers promise to indemnify the insured: that is, they promise to put them back into the situation they were in before the loss. It is obviously not a principle of life insurance.

In practice, the indemnity on cargo insurance policies is expressed as an amount of money, the insured value of the goods. While it is possible that the insurers could replace lost or damaged goods with exact equivalents, it is clearly impractical, and therefore cargo insurance is invariably based on valued policies.

The UK Marine Insurance Act 1906, a model for most others, specifies that the insured value of the goods must be the 'prime cost plus all expenses incidental to shipping plus charges of insurance'; in practice the typical insured value is CIP or CIF plus 10 per cent.

The additional 10 per cent is there to represent the buyer's potential profit. After all, the seller's profit is in the ex-works price and if the goods had arrived, then the buyer would presumably have made a profit on top of the CIP/CIF price they have agreed to pay. The insurance company is in fact indemnifying both parties.

This seems even more logical when you consider the situation in which the buyer is making the claim. They claim the full CIF/CIP price that they have paid the seller plus a percentage to cover their lost profits. In this respect it is perfectly acceptable to the insurers to insure goods for CIP plus 20 per cent or CIP plus 30 per cent, as long as they are consistent, because the premiums are also calculated on the insured values.

It is possible to agree an 'excess' on the value, in which case the exporter will always bear a percentage of the loss, and have no claim if the loss is below the excess amount. Alternatively a 'franchise' amount might be agreed, in which case a loss below the amount would preclude a claim, as with the excess, but losses above the amount specified would be met in full; that is, the exporter would not carry any part of the loss so long as it exceeded the franchise percentage.

Uberrimae fidei (utmost good faith)

Once again, this is a principle that applies to all forms of insurance. The insurers are almost totally dependent on the insured to disclose any relevant information regarding the insured risks. Thus a person taking out a life insurance policy who failed to disclose a serious medical problem would find that the policy could be 'voided' by the insurers. There is an important application of *uberrimae fidei* to the type of open policies commonly used for cargo insurance.

Imagine the situation in which an exporter makes a shipment by road to Germany at the beginning of June and it arrives intact during the second week of June. At the end of June the seller declares all the month's shipments to the insurance company in order for them to calculate the premiums. However, the safe arrival of the German consignment could persuade the seller not to declare the shipment because, after all, the insurance was not actually required for that consignment.

This would be a clear and serious breach of good faith and, if deliberate, would almost certainly lead to the policy being voided, that is, cancelled by the insurers. It is obviously inequitable for the insured to avoid paying premiums on goods that they already know have arrived safely. Goods are declared 'safe or not safe, lost or not lost'.

Good faith works both ways. Imagine the situation in which the goods are actually written off due to a road accident on their way to Germany. The insurance company's good faith is that they accept the claim, at the end of June, even though the loss occurred before declaration, ie before they knew of the consignment.

Subrogation

In the event that loss or damage occurs due to an insured risk, then a claim will be made on the insurance company. If we assume that the claim is successful, then the insured will regard the matter as closed. However, if nothing else happens we have a carrier who may well be liable for the loss or damage but who has apparently avoided any liability.

It is the principle of subrogation that avoids this outcome, in that it allows the insurance company to take action against liable carriers in the name of the insured. The exporter, or importer, must maintain any rights of action against carriers by avoiding giving clean receipts and advising loss or damage as soon as is possible, ideally within three days, but these rights are subrogated to the insurance company once the claim has been paid.

It is very fair to the insured in that the claim must be paid first. The insurance company cannot make a claim on the carrier and only pay the insured if the action against the carrier is successful. The insured will have a valid claim irrespective of the carrier's liability. Also, in the unlikely event that the insurers actually receive more in their claim on the carrier than they have paid to the insured, then the insured receives the difference.

The whole issue becomes somewhat more complicated because the carriers will often have taken out insurance to cover their liability to the owners of the goods. This is known as a goods in transit (GIT) policy, and valid claims will be met by the carrier's insurance company. What this means is that claims against carriers are often made by insurance companies and that disputes may well be settled between the two insurance companies involved.

Contingency (seller's interest) insurance

Many exporters find that there are situations where they are making export shipments for which the buyer is responsible for cargo insurance. The most obvious cases would be CPT or CFR shipments, although the same situation applies to FCA and FOB sales. In some markets CPT/CFR shipments are very common as the importer's country have a requirement that cargo insurance is taken out with one of their national insurance companies, rather than a foreign company in the seller's country.

The risk here is that loss or damage can occur and the buyer refuses to take up the goods or documents, it may even be that the buyer has not actually insured the goods. If the buyer attempts to avoid liability – and legal action is often pointless – it can lead to a substantial loss to the exporter. Seller's interest insurance, sometimes called contingency insurance, covers the contingency that the buyer is responsible for insurance, loss or damage occurs, and the buyer has failed to insure. In such a case, and for a relatively small premium, the seller would be able to make a claim. It is often important that the existence of such cover is not revealed to the buyer.

Proximate cause

It is perfectly reasonable for insurance companies to prefer that claims are made for loss or damage due to risks that are actually covered by the policy. In fact, many claims fail simply because the cause of the loss is not an insured risk. Just what the insured is not covered for is listed below, but first the principle of 'proximate cause' need to be explained.

When a loss occurs it is often the result of not one clear event but of a series of events that, cumulatively, lead to a loss. What the insurers must do is establish the actual cause of the loss, what they describe as the 'active, efficient cause', that is the proximate (closest) cause.

As an example of this in action, consider a situation in which a road vehicle is in collision during transit. If goods are damaged in the collision, then there is a valid claim as collision is an obvious insured risk. However, if the goods are not damaged but the vehicle is, and this results in a delay of the journey for repairs, and the Christmas cards arrive at the wholesalers on Boxing Day, then there is no claim because delay is not an insured risk. It is therefore important to investigate the process of events leading to a loss, and thus establish the proximate cause, and then ensure that this is an insured risk.

Rather than list what risks are insured it is actually easier to identify those that are specifically excluded from the (A), (B) and (C) policies.

You are not insured for:

Delay

As we have seen above, if any loss occurs because of the late arrival of the goods, then there is no claim. It may be in this case that action is possible against the carrier, the transport conventions defining what would be considered unreasonable delay in delivery, but not against the insurers.

Wear and tear

The exporter has to plan for predictable factors that could lead to loss, perhaps of value, to the goods. Normal wear and tear is never covered by the policy and the exporter has to prepare for the possibility of, for example, a rough sea voyage. In fact, the consequences of 'the ordinary action of the wind and waves' is not covered. It is, after all, no surprise that it gets a bit windy in the North Atlantic.

Inherent vice

This describes things that goods are likely to do and are therefore predictable. For example, it is obvious that metal has a tendency to rust, particularly in damp conditions, and the exporter must take steps to avoid such damage by priming or the use of silicone gels or shrink wrap, rather than rely on the insurance policy. Similarly, cotton can rust, fishmeal ferment, concrete set and perishables go off, all of which must be managed by the exporter.

Ullage

This is almost a form of inherent vice but is specifically applied to liquids. In the context of cargo insurance it describes loss of liquid due to evaporation or 'ordinary leakage or loss in weight or volume', which is excluded from policies.

Wilful misconduct of the assured

This may be obvious but is extremely important in that the documentation supporting claims must prove that the claimant has acted prudently and that the loss is not the consequence of their direct actions or their negligence. A clear example would be to attempt to make a claim for damaged goods that included bills of lading that were claused 'inadequate packing'. Any claims where there is evidence of insufficient or unsuitable packing are likely to fail.

Claims documents

Assuming the claim is actually being made for the consequences of an insured risk, the second reason that claims may fail is that they are not correctly documented. The insurance companies do not require excessive documentation and ask for nothing that is not relevant to the claim. The documents typically requested would include:

Original policy or certificate
Bearing in mind that the policy is proof of interest (ie insurable interest) this is essential. It also describes the subject matter, insured value and appropriate clauses.

Invoices and packing specifications
Needed to assess the percentage of a part loss and specifically where lost or damaged goods were packed.

Original bill of lading or other transport document
Proves the goods were in apparent good order and condition when shipped, and evidences the contract of carriage should action be later taken against the carrier.

Survey report or other evidence of loss or damage
An independent report of the nature and extent of the loss should ideally be produced by an approved agency, eg Lloyd's agent.

Landing account/weight notes at destination
The carrier's or stowage broker's record of the out-turn of the goods at destination. Useful for identifying where damage took place in the container or on the vessel or haulage unit.

Any correspondence with the carrier/other parties
Obviously the insurers wish to maintain any legal rights against other parties and insist that the insured do not give them away.

Not an unreasonable set of documents to require and every one there for a specific, and understandable, purpose.

22
Credit insurance

Assuming the exporter is able to actually get the right goods, in perfect condition, to the right place at the right time, the problems are not yet over – because it may be that the buyer, for a variety of good and bad reasons, does not pay for them. The management of this credit risk is a task that occupies an increasing amount of the time and resources of the typical exporter as the credit risk in world markets increases.

There is little doubt that the credit risk faced by international traders is greater than it has ever been. In many markets, particularly Third World countries, there is a probability of delay in payment and a distinct possibility of non-payment. In fact, something like 75 per cent of the countries in the world would be bankrupt if they were companies, in that their liabilities far exceed their assets.

This is the result of recurring world recessions, not least those generated by the bank failures of the late 1990s, which affect developed and developing countries alike, and, in particular, the increasing problem of Third World debt, much of which is unsustainable, ie interest payments cannot be made, let alone any repayment of capital amounts. Add to this the overall drop, with certain short-term exceptions, in the majority of basic commodity prices in world trade, increasing the economic problems of the developing countries whose export earnings are based on primary and extractive products, and it is clear that world trade has enormous financial problems.

It may be useful to briefly examine the origins of such widespread credit risk, particularly in developing countries. There is much that is taken for granted by traders in developed countries like the UK and USA.

A UK company wishing to buy goods from an overseas supplier can invariably trade in pounds sterling. Even if the supplier does not wish to accept pounds sterling, then they can easily be converted into US dollars or into euros by the importer or the exporter. A US company would also be happy to accept such 'hard' currencies in payment.

The situation is not the same, for example, for a Ghanaian trader. It is highly unlikely that any supplier would be prepared to accept Ghanaian currency, the cedi (GHC), as payment for goods, as the buyer's cedis cannot be converted into other hard currencies, being a non-convertible 'soft' currency.

So how does a Ghanaian buy and pay for your goods as an exporter? If they are lucky they are able to earn hard currencies from their own exports.

Some countries would be underdeveloped if it were not for the good fortune they have in owning resources, invariably natural resources, which earn them hard currency. The Middle East is a perfect example of a group of countries that are rich because of natural resources.

Some other developing countries, which at one time were able to export commodities at good market prices, have found that an overall downturn in world commodity prices has severely reduced their earnings.

Finally, there are many countries that have no valuable resources or are unable to exploit them, and in fact have trouble feeding themselves. In the last two cases the only way that funds can be made available to pay for imports is to borrow, and Third World debt is the core of the credit-risk problem. We are now in a situation in which many overseas countries cannot even service their debts by making interest payments, and where millions of US dollars' worth of loans are being written off by Western banks.

In such a situation the exporter has to be extremely careful in managing the risk of non-payment.

In Part 8 we will examine the range of alternative methods of payment available to the exporter that can provide varying degrees of security, from the most secure, cash in advance, to the least secure, open account. The security that the exporter enjoys is obviously improved further by a sensible approach to credit control, involving the proper use of credit information, credit limits for individual buyers and operative blacklists. All of this can be made much easier by the operation of a credit insurance policy.

The basic risks can be broken down into two categories:

- Buyer risk: default, dishonour, insolvency, failure to take up goods.
- Country risk (sovereign risk): government action, eg failure to transfer currency.

The exporter's assessment of risk must take into account both aspects.

Credit risk insurance is provided by a number of specialist organizations, of which one of the most important is the UK Export Credit Agency's (ECA) Export Credits Guarantee Department (ECGD). This remains a UK government department concerned only with contracts with credit periods over two years and generally with project finance. This includes a range of pre-shipment and supplier credit arrangements that relate to the sometimes complex payment schemes associated with overseas projects.

Most countries have their own ECAs, eg:

- Ex-Im Bank: USA;
- Coface: France;
- Euler Hermes: Germany;
- SERV: Switzerland;
- EDC: Canada;
- Nexi: Japan.

There is an increasing number of private companies offering international credit insurance who can supply almost any form of cover subject to the agreement of appropriate premiums. Some are also their country's official ECA. They include Atradius (formerly Gerling NCM Credit Insurance Ltd). Atradius is the largest in the UK and typically offers a comprehensive short-term policy covering credit periods of up to two years. Cover is available for both buyer and sovereign risk subject to the seller operating within either written credit limits from the insurers or discretionary limits that can be calculated from the company's trading experience.

The limits are obviously affected by the method of payment in use. Generally Atradius would require a fair spread of an exporter's business but is prepared to negotiate premiums for selective contracts, which could include pre-shipment as well as post-shipment cover. It insists that the seller bear a percentage of the loss, providing payment cover themselves of between 80 and 90 per cent. The purpose of the exporter's exposure is to maintain some interest from the seller in recovery of the debt. As with contingency cargo insurance, the existence of a credit insurance policy should not be revealed to the buyer.

Other providers of short-term export credit insurance include:

- Lloyd's Underwriters (of course);
- Euler Hermes;
- Zurich Surety, Credit and Political Risk (USA);
- Zurich Versicherung (Germany);
- Coface (France);
- AIG UK Ltd;
- AXA-Winterthur (Switzerland);
- CESCE (Spain);
- Credit Guarantee (South Africa);
- Ducroire-Delcredere (Belgium);
- GCNA (Canada);
- Mitsui Sumitomo (Japan);
- PICC Property and Casualty Company (China);
- SACE BT (Italy);
- Sompo Japan (Japan).

Generally, credit insurance policies operate in a similar way to the open cargo insurance policies examined in Chapter 21, although each insurer will make its own particular administrative arrangements. Typically, premiums will be negotiated in advance, in some cases being averaged over all customers and markets, and it may be that a fixed fee or advance payment of a percentage of premiums is required.

Insurance and the exporter

The typical exporter will operate both cargo and credit insurance policies and therefore conduct business in the knowledge that such security exists in the event that things go wrong that are, of course, outside their control. However, it is very important to understand that:

- The security operates only in the situation where the exporter is not at fault. We established earlier that, pretty obviously, there is no cover where the loss is due to the misconduct of the exporter, but the situation may not always be clear cut. For example, there may be a situation in which the seller considers that they have fulfilled all contractual obligations, but the buyer disagrees. A typical example would be a dispute regarding the quality of goods supplied. In such a case there is not necessarily clear misconduct on the seller's part but, nevertheless, the insurance companies will not entertain a claim until the contractual dispute is settled. If, however, the sellers can prove to the satisfaction of the insurers that the buyer's complaint is simply an excuse for delay or dishonour, a not uncommon scenario, and that they have fulfilled the contract, then a claim will be accepted. The moral is that exporters do need to maintain a high quality of administration, and the documentation evidencing it, to ensure that they can prove performance of all their contractual obligations.

- The insurers expect the insured to minimize not only the possibilities of loss but also the consequences of losses when they happen. An example of this, mentioned earlier, is the fact that claims on carriers for loss or damage should be made as soon as possible, and certainly within three working days. The basic and very important principle is that the insured must act as 'a prudent man uninsured'. With apologies for the phrase's gender (this is a quote from Lloyd's underwriters in the 1600s) the phrase does concisely describe the expectations of the insurers. The policy is not a safety net for a lack of concern on the seller's behalf, and all insured parties must conduct their business as if an insurance policy does not exist.

23
Exchange risk management

It is becoming increasingly common for developed countries to do business with overseas buyers in currencies other than their own hard currency. The currencies used would invariably be the 'hard' convertible currencies of developed countries, in particular pounds sterling, US dollar, euro and perhaps Japanese yen and Swiss francs.

In the cases where the UK exporter chooses to deal in pounds sterling or the US exporter deals in US dollars with overseas customers, there is a clear possibility of risk for the buyer in that the cost of the currency in which they need to pay, in terms of the amount of their own currency needed to buy it, may well increase due to fluctuations in the relative values of the two currencies. It is a fact of modern commerce that the exchange rates of currencies are subject to sometimes large movements.

Because of the importance of the balance of payments to the value of a country's currency relative to others, there is a perfect logic to the economic theory that describes the corrective mechanism that controls such fluctuations. To use the UK as an example, if the pound weakens against other currencies, ie becomes worth less in that it takes more pounds to buy the same amount of foreign currency, then UK exports become cheaper to foreign buyers – and therefore UK exports increase, the balance of payments deficit reduces and the pound strengthens. The reverse situation is that a strengthening pound makes exports more expensive to the buyers and the reduction in exports leads to a weakening pound. Wonderful in theory until one considers the fact that many UK exporters, especially the bigger ones, choose to invoice in other currencies and the situation above operates in reverse. For example, the exporter receiving US dollars, with a weakening pound, actually benefits from the change.

Movements in exchange rates are broadly subject to supply and demand within the market for currencies. This is affected by the demand for trading currency, ie an increase in US exports can lead to an increased demand for US$, but also by the differences in interest rates from one country, and one currency, to another. The higher the interest rate available, the more that currency will be demanded.

The simple risk faced by the exporter is that the calculated export price, based on predominantly pounds-sterling or US-dollar costs, which is then converted to a foreign currency price at the current exchange rate, has to be calculated some time in advance of the eventual receipt of those funds, and the eventual revenues may well be less than was planned.

Assuming that the decision is taken to invoice some overseas buyers in their own currencies, then the exporter has a number of options in relation to the management of the risk. We will now examine these.

Do nothing

Not a very dynamic approach but nevertheless one that could be justified. It is simply the case that the exporter may well be prepared to accept whatever the exchange rate happens to be when the foreign currency payment is actually received. The rate on that day, which is known as the spot rate, may actually favour the seller if their currency has weakened against revenue currency. It also has the advantage of simplicity, which makes it very attractive to many traders.

However, we must accept that the opposite situation could apply, and there is a clear risk that the seller could lose substantial revenues, possibly even sustain losses, should the exchange rate movement go against them. This is a particular problem where the amounts involved are large and if the profit margins are small. Therefore the average exporter looks for ways in which to minimize or remove the risk.

Currency accounts

The most obvious way to remove the exchange risk is not to exchange at all. That is, the seller simply keeps the foreign currency in foreign currency accounts. The absence of exchange control regulations within most developed countries means that the exporter can maintain domestic accounts in any currencies. In many cases it will also be possible to hold foreign currencies in accounts overseas.

The typical regular exporter in a developed country may maintain multi-currency accounts in US dollars, pounds sterling and euros. Apart from the fact that any exchange risk is eliminated, it may also be the case that the interest earned on such accounts, which would depend on the type of account, could be superior to interest rates paid on other currency accounts. It may even be possible to borrow foreign currencies at beneficial rates.

However, the main benefit of currency accounts applies to the situation in which a company is selling and buying in foreign currency. The ideal situation would be where the receipts and payments actually balance each other out, but there are still great benefits even when there is no balance, any shortfall being made up by borrowing currency and any surplus being held in interest-bearing accounts. Also, there is often the option to take advantage of movements in spot rates by exchanging currency where there is a revenue benefit.

Forward exchange contract

It is possible to approach a bank and be given a rate for selling (your receipts) or buying (your payments) foreign currency at a future time. What this does is to guarantee an exchange rate to the trader at the time when prices are being calculated and allows them to rely on that rate irrespective of the actual spot rate at the time of the exchange. The banks will quote forward rates for anything from one month to five years, but the standards periods are 3, 6 and 12 months.

The rates banks offer differ depending on whether the bank is buying or selling the currency and will be expressed as a 'premium' for currencies strengthening, which is deducted from the spot rate, or 'discount' for weakening currencies, which is added to the spot rate.

Let us look at some of the basic rules for the calculation of a forward exchange transaction.

You are the bank

This is to say that all rates are quoted and calculated from the point of view of the bank:

Banks buy high and sell low

Again this is logical from the bank's point of view.

Add a discount

This will represent a currency that is weakening, ie its value is falling against the contract currency.

Deduct a premium

This will represent a currency that is strengthening, ie its value is rising against the contract currency.

The great advantage of forward exchange contracts is the fact that the exporter knows exactly what rate will be used when the currency is eventually received and converted. However, there are potential problems in that the contract must be met even if the payment has not been received from the overseas buyer. This would entail the exporter having to purchase the correct amount of, say, US dollars, at the spot rate, in order to meet the forward contract, and then having to convert the eventual dollar payment, again at spot. It also means that the exporter cannot take advantage if the actual spot rate is better than the forward rate.

In the cases where the exporter has some doubt about the exact time payment would be received, then it is possible to negotiate an 'option forward'. This would fix a rate that could be taken up over a period of time, eg one to three months, and therefore give an element of flexibility to the timing of the exchange. However, this does not give the exporter the option to take up the forward rate or not; the forward exchange contract *must* be honoured at some time during the period allowed. Also, the bank will attempt to quote a rate that will be the best for it over that time period.

As an example of an option forward exchange contract, let us suppose that we contract to sell 100,000 euros to the bank in exchange for pounds sterling, the euros to be available some time between the beginning of Month 1 and the end of Month 3:

- spot rate: 1.41–1.44;
- 1 month forward: 1.49–1.54;
- 3 months forward: 1.57–1.63.

Remember: you are the bank – and the bank buys high and sells low, and will take the most favourable rate to itself for the period of the option: it will take the lowest selling rate and the highest buying rate. Thus:

- Option rate (1 to 3 months): 1.49–1.63.

The euros are sold to the bank, which converts them at the buying rate of 1.63 to the pound. The exporter thus receives £61,349.69 (less bank charges).

Note that these figures above are for demonstration purposes only and have been simplified for clarity. They do not relate to actual spot or forward rates, which would normally be defined to four decimal places and would not exhibit such large ranges in value.

Currency option

In this case the exporter does have the option to take up the forward rate or to ignore it and convert at spot if that is more favourable. There will still be a fixed forward rate, known as the 'strike rate', and either a stated date or a time period for that forward rate to be taken up. In return for the option to take the forward rate or ignore it, the exporter (or importer, of course) will pay an 'up-front' premium, the amount of which is dependent on the strike rate agreed and the time period.

Contrary to popular belief, the forward rates used in the above contracts are not the banks' guess of what the rates will be in the future, but are simply a spot rate adjusted to take into account the differences in the interest rates for the two currencies and effectively compensates the party who has held the currency with the lower interest rate for the period of the contract.

Summary

We started Part 7 by examining the range of risks faced by an exporter and have attempted to identify the ways in which the typical exporter deals with such risks. In brief they are:

- Physical loss/damage: Cargo insurance policy.
- Non-payment: Credit insurance policy.
- Loss on exchange: Currency accounts or forward exchange contracts.

However, none of the solutions mentioned above is compulsory. Traders have a perfect right to choose not to insure against these risks and may have good reasons not to. If, for example, the costs of the premiums on a credit insurance policy actually exceed the claims, then it could actually be more cost effective not to insure. This should also be coupled with the fact that the better the level of professionalism displayed by the trader, notably in terms of shipping the goods, credit control and payment collection, then the less important becomes the safety net of the insurance policy.

PART EIGHT
Finance of international trade

24
Business finance

Legal entities

The person or people running a business may organize it in one of three basic ways, all different both from legal and tax points of view:

- as a sole trader;
- as a partnership;
- as an incorporated company.

Sole trader

The sole trader is a one-person business, in many cases the individual who started the business. It is easy to set up as there are no legal formalities, except for the registration of any business name to be used. This means that they are the most common form of enterprise in most developed countries.

The sole trader will have to provide the capital for the business – from their own resources or a loan from the bank or from various forms of government funding for small firms.

Advantages:

- easy to establish, with minimal capital required;
- all the profits of the business (after expenses and taxation) go to the owner;
- as the owner works for themselves, it is a good incentive to run the business efficiently;
- no decisions have to be shared – nor do the profits.

Disadvantages:

- all debts of the business are the owner's responsibility;
- the owner has 'unlimited liability';

- there may be tax disadvantages;
- if the owner becomes ill, the business is at risk;
- it can be difficult to raise extra capital for expansion.

Partnerships

The original UK Partnership Act of 1890 defines a partnership as 'the relation which subsists between persons carrying on a business in common with a view of profit'. This simply means that a partnership is made up of members who are in business and whose aim is to make profits.

Advantages:

- easy and cheap to set up;
- usually more capital is at the disposal of the partners;
- the partners can pool their knowledge, experience and resources;
- no legal formalities are required to set up a partnership, but an agreement is highly desirable;
- in case of illness there exists a better chance of continuity;
- profits after tax are divided among the partners as agreed in any partnership agreement.

Disadvantages:

- unlimited liability, which means that the partners may be personally liable for any business debts;
- there is always the risk of relationships breaking down between partners;
- the actions of one partner are binding on the others;
- when one partner dies, there may be problems because the family of the deceased person may choose to take out their capital from the business. In this case the partnership may have to be wound up or dissolved.

In addition to what might be termed a general partnership, as described above, many countries also now recognize the concept of a limited partnership, which is similar to a general partnership except that in addition to one or more general partners (GPs), there are one or more limited partners (LPs). It is a partnership in which only one partner is required to be a general partner. The GPs are, in all major respects, in the same legal position as partners in a conventional firm, ie they have management control, share the right to use partnership property, share the profits of the firm in predefined proportions, and have joint and several liability for the debts of the partnership.

A more recent development is the concept of the *limited liability partnership* (LLP), which is a partnership in which some or all partners (depending on the jurisdiction) have limited liability. It therefore exhibits elements of partnerships and corporations (see below).

In an LLP one partner is not responsible or liable for another partner's misconduct or negligence. This is an important difference from a limited partnership. In an LLP, some partners have a form of limited liability similar to that of the shareholders of a corporation. In some countries, an LLP must also have at least one general partner with unlimited liability. Unlike corporate shareholders, the partners have the right to manage the business directly. An LLP also contains a different level of tax liability from that of a corporation.

Limited liability partnerships are distinct from limited partnerships in some countries, which may allow all LLP partners to have limited liability, while a limited partnership may require at least one unlimited partner and allow others to assume the role of passive and limited liability investors. As a result, in these countries the LLP is more suited for businesses where all investors wish to take an active role in management.

There is considerable confusion between LLPs as constituted in the USA and treated as partnerships for tax purposes, and LLPs introduced in the UK in 2001 and adopted elsewhere. The UK LLP is, despite the name, specifically legislated as a corporate body rather than a partnership.

Incorporated companies

An incorporated company, in some countries referred to as a 'corporation', is one that has its own legal personality. This 'legal person or identity' has implications for the way companies keep their accounts and for the terminology used. Because a company is a 'distinct legal person' it can own things, it can buy and sell in its own right and it can owe money. It can sue and it can also be sued, taken to court, and even fined by the court if found liable.

The financial accounts of a business are the accounts of the company; they are not the accounts of the owners (ie the shareholders) of the company who are legally quite distinct. This is why the capital of the company, comprising money invested by the shareholders, is shown as a liability in the balance sheet, ie the company owes the money to the shareholders.

The owners of the company are the so-called 'members' or shareholders, who have a role to appoint the directors of the company. The shareholders have no liability for the debts of the company beyond payment in full at the face value of the shares they hold. Control is usually organized on the basis of one vote per one share. The profits earned by the company may be retained by the company or distributed to the shareholders as dividends.

Advantages:

- a company is a separate legal entity: it is distinct from the people who run it;

- limited liability means that the owners are not responsible for the debts of the company except in cases of fraud or personal guarantees;
- losses can be carried forward and offset against profits in good years;
- in the eyes of the public a company may be seen as more reputable;
- ownership is transferable;
- certain tax advantages may exist.

Disadvantages:

- closer regulation by law;
- more complicated accounts than other forms of business organization;
- more expensive to set up.

In the UK there are three basic types of incorporated companies:

- private limited company;
- public limited company;
- quoted public limited company.

Private limited companies

Those companies with 'Limited' (Ltd) after their name. They may not offer shares to 'the public at large' and share transfers between members are restricted. The shares can only be sold privately (thus *private* limited company) and with the agreement of the other shareholders.

Private limited companies only have to publish their accounts in a summarized form; thus they are able to retain some privacy. The accounts have to be available if the public asks for them.

Public limited companies

Denoted by 'plc' after their name, these companies may offer their shares to the public. Individual shareholders may sell them without restriction, but these companies must have a minimum share capital of £50,000. Plcs are the largest type of company in the private sector.

The shareholders have the right to attend, vote and speak at the company's annual general meeting (AGM) and to elect the board of directors and the chairman.

Quoted public companies

The shares of most public companies are traded ('quoted') on stock exchanges. The price at which such shares are bought and sold is quite distinct from the nominal or 'par' value of such shares. The price represents the market's expectation of future dividends or increases or decreases in the market price of the shares.

The legal concept of incorporation is recognized all over the world, though with differing descriptions. In the USA, most (but not all) corporations are identified by the term 'Incorporated' (Inc) added after the business name, such as 'Texas Instruments, Incorporated', or by putting the word 'corporation' in the name of the company, as in 'Netscape Communications Corporation'.

In Germany, Austria and Switzerland, GmbH ('Gesellschaft mit beschränkter Haftung', meaning 'limited liability business association'), as well as AG ('Aktiengesellschaft', meaning 'business association with shares') are the most common comparable concepts.

In France, Switzerland, Belgium and Luxembourg, the term 'SARL' ('société à responsabilité limitée', meaning 'company with limited liability') or SA ('société anonyme', meaning 'anonymous partnership') is used. Spain, Portugal, Poland, Romania and Latin America use the title 'SA' ('anonymous partnership') or 'Limitada' (Ltda).

Sources of funding

The main sources of business finance are:

- retained profit;
- short-term finance: usually from banks in the form of loans or overdraft facilities;
- long-term capital market: the trading of stocks and shares takes place within stock exchanges.

A significant source of funds for businesses is retained profit. After paying a proportion for corporation tax and a proportion to shareholders as dividends, the remainder is designated as retained profit. Profits retained in the business are shown in the balance sheet as reserves.

Businesses can also raise finance from external sources but, naturally, this always involves a cost. Besides banks, where a business can raise finance in the form of an overdraft, a secured loan, or a mortgage, finance can also be raised from other financial institutions or the general public.

There are two ways of doing this:

- by issuing shares, ie invite the general public or financial institutions to become shareholders;
- by issuing debentures or some other form of debt instrument, ie borrow from the general public or financial institutions.

Equity or share capital

A combination of share capital, long-term loan capital and short-term facilities (eg an overdraft from a bank) is the most common arrangement.

Ideally, a significant proportion of the company's finance will be provided by ordinary shareholders, as this is permanent capital invested in the company, which will not normally be paid back.

Ordinary shares

Ordinary shareholders have a share in any profits that have been made that year after tax has been deducted and interest on any loans paid. If the directors agree, the shareholders are paid a share of the profit in the form of a dividend. A dividend is simply the sum of money payable to a shareholder.

Preference shares

These shares have a fixed rate of dividend, expressed as a percentage of nominal value, which is paid before the dividends of an ordinary shareholder. Preference shareholders do not have a right to a vote.

Cumulative preference shares

A company may not earn enough one year to be able to pay a fixed rate of dividend on its preference shares. With a cumulative preference share any shortfall is carried forward to the next year.

Debt or loan capital

Debenture or secured loan stock

Debentures are the written acknowledgements of debt, and are documents given to people or institutions who lend money to companies. The document will inform the lender:

- when they can expect to be repaid;
- how much in interest they can expect to receive.

Debenture holders do *not*:

- own the company;
- have a vote;
- have a say in running the business.

However, they do have:

- a right to receive their interest every year or half yearly;
- a right to sell their debentures on the market.

Their interest is paid out before anything is paid to the holders of preference and ordinary shares.

Security usually comes in the form of a floating charge over the assets of the business, which gives the holders of the debenture the right to appoint an administrative receiver in the event of default. The advantage, from the borrower's point of view, is that the rate of interest is usually significantly lower on a debenture than on an overdraft.

Unsecured loan stock

Unsecured loan stock is also a tradable debt instrument but is similar to preference shares, although it ranks above preference shares in a liquidation. Loan stock is used commonly in structuring venture capital deals and in situations in which loans to larger companies are syndicated among a number of banks.

Convertible loan stock gives holders the right to convert the whole or a part of their stock into ordinary shares at predetermined dates and prices.

Working capital

The funds needed to finance the business can be divided between fixed capital and working capital.

Fixed capital is that which has been used to buy fixed assets such as machinery and buildings, which cannot be converted quickly into ready cash.

Working capital is the difference between the current assets and current liabilities of the business, ie the funds that are left after all debts are paid and are therefore available to run the business by paying salaries, suppliers, etc. It can also be called 'the circulating capital' of the business because of the way some of the resources of the business circulate around through the various types of current assets.

Some definitions

Fixed assets

Assets that the firm buys and are not for processing or resale, eg plant, equipment, buildings, vehicles, etc. In most cases they are subject to depreciation.

Current assets

These are the things that belong to the business, just like fixed assets, but they are not permanent: stock, work in progress, debtors and cash.

Current liabilities

These are the amounts that a firm owes, eg overdraft, trade creditors.

Stock

Can be made up of raw materials, work in progress and finished goods. Excessive stock levels are an inefficient use of resources.

Debtors

Those who owe money to the company. A willingness to wait to be paid, eg letters of credit in the form of termed payments, may give a marketing advantage and, in exporting, may be a significant factor.

Trade creditors

Those whom the company owes in the course of its business. The longer we can take to pay, the longer we can use that cash for other, profitable purposes. But when a company hits a cash crisis it is often at this point that suppliers decide, perhaps unexpectedly, to stop deliveries or even start legal proceedings.

Short-term investments

These are easily realizable investments. However, the percentage return on this type of investment will be lower than other less flexible investments.

Overdraft

It is attractive and profitable to run a business using the bank's money – but there are limits on the facility the bank will allow and they can always withdraw or reduce such a facility. The bank's security is a legal floating charge over all the assets of the business.

Exports and working capital

An exporter needs to watch working capital even more closely for two reasons:

- The time involved in shipping goods to distant customers (and for remittances to get back into the exporter's bank) means that the debtors figure is likely to be larger for the equivalent volume of home business.
- A large debtors figure may stay large because of increased bad debts and the difficulty of chasing delayed payments in overseas markets.

The solution to this problem is the technique called 'trade finance' or in the case of an exporter, 'export trade finance.'

These techniques include:

- negotiating or discounting bills of exchange;
- documentary letters of credit;
- forfaiting;
- factoring;
- international credit unions;
- facilities provided by export credit agencies (eg ECGD).

Financial reporting

Accountants follow agreed principles when recording the transactions of a business. This enables the management and others to monitor the progress of the business through examination of a variety of sources of data.

These sources are:

- the balance sheet;
- the profit and loss (P&L) account and other related documents;
- management information (management reports), which includes more frequent reports than the balance sheet and the P&L account.

Balance sheet

A balance sheet shows what the company owns and what it owes at any one moment in time.

A simple (horizontal) structure would be as shown in Table 24.1.

TABLE 24.1   Horizontal balance sheet layout

Sources of finance	Fixed assets
Current liabilities	Current assets
Total	Total

A balance sheet always balances because everything the company owns must have been paid for by money acquired from elsewhere: from shareholders or banks or the sale of current assets such as stock, etc.

It is now more usual to use a vertical layout as in Table 24.2.

TABLE 24.2 Vertical balance sheet layout

Sources of finance	Total
Fixed assets	
plus	
Working capital (ie current assets minus current liabilities)	Total

Profit and loss account

It would be quite possible to add together all the expenses of a business incurred during an accounting period, deduct the total from the sales revenue for the same period and arrive at the profit figure. That would not tell us very much, so the profit calculation is broken down in steps:

- Cost of manufacture: this is the total expense involved in purchase and manufacturing of goods for sale.
- Gross profit: this is the profit earned by the business through trading (the trading account).
- Net profit: from the gross profit we can deduct all the incidental expenses of running the business to calculate the net profit.

Table 24.3 illustrates a simple layout.

TABLE 24.3 Profit and loss account layout

Opening stock	Sales revenue
plus	
Purchases	
minus	
Closing stock	
Cost of goods sold	Gross (trading) profit
minus	
Expenses	Net profit

Management information (reports)

Sales orders

An 'orders received', or a weekly or monthly sales summary report. Year-to-date and budget comparison figures are commonly included.

Cash flow forecast

Shows the value and timing of revenue and expenditure for a period. The relationship between cash flowing in and out of a company is particularly important to small companies.

Credit status

A report showing the payments record of existing customers and highlighting delays in payments as part of a credit control system.

Outstanding orders

This report will assist sales administration when handling enquiries from customers. More importantly, variations in the size of the 'order book' will give early warning of future dangers. A decrease in orders indicates a decrease in cash receipts in several months' time; an increase suggests a factory overload and delayed dispatches arising fairly quickly.

Sales analysis

A regular monthly or more frequent sales analysis will alert management to changes in market conditions or sales performance. Investigations can be made and corrective action taken before damage is done to the commercial prospects of the business.

Stock levels

A good stock control system will incorporate sales orders received to show both 'allocated' stock and 'free' stock.

Dispatches

Year-to-date totals and budget variances give strategic guidance to management. Comparison with promises shown in previous dispatch schedules highlights immediate problems within the company.

Debtors ledger

Ledger entries will indicate who has bought what, how frequently, and the promptness of payment.

Aged debtors report

This analysis will rate customers according to the age of outstanding, unpaid bills, and by reference to individual allowed credit limits.

Business costs

Costs can be divided into two categories:

- costs that are either direct or indirect;
- costs that are either variable or fixed.

Direct costs and indirect costs (overheads)

Direct costs are those costs directly attributable to an individual cost unit such as a manufactured unit or a production run, eg materials, labour.

All other costs that are not directly related (to a cost unit) are called 'indirect' or 'overheads', eg light and heat, rent and rates.

Variable and fixed costs

Variable costs are all those which increase or decrease if more or less of a cost unit (product or service) is produced. The essential point here is that the term 'variable cost' is applied only to those costs that must vary if the production volume changes. A typical example would be the cost of components purchased for assembly. In the simplest cases, variable costs vary in direct proportion to the volume of products or service. If the volume doubles or halves, so does the cost.

All other costs that are not variable are 'fixed', that is they do not change as volume changes. Examples are salaries (as opposed to wages per hour), rent, advertising expenditure. Such costs are sometimes referred to as 'sunk costs' in that the business must pay them irrespective of the level of business.

Unfortunately, not all costs fall into these categories so neatly.

Direct fixed costs

The depreciation charge on a machine that has been purchased to produce only one specific product and no other. The depreciation charge is direct to that cost unit (the product) but is fixed. It could remain the same whether a lot or a little is produced.

Variable overhead

The factory's electricity bill. If the factory shuts for a week the consumption would be zero; if the factory went on to double shift the consumption would double. Clearly the electricity cost is a variable one. But since electricity is used by all the activities of the factory, for all the products, the cost is an indirect or overhead cost.

Budgets

A budget is a tool for management control. The quality of any budget is only demonstrated when management can use it to control the business in such a way that it successfully achieves its objectives.

A budget is a set of interrelated business plans for an organization, exhibiting quantified and feasible plans of action and forecasts of results, together with the premises or beliefs on which those plans are based.

There are at least four ways in which a properly prepared budget will help management to run the business:

Strategy
The preparation of a budget will enable managers to see if the company's strategy makes sense. It allows examination of the practical details of that strategy and the assumptions (mainly about markets) on which that strategy is based.

Numbers
By quantifying the various forecasts, management can see if the business is likely to achieve its objectives, in the light of assumptions about the business environment.

Risks
By highlighting potential problems or areas of risk, management can estimate the sensitivity of forecast profits to errors in the basic assumptions on which the budget is built.

Monitoring
By providing performance targets, management are able to monitor progress and concentrate on those aspects of the business where the 'actuals' have diverged from the budget figures.

Does it matter?

Where actuals diverge from budget the managers can decide whether they are:

- small enough to be ignored;
- the natural effect of other changes that are already being attended to, suggesting that some of the basic budget assumptions may be wrong;
- of unknown significance until the budget figures have been reworked.

In the case of significant variances from the planned figures, a well-prepared budget will give a good practical guide to the correct remedial action. In some cases the necessary counter measures may be simple and obvious; in other cases the whole company strategy may have to be rethought.

Five rules of budgeting

A budget is not a licence to spend money, but part of the process of delegating responsibility.

When preparing a budget or any other type of business plan, always start with the sales forecast.

Implementing the budget involves:

- motivation, so that everyone is working to the same objectives;
- communication, so that people can talk to each other about it;
- monitoring, or 'How are we doing so far?'

The actual figures will always be different from the budgeted ones; it is the size of the variance that matters.

Budgeting is a continuous, rolling process, so it is always a case of 'Monitor, revise, monitor,' and so on.

Absorption costing and marginal costing

Absorption costing

An absorption cost is the total cost divided by the number of units produced. If we want to know the cost of a product or batch, there is no problem with the direct costs. We simply take all those costs directly attributable to that product or batch and add them up. It is the indirect costs that can pose a problem.

If these can be 'apportioned' in some way to each cost unit, then the total costs attributed to all the cost units together will equal the actual total costs of the business. This process of spreading the indirect or overhead cost over the range of cost units is what absorption costing does.

The problem with absorption costing

When indirect costs are apportioned to each cost unit, the calculations must include some *assumption* about volumes of production and sales. The more we expect to produce of a product, the more thinly these overheads can be spread – and the lower the calculated cost for the product.

If our assumptions about volumes turn out to be wrong, the cost figures will be wrong, ie overheads will be over- or under-absorbed.

Also, an arbitrary allocation of indirect costs over a number of different products or production departments can directly affect their apparent profitability.

Marginal costing

A marginal cost is the cost of producing one extra unit, and will therefore be made up of variable costs. It is not about absorbing overheads. It only considers the variable costs associated with a product.

A marginally costed product can be sold at a marginal price, which will be lower than a full absorption price. A product that looks to recover only its variable (direct) costs will make no contribution to the fixed (indirect) costs of the business.

This is, unfortunately, a method sometimes used to lower the prices of excess-capacity goods dumped in overseas markets and should not be part of any long-term export strategy.

Contribution

Because we can measure very accurately the direct costs of a single unit and because of the problems associated with the allocation of indirect costs to that unit, contribution is often used as a more accurate measure of a unit's profitability.

Contribution is revenue minus direct costs and is therefore an accurate figure. The assumption is that, subject to an appropriate allocation of indirect cost, the unit that generates the greatest contribution will also generate the greatest profit.

It is called contribution because it 'contributes to the indirect costs and thereafter to profit'. In other words, contribution is indirect costs plus profit.

25
International payment methods

As the majority of companies trading internationally are profit making, or are at least attempting to be profit making, it is fairly obvious that the receipt of payment is essential to that purpose. It is clearly the responsibility of the exporter to operate in a way that maximizes, and ideally guarantees, the possibility of payment being received in full and on time.

This primarily relates to the choices made regarding the terms and methods of payment used for particular countries and customers. Also, as will become obvious when we examine these methods, the whole export order process needs to be carried out correctly in order to ensure collection of payment. In particular, the documentary procedures, and the quality of documents they produce are very often the deciding factor as to whether the money is paid or not.

To clarify the distinction made above:

- Terms of payment are the time allowed for payment to be made, ie the credit period allowed. This is usually expressed as sight payment, where no credit period is allowed, or in blocks of 30 days, eg 60, 90, 180 days, etc, following a date specified in the contract, which could be from sight of documents or from date of shipment or from the invoice date.

- Method of payment is the means by which the money will be paid, and the exporter has a range of choices that offer varying degrees of security.

Figure 25.1 ranks the basic methods of payment from the least secure to the most secure (from the seller's point of view).

FIGURE 25.1   Payment methods ranked according to security

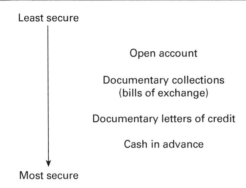

Least secure

Open account

Documentary collections
(bills of exchange)

Documentary letters of credit

Cash in advance

Most secure

The trader obviously has to make a choice as to the appropriate terms and method of payment right at the beginning of the process when the quotation is first made, and this choice will be affected by a variety of factors.

The market

Certain methods of payment are clearly more common than others in particular markets, so the exporter invariably has a 'rule of thumb' as to the usual method for a particular market. In this context it is no surprise that for high-risk markets, for example West Africa, cash in advance is not uncommon and letters of credit are very common. On the other hand, a developed market like Germany exhibits a preponderance of open account contracts.

Companies like Standard & Poor's and Moody's can provide long-term ratings of countries and also large corporations like banks. For the typical exporter, shorter-term ratings are obtainable from Dun & Bradstreet and other specialized agencies.

The buyer

Irrespective of the traditional and accepted method of payment in a particular country, the seller's perception of the buyer risk, or lack of it, can override any rule of thumb.

Criteria that would affect this decision include:

● previous experience;
● trade references: from other companies with which the buyer is trading;
● bank report: may not give much detail;

- credit report: more detail but more expensive;
- agent's report: may look to present a better picture than is accurate;
- credit risk insurers: see Part 7.

The competition

This does overlap with the two factors mentioned above in that the typical method of payment adopted in a market is clearly the one most likely to be offered by the competition in that market. It could be the case that the competition faced by a particular exporter is prepared to use terms and methods of payment as a marketing tool. That is, they are prepared to agree longer credit periods or less secure and often cheaper methods of payment in order to win or hold business.

Any decision regarding the terms and method used must be based on the application of all the above factors and underpinned by a very clear understanding of the operation of the various methods, the risks involved and the ways in which good management can minimize those risks.

Cash in advance or with order

The most secure method of payment for the exporter, if you can get it. It is because of exporters' perceptions of an increased credit risk in world trade, and the fact that they do not regard letters of credit as an absolute guarantee, that there has been a clear increase in the incidence of advance payments in the last 20 years.

It is increasingly the case that overseas buyers in certain high-risk countries also accept it as the normal method of payment, subject, of course, to their exchange controls. In this context many African markets are regularly paying in advance. In the case of large projects, it is not unusual for a percentage of the payment to be made in advance, the balance often being paid in instalments.

The money can be transferred just as for an open account payment, the only difference being that the transfer takes place before shipment (or even before manufacture) against a pro-forma invoice (see Chapter 14) rather than a final invoice.

Open account

The least secure method of payment and therefore only used regularly in low-risk markets. It is thus quite common in Western Europe and the USA.

The seller will send the goods and all the documents direct to the buyer and trust them to pay on the agreed date.

It is important that it is made absolutely clear:

When payment is due

This may be on receipt of documents or goods, which would invariably be sent direct to the buyer, or after a credit period of typically 30, 60, or 90 days after a specified date, eg date of invoice.

Where the payment is going

An export invoice should specify:

- full company name;
- full business address;
- name of bank;
- name of account holder;
- bank branch address;
- account number;
- bank sort code;
- bank identifier code (BIC, ie SWIFT address);
- international bank account number (IBAN).

How the payments will be made:

- cash
  Because of the problems associated with money laundering in world trade, ie illegally earned money being used to buy goods for legitimate sale, it is advisable that cash is refused for anything other than small amounts from individuals.

- buyer's cheque
  Apart from the chance of the cheque bouncing, the real problem is that the cheque will have to be returned to the buyer's country to be cleared, and this can often take anything from one to six weeks.

- banker's draft
  In effect, a cheque drawn by one bank on another is more secure than the buyer's cheque and will clear in the seller's country. The time delay in the draft being raised and posted to the seller followed by clearance still occurs.

  All of the above are increasingly uncommon now because of the development of electronic means of fund transfer.

International transfer

An international transfer represents the fastest way of making payment and results in the exporter receiving cleared funds direct into their bank account. In fact, there are three ways in which transfers can be made:

- mail transfer;
- cable/telex transfer (often known as TT or telegraphic transfer);
- SWIFT (Society for Worldwide Inter-bank Financial Telecommunications).

The last method is the fastest and therefore most common. It is an automated inter-bank system similar to BACS in the UK and offers a secure and rapid method of financial transfers between international departments of banks. In some cases, like Western Europe, SWIFT may be used automatically.

It is very much in the seller's interest to minimize the delay between the buyer paying and the funds being cleared and available. The delay is sometimes referred to as 'float time' – and banks make a lot of money out of float.

Factors

It is possible for exporters to actually avoid the problems of collecting overseas debts by factoring them to specialist financial institutions. The factors will take over the invoices of the exporter and pay a percentage of their value.

This is calculated on the trader's average credit period and level of bad debts, and is often paid at the end of an agreed period from the invoice date. The exporter is therefore able to accurately predict receipts with all the cash flow advantages that entails.

It may be that these payments are made with or without recourse should the buyer not pay on time. The larger factors operating internationally are obviously very adept at credit control and debt collection.

This will invariably cost more than if the exporter were to successfully collect their own debts, and perhaps we do not wish to pass our debt collection procedures on to third parties who do not consider customer relations or the business implications. It does smack of 'passing the buck'.

Documentary collections

The use of bills of exchange, sometimes called drafts, introduces a new documentary requirement for the exporter in that the bill of exchange will be drawn up by them in addition to the other shipping documents. The security that bills of exchange offer is based on the fact that the procedures involve the banks in arranging for collection of payment from the buyer on behalf of the seller.

The exporter, having agreed such a method of payment with the buyer, will draw up a bill of exchange, which will form part of the document set that will be sent to their bank. The bank will send the documents to a bank in the buyer's country, often the buyer's bank, who will negotiate payment. The procedure is illustrated in Figure 25.2.

FIGURE 25.2 Processing the bill of exchange in export trade

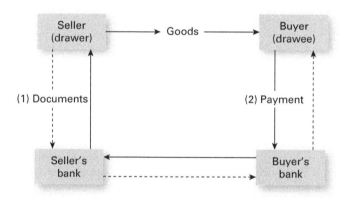

The layouts of bills of exchange do vary but a traditional blank bill is shown in Figure 25.3.

FIGURE 25.3 Traditional blank bill of exchange

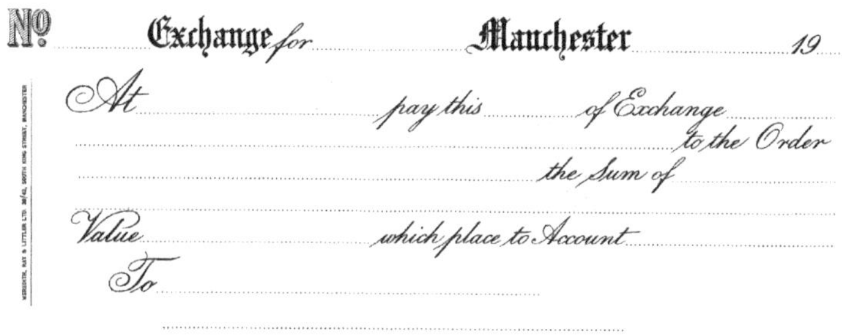

However, this document format could be seen as rather old fashioned and it is not necessary to use a particular printed form. A much simpler layout, as shown in Figure 25.4, would be just as acceptable.

FIGURE 25.4 Typical blank bill of exchange

Elton Paper Mill
Bury, Lancashire

Date......................

....

THIS FIRST OF EXCHANGE (SECOND OF THE SAME
TENOR AND DATE BEING UNPAID) PAY TO J R CROMPTON PLC,
OR ORDER, THE SUM OF

FOR VALUE RECEIVED.

For and on behalf of
J R Crompton PLC

.....................................Director

..................................Authorised
Signatory

The reason why a bill should contain the words 'first of exchange second unpaid' is that it is common for two, or even three, bills to be drawn up. This is based on the same rather antiquated logic of having two or three bills of lading (see Chapter 18), designed to ensure that at least one arrives successfully at destination. The second bill will contain the words 'second of exchange first unpaid'.

Once the exporter has drawn up the bill(s) of exchange and assembled the full set of shipping documents, they are then sent to their bank along with the appropriate completed letter of instruction. The major banks use their own versions of instruction forms, most of which are presented in the form of tick boxes, and they will include clear reference to the procedures followed not only by the UK bank but also the overseas bank.

The documents will be dispatched either to the seller's bank's correspondent or the buyer's bank, who will make the collection.

The point is that a bill of exchange is defined in terms of the information it contains rather than the way it is laid out. The following definition, from the English Bill of Exchange Act 1882, is supposedly the finest legal definition in the English language:

> ...an unconditional order in writing, addressed by one person (the drawer) to another (the drawee), signed by the person giving it, requiring the person to whom it is addressed to pay on demand, or at a fixed or determinable future time, a sum certain in money to, or to the order of, a specified person or to bearer (the payee).

The expressions in brackets are the titles the banks would use to identify the parties. The exporter is the drawer in that they actually draw up the bill of exchange and the importer is invariably the person to whom it is addressed, and therefore the drawee. The drawee is the payer or acceptor of the bill and the money will be paid, at the specified time, to the payee, who is usually the exporter but could be another party or even the bearer, ie the person holding the bill to claim the funds.

Bills are either drawn up at sight (Figure 25.5) or at a number of days after sight or another determinable future time (Figure 25.6).

FIGURE 25.5 Typical blank sight draft

No. 120

Exchange for £12,560 200--

AT SIGHT... *of this* FIRST BILL *of Exchange*

(SECOND .... *of the same tenor and date being unpaid) pay to the*

order of OURSELVES .... *the sum of*

TWELVE THOUSAND FIVE HUNDRED AND SIXTY POUNDS ONLY

                                              FOR AND ON BEHALF OF

To   ADAM STEVENS LTD   RICK O'SHAE LTD
        NEW YORK USA

                                              Director

In the case where the amount is payable at sight, ie no credit period will be allowed, the overseas bank will require the buyer to pay the due amount at sight of the documents. The reason this provides security for the seller is that the bank will not release the documents to the buyer unless payment is made. This is referred to as documents against payment (DP) and the buyer will not be able to take possession of the goods without first paying for the documents, particularly if a bill of lading is part of the document set.

A typical 90-day bill is shown in Figure 25.6.

Where the exporter has agreed to allow a credit period, for example 90 days, then the bill is referred to as a termed bill or usance bill. The latter description denotes the fact that the buyer has a period of use of the goods before having to pay. The credit term allowed in the bill can run from the date of shipment (as evidenced by the transport document), the date of the bill or even the date of invoice.

In the case of a termed bill, the overseas bank will not collect payment in return for the documents but will instead release the documents against acceptance of the bill. This usually requires only a signature, of the drawee, and often a company stamp. The credit term of the bill is known as the tenor and when this expires, ie 90 days later, the bill is said to have matured and

FIGURE 25.6   Typical termed or usance draft

No. 156

Exchange for £18,240 200--

AT 90 DAYS .... *after* ... DATE .... *of this*   FIRST BILL   *of Exchange*

(SECOND .... *of the same tenor and date being unpaid) pay to the*

order of   OURSELVES .... *the sum of*

EIGHTEEN THOUSAND TWO HUNDRED AND FORTY POUNDS ONLY

	FOR AND ON BEHALF OF
To FERNANDO BROS. LTD	IVOR BIGGEN LTD
CARACAS, VENEZUAELA	Director

---

will be presented for payment. This procedure is described as 'documents against acceptance' (DA).

It is important to appreciate that in the case where documents have been released against acceptance there will be no automatic payment transfer when the bill matures. The buyer must still make the payment and it is perfectly possible for dishonour to take place.

In the cases where there is non-payment of a sight bill, or non-acceptance of a termed bill, or non-payment of an accepted bill on maturity, it is important in many markets that a protest is made. While this procedure does not apply in every country overseas, there are many in which the lack of a protest will lead to a loss of all legal rights against the buyer.

As any protest must be made the next working day (in practice three days' grace are allowed), it is important that the banks are instructed in advance.

Even in the cases where the exporter has little desire to take legal action, the protest can be sufficient to prompt payment from a buyer who is simply playing for time. Also, lists of protested bills are published in the financial press or bank gazettes of some countries and buyers will usually wish to avoid this. Finally, most credit insurance companies will require protest to be made as part of their policy requirements.

Figure 25.7 reproduces an example of a protest which was actually made in Nigeria. Only the names have been changed to protect the guilty.

The above procedures describe what are known as documentary collections in that the bank handles the set of shipping documents as well as the bill of exchange. It is possible to arrange for what are known as clean collections in which the documents are sent direct to the buyer, rather than to the bank, the bill of exchange being handled by the banks in the normal way. This is only used where there is a large element of trust between seller and buyer, and the bill is simply a convenient way to collect and transfer the payment.

FIGURE 25.7 Protest for non-payment (example)

By This Public Instrument

Be it known and made manifest that on the......22nd......day of......JUNE......
in the year......ONE THOUSAND NINE HUNDRED & SEVENTY NINE...... I Frank Odunayo
Akinrele, Notary Public, duly authorised, admitted and sworn, practising in Lagos, Nigeria,
West Africa do hereby certify that on this the......22nd......day of......JUNE......
IN THE YEAR OF OUR LORD ONE THOUSAND NINE HUNDRED & SEVENTY NINE

at the request of......ARAB BANK NIGERIA LIMITED (BALOGUN SQUARE)......
of the Colony of Lagos, Nigeria, Bankers and holders of the original Bill of Exchange a
true copy of which is on the other side written, I, Frank Odunayo Akinrele of the said
Colony, Notary Public, duly authorised, admitted and sworn, did cause the said Bill of
Exchange to be taken to No......26 Kingoady STREET, LAGOS NIGERIA......and to
be produced and exhibited to...XYZ **ELECTRICAL STORES LIMITED**......
on whom it was drawn, at No...**26 Kongoday Street,** LAGOS NIGERIA

......and cause to be demanded
payment thereof,......When **J. Smith** (Jr.) Brother for and on behalf of......
XYZ **Electrical Stores Limited,** , Said:- "My Director is not in office
but he will be informed to make necessary arrangement for payment."

and so, I am unable to obtain payment of the said **Bill of Exchange**.

Whereupon, I, the said Notary, at the request aforesaid, did cause protest to be
made and by these presents do solemnly protest against the drawers of the said Bill of
Exchange and all other parties thereto, and all others concerned for Exchange, re-exchange,
and all costs, damages, charges and interest present and future for want of payment of the
said Bill of Exchange.

Thus done and protested at Lagos in the presence of:-

T.A.O. ADEYEYE
130. Broad Street,
Lagos Nigeria

Dated the......22nd......day of......JUNE IN THE YEAR OF OUR LORD
ONE THOUSAND NINE HUNDRED AND SEVENTY NINE...
......Which I Attest,

Public, Nigeria

It is even possible to simply instruct an overseas bank to release the documents against payment without including a bill of exchange. This is known as cash against documents but does not provide the security of a sight draft and operates according to local practice rather than a set of rules.

In this respect the advantage of both clean and documentary collections is that the banks handling such collections invariably operate under the same set of procedural rules. These are known as the uniform rules for collections and are a publication of the International Chamber of Commerce (ICC publication no. 522), available from your local Chamber of Commerce.

Avalised bills of exchange

As we have seen, a termed bill accepted by the drawee is not a guarantee of payment on maturity, but it is possible to arrange for the accepted bill to be avalised by the buyer's bank. This must be arranged in advance and involves the bank adding their 'pour aval' (for value) endorsement or guarantee to the accepted bill. In such a case the exporter has a bank's promise to pay rather than the buyer's. This is not as secure as a letter of credit in that the buyer must accept the bill of exchange first, but it does have the great advantage of producing an accepted bill that can be *discounted*.

This describes the process whereby it is possible to receive a discounted amount of the bill value at the time of acceptance rather than wait for it to mature. The 'pour aval' on the bill means that a number of agencies will be prepared to advance funds. In particular, there are financial institutions who specialize in what is known as 'forfaiting' and who will advance funds at good rates. Such forfaiters will also become involved in long-term forfaits of high-value bills over long periods of time.

26
Documentary letters of credit

Most exporters will feel that a promise from a bank to pay is an improvement on a promise from the buyer, and we have seen above that the addition of a bank's pour aval on an accepted bill of exchange gives distinct advantages. The ultimate form of bank guarantee used in international trade is that of the letter of credit (LC), which, in simple terms, is a letter from a bank promising to pay an amount of money.

However, the typical operation involves the use of documentary letters of credit, which promise to pay only if the documents stated on the LC are provided by the exporter. In this respect they are very much conditional guarantees of payment.

The procedure, which begins with the seller and buyer agreeing payment by LC, requires the buyer to arrange for the LC to be opened by their bank at the time the order is placed. From the exporter's point of view the LC would need to be received before the order was accepted and checks on its acceptability would take place right at the beginning of the order process.

The buyer will instruct their bank, known as the opening or issuing bank, to raise the LC and agree with them the specific documentary requirements. The LC will then be passed to the exporter, known as the beneficiary, through the issuing bank's correspondent bank in the exporter's country.

The bank in the seller's country may simply pass the LC to the exporter, in which case they are the advising bank and the exporter has the issuing bank's promise to pay subject to the provision of the required documents. It may be that the advising bank (or even a third bank) adds its confirmation to the LC, ie its own promise to pay, and will be referred to as the confirming bank. As we will see later, the exporter may feel that the confirmation of a bank in their own country is an improvement on the foreign issuing bank's promise.

Once the LC is received by the exporter, it is important that it is checked immediately to ensure that the documentary requirements, and the time periods allowed, are acceptable. If amendments are required, it is advisable to request them immediately from the issuing bank, through the advising or confirming bank.

This procedure is shown in Figure 26.1.

FIGURE 26.1   LC process

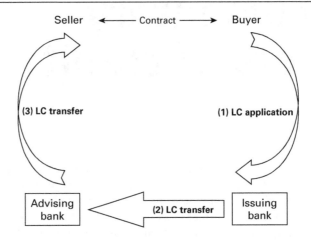

Assuming that the LC is acceptable to the exporter, they will then proceed with the manufacture, packing and shipping of the goods in order to produce a set of shipping documents in compliance with the LC. These documents will be presented to the advising or confirming bank in the seller's country, who will check that they comply with the LC requirements and, assuming they find no discrepancies, they will pay the exporter.

Unfortunately, the reality is not always quite so simple and in fact the statistics show that between 60 and 80 per cent of document sets presented to banks in developed countries against LCs are rejected because of documentary discrepancies. They actually go wrong more often than they go right. To see why such problems are experienced, it is necessary to look in more detail at the LC process.

Documentary requirements

Figure 26.2 is an example of a typical letter of credit. The norm now is that the exporter will see a hard copy of the SWIFT-transmitted LC, perhaps preceded by an e-mailed pre-advice. This is based on a standard format and fields for all LCs.

FIGURE 26.2   Typical letter of credit

Issuing bank		Shinhan Bank, Seoul
Form of doc: LC	40A	Irrevocable
Doc LC number	20	1234
Date of issue	31C	1/1/2010
Expiry	31D	31/3/2010
Applicant	50	Korea Importing Company
		Changwon City, Kyungsangnam-do, Korea
Beneficiary	59	Shady Lane Exporting Co, Manchester
Amount	32B	GBP 12,027.25
Available with/by	41D	Any bank by negotiation
Drafts at	42C	90 days after sight
Drawee	42D	Shinhan Bank, London
Partial shipments	43P	Prohibited
Transhipment	43T	Prohibited
Loading in charge	44A	UK port
For transport to	44B	Busan port
Latest date of shipment	44C	10/3/2010
Description of goods	45A	1000 units of widgets CIF
Documents required	46A	Signed commercial invoice. Packing list. Full set clean on board. Ocean bills of lading made out to the order of Shinhan Bank, Seoul, marked freight prepaid, notify applicant. Certificate of origin. Original insurance policy endorsed in blank for the invoice value of the goods plus 10%, covering institute cargo clauses (all risks or 'A') including institute war clauses and institute strikes clauses.
Additional conditions	47A	All documents must be issued in the English language; if they are not, they may be disregarded. All presentations received by us with discrepancies will attract a fee of GBP25.00 per presentation. This charge, unless otherwise stated by us, will be for the account of the beneficiary.
Details of charges	71B	Charges for beneficiary's account except opening bank's charges.
Presentation period	48	Within 21 days after date of shipment but prior to the expiry of the LC.
Confirmation	49	Without
Advise through	57D	Bank of Scotland International, Trade Services Princes House, 55 West Campbell Street, Glasgow G2 6YJ Swift: BOFSGB2S

The average LC will require:

1 Drafts (bills of exchange), which are often drawn on the issuing or the confirming bank. That is to say that the drawee on such bills will be a bank rather than the buyer.

   The bills will reflect whether the LC is payable at sight or contains a credit term, as can be seen from Figure 26.2, which requires a 90-day bill drawn on Shinhan Bank (42C and 42D). In both cases the bill will contain a clause referring to the relevant LC.

   Assuming that no documentary discrepancies are found, the bank will pay against the sight draft or will accept the termed draft. These bills are known as bank bills and such a bill, drawn on and accepted by a first-class bank, would be 'good paper' in that a discount of the bill would be very easy. The acceptance, for example by HSBC, of a bill due to mature in 90 days would be seen as an absolute guarantee of payment on maturity. In fact HSBC would be happy to discount their own accepted bills.

2 Export invoices will be required in a prescribed format and in sufficient numbers. Any required certifications and legalizations must be arranged and it may be that certificates of origin or other status documents are requested.

3 Insurance policy or certificate, which will be necessary if the contract is one that requires the exporter to arrange for the cargo insurance ie CIF, CIP. Such cover must be for the risks and the amount specified.

4 Transport documents, which could be bills of lading, air waybills, road or rail consignment notes (see Part 5), or even freight forwarder's receipts.

The above represent the typical documentary requirements on a LC but there could obviously be a number of additional documents, depending on the specific consignment involved. These may include packing specifications, consular invoices, inspection certificates, clean reports of findings, standards certificates, black-list certificates, phytosanitary certificates, veterinary certificates, halal certificates, etc.

The LC will also impose other conditions on the exporter, most noticeably the strict time limits imposed on shipment and document presentations, and will allow, or not allow, transhipment and part shipment. Obviously there will be a fixed value that cannot be exceeded.

The problems arise when the exporter presents the documents, against the LC, to the advising/confirming bank, who will examine them to assess whether they comply with the LC requirements. The banks operate on what is known as the 'doctrine of strict compliance', which means that they insist that the documents comply exactly with the LC requirements.

As illustrations of how far the banks will take the doctrine of strict compliance, the following are examples of typical bank rejections:

- ABC Engineering Ltd are described as AVC Engineering Ltd on the LC. Despite the fact that they are obviously the beneficiaries of the LC, they would have to have the LC amended or produce a letterhead with their name spelt wrongly.
- '20,000 rells' of insulating tape are defined on the LC and the exporter uses the correct description, 'rolls', on the invoice, which the bank, of course, reject. In their defence they would say that there may be a technical trade expression that distinguishes rells from rolls.
- A quantity of 5.000 kgs industrial laminate is described as 5,000 kgs on the invoice and the bank reject for an incorrect description. (You will have noticed that there is a full stop instead of a comma.)

The above examples, which mostly relate to word descriptions, are the result of the detailed examination that the exporter's documents receive when presented; there are many other reasons for rejection, which are mentioned below.

The justification of such a level of compliance is that, if payment were made by the bank in the seller's country, they having found no discrepancies, then it is probable that the issuing bank would find such discrepancies and therefore refuse to reimburse the paying bank.

The situation is even worse for the confirming bank, who will pay the exporter without recourse and will not be able to recover any funds should the issuing bank not pay.

The banks do not operate willfully or independently in rejecting documents presented to them but apply a very strict set of rules, originating with the International Chamber of Commerce (ICC), which are known as the 'Uniform Customs and Practice for Documentary Credits' (UCP). The latest version was published by the ICC in July 2007 and is ICC brochure 600 (replacing the previous 500), and the rules are therefore referred to as UCP 600.

The first solution for the exporter is to attempt to ensure that the LC is acceptable when it is received. A number of organizations, including the banks, will provide LC checklists, which can be useful for this purpose, and an abbreviated version would be along the following lines:

- Is the LC irrevocable?
- Is it confirmed by an acceptable bank?
- Are your name and that of your customer complete and spelled correctly?
- Do expiration and shipping dates give sufficient time to arrange shipment?
- Is the LC amount sufficient to cover the order value and the currency as agreed?
- Are the description and quantity of goods correct?
- Are partial shipments permitted?

- Is transhipment permitted?
- Is shipment permitted from any place or only one named place?
- Does the named destination you quoted agree with the LC?
- Can you obtain properly executed documents to conform with the LC?
- Can you produce and submit the documents in the time allowed? (If no fixed time is specified, you have 21 days from the date of shipment.)
- Is any specified agency required to issue any of these certificates?
- Can you comply with insurance risks required and is a policy or certificate required?

On presentation:

- Have all the required documents been provided?
- Are there sufficient data in the documents to show that they all relate to the same transaction?
- Are the following points consistent throughout the documents and LC:
  - amount of LC?
  - description of goods (quantity, weight, dimension)?
  - Shipping marks and import licence number?
- Are the documents signed where required?
- Have the correct number of originals and copies of documents been provided?

Bill of exchange checklist:

- Have you supplied the required number of bills?
- Is the amount correct, ie in agreement with invoice amount (unless LC specifies otherwise, eg 90 per cent of invoice amount)?
- Has it been manually signed and if signed 'for', 'pro' or 'per' a company, is the capacity of the signatory shown? (Not required if 'pp' or 'per pro' is used.)
- Is the tenor correct (at sight, at 120 days' sight, etc)?
- Is the drawee correct (as stated in the LC)?
- Is the payee correct, and if you are the payee, have you fully endorsed the reverse?

Bill of lading checklist:

- Has it been issued by a shipping company? (It must indicate the carrier on its face.)
- Is special authorization included in the LC if any of the following applies?

- bill is not 'clean' (marked to the effect that packaging and/or goods are defective);
- bill is a charter party bill of lading, a forwarding agent's bill of lading or a received for shipment bill of lading.
- Are consignee's name and address correct?
- Are notify party's name and address correct?
- Are ports of departure and destination correct (ie same as the LC)?
- Is it correctly marked 'freight paid', 'freight collect', etc?
- If issued to order of shipper, is it suitably endorsed?
- Are any alterations or notations suitably authenticated?
- Have all originals been duly signed by the carrier or an agent? If by an agent, is there an indication of the name and capacity of the party on whose behalf that agent is acting?
- Have any non-negotiable copies been provided where required?
- Has the correct number of originals been provided? (Most LCs call for a full set.)

Air transport document checklist:

- Is special authorization included in the LC if any of the following applies?
  - Air transport document not 'clean';
  - Air transport document is a forwarding agent's air transport document.
- Are consignee's name and address correct?
- Are notify party's name and address correct?
- Are airports of departure and destination correct?
- Are any alterations or notations suitably authenticated?
- Is it correctly marked 'freight paid', 'freight collect', etc?
- Is it stamped with carrier's stamp, showing flight number and departure date, if requested?
- Is it the original for consignor?

Multimodal transport document checklist:

- Are consignee's name and address correct?
- Are notify party's name and address correct?
- Is it correctly marked 'freight paid', 'freight collect', etc?
- Are any alterations/notations suitably authenticated
- Has it been properly signed?

Commercial invoice checklist:

- Is the description of goods *exactly* as stated in the LC?
- Is the price of goods *exactly* as stated in the LC?
- Is it correctly addressed (to the importer or other party specified in the LC)?
- Are the terms of shipment correct (FCA, CIP, etc)?
- Have separate charges, eg for packing, consular fees, been included that are not specifically permitted by the LC?
- Do identifying marks and numbers agree with the LC?
- Does the LC require that an import licence number be shown?
- Is a special declaration or certification required?
- If signed invoices are required, does a signature appear on all copies?
- Have you supplied the correct number of invoice original and copies?

An understanding of the most common discrepancies that banks find in examining documentary LC presentations can be instructive in terms of the exporter avoiding common rejections. A current 'top ten' would be:

1   late shipment;
2   documents not presented in time (within time allowed or 21 days);
3   absence of documents requested in the LC;
4   claused bills of lading/carrier receipts;
5   no evidence of goods 'shipped on board';
6   description of goods on invoice differs from that on the LC;
7   documents inconsistent with each other;
8   insurance not effective from the date of shipment;
9   bill of exchange not drawn up in accordance with the LC;
10   invoices or CofO not certified as requested.

It can be seen from the above that the bank not only checks the documents against the LC, but also against each other. This means that rejections can happen even when there is no specific breach of an LC requirement. An example of this would be a case where the shipping marks shown on the invoice differ from those on the bill of lading. The bank would reject the documents even though a specific shipping mark is not mentioned on the LC at all.

In the event that documents are rejected by the bank, the exporter has a number of possible strategies:

- The discrepancies can be corrected and the documents re-presented to the bank (the 60–80 per cent statistical rejection rate in the UK is on first presentation and it is often possible to re-present and obtain payment on second presentation). Another example of bank practice is illustrated by the fact that, if the original errors are corrected and the documents re-presented to the bank, it may well accept that the original causes of rejection are now acceptable but could reject because the time limit for presentation of documents (time specified in the LC or 21 days) has by then expired.

- In the event that the errors cannot be corrected, the exporter must except that the security of the LC has been lost. The bank may simply contact the buyers, via the issuing bank, and inform them of the nature of the discrepancies. The buyers then have the right to accept or reject the documents as they see fit.

It may be that the documents themselves are dispatched to the issuing bank 'for collection', which means that we have reverted to a bill of exchange to collect payment, or even that the documents are sent to the overseas bank for the buyer to inspect 'in trust'. In either case the buyer has the right to reject the documents and therefore reject the goods.

It is possible for the paying bank to pay 'with recourse' and usually against a form of indemnity from the exporter, although this may only be available for certain discrepancies, such as late (stale) documents.

The fact that the goods are actually on the way to, or have even arrived at, the destination merely adds to the problems of the exporter. To take this just a stage further, the situation in which goods have arrived at destination and the buyer has legitimately rejected the documents is a very difficult one for the exporter. The worst consequence is that, if the goods are not cleared (into the importing country) or re-exported (returned to the exporting country), then they will eventually be auctioned off. The more congested the overseas port or depot is, the sooner this will happen. It could easily be only a matter of weeks rather than months. In such a case there is a clear hierarchy in terms of the distribution of the auction revenues. Top of the list?

- Customs and Excise (you guessed it).

Followed by:

- demurrage charges (fines for delay);
- other warehousing and storage charges;
- auctioneer's fees;
- any other receiving authority charges;
- any outstanding carrier's charges.

And last and very definitely least:

- the owner of the goods, ie the exporter.

A situation to be avoided at all costs, particularly if the person who picks up the goods at auction just happens to be the original buyer who rejected the documents in the first place.

So the security of the letter of credit brings with it a clear responsibility for the exporter to produce a set of documents that comply exactly with the LC and with each other. Should discrepancies occur, it is almost guaranteed that the bank's checking system, which may involve two or three separate examinations, will find them and the security of the LC is lost. The documentary letter of credit is very much a conditional guarantee of payment.

Types of letters of credit

Irrevocable

An irrevocable LC cannot be cancelled or amended without the consent of all parties. It is irrelevant if the buyer changes their mind or even goes out of business. The only thing that can invalidate the LC is if the issuing bank goes out of business or a government moratorium means that trading must cease with a particular country.

Revocable

It is possible, but unusual, to trade with revocable LCs, which, as the name suggests, can be cancelled or amended by either party. The obvious problem for the exporter is the possibility of the buyer simply cancelling the guarantee. The UCP 600 states that LCs will be regarded as irrevocable unless they state that they are revocable.

They are used only where the parties are closely related and as a means of efficient funds transfer, not as security of payment.

Confirmed

As mentioned above, it may be in the exporter's interests to obtain the promise of a bank in their own country to pay, by adding their confirmation to the LC, in addition to the issuing bank's promise. Whether this is insisted upon or not should depend on an informed assessment of the reliability of the issuing bank and not simply as a blanket request.

Transferable

In the cases where a 'middleman' operates between a manufacturer and an end user, it is possible for an LC to be raised showing the agent as the beneficiary but also allowing the transfer of a percentage of the LC to the manufacturer. The difference is the agent's profit, and the manufacturer must meet the conditions of the LC to obtain their payment, just as the agent must.

In similar situations it may be that the first LC, paying the agent, is used to raise a second LC for a lesser amount, paying the manufacturer, with identical documentary requirements. These are known as 'back-to-back' LCs.

Revolving

Where a series of identical shipments is to be made, it is possible to raise one LC to cover all of them rather than a separate LC for each shipment. They are known as revolving because after payment against a shipment, the amount payable is reinstated for the next shipment.

Deferred payment

These are becoming increasingly popular where an LC term has been agreed but the parties wish to avoid raising a bill of exchange under the LC. This will usually be because the bills attract stamp duty in the issuing country. When correct documents are presented, the bank does not 'accept' a bill of exchange but instead gives a 'letter of undertaking' advising when the money will be paid.

Standby LCs

This type of LC is unusual in that both parties hope it will never be used. They are used in two situations:

- Where the seller is trading on open account but requires some security of payment. They are raised by the buyer as a normal LC but require the issuing bank to make payment to the seller only on presentation of documents evidencing non-payment by the buyer within the open account agreement. That is to say, as long as the buyer continues to pay on time under the open account, the LC will not be drawn on.

- To replace performance bonds (see Part 4) issued by the buyer and required under most tender procedures. They have the advantage over normal bonds of being regulated by the UCP 600 rules. They are well known in the USA and becoming increasingly common in many markets.

Summary

The documentary letter of credit is an important and very common method of payment in international trade, primarily because of the security it offers to the exporter. However, we must accept that the security of the bank guarantee inherent in the LC is tempered by the documentary conditions imposed.

It is an unfortunate fact that the majority of presentations to UK banks are rejected on first presentation because of documentary discrepancies, as is the case in most developed countries. It is vital that exporters not only establish systems that eliminate documentary errors but that they also understand the 'rules of the game'.

The banks do not invent reasons for rejection; they genuinely play by the rules, and the rules are the Uniform Customs and Practice for Documentary LCs (ICC brochure 600). Copies are available from Chambers of Commerce or the ICC website at **www.iccbooks.com**.

Countertrade

Over the last few decades there has been an enormous increase in countertrade throughout the world, and the breakup of the state-planned economies of Eastern Europe only served to accelerate this development. Some estimates suggest that in anything up to 33 per cent of world trade, countertrade at least forms part of the negotiations, although final payment might actually be made in currency.

It is obvious that the severe hard-currency shortages experienced by many developing countries lead to countertrade being seen as the only way in which international trade can occur in some situations.

The expression 'countertrade' actually covers a variety of possible procedures, which include:

Barter
The direct exchange of goods for goods. Overseas markets with excess
    commodities trade them for negotiated quantities of imported goods,
    with no cash changing hands. It is not uncommon in Africa and Latin
    America, and is preferred by some oil-dependent economies. There
    are specialist consultants who will handle the disposal of the bartered
    products on behalf of the exporter.

Counter purchase
As a condition of securing the export order, the seller undertakes to
    purchase goods or services from that country. Two contracts are
    agreed, one sale and one purchase, and payments are made on
    negotiated cash or LC terms. The counter-purchase contract can be
    anything from 10 to 100 per cent (or even more) of the value of the
    export sale.

Buy back
A form of barter in which the supplier of capital equipment, such as
    manufacturing plant, agrees to accept payment in the form of the
    output of the manufacturing unit. An important variation of this is
    practised by IKEA, who establish factories, mostly in Eastern Europe,
    based on Western European equipment, and buy back the

production. This has the distinct added advantage that the small-to-medium-sized European manufacturers supply equipment direct to, say, Poland but receive payment from IKEA.

Offset

A condition of the export would be that materials and components originating in the importing country are incorporated in the finished product that they eventually receive. This is particularly relevant to high-technology products such as aircraft and defence systems and may even involve the exporter participating in the establishment of production units in the overseas market.

Evidence accounts

Traders with significant levels of business in certain markets may be required to arrange an equivalent amount of counter-purchased exports from that country. For example, a multinational company with a local manufacturing subsidiary may be required to balance the import of materials and equipment with equivalent exports. The evidence account attempts to record the balance of imports and exports over a period of time.

27
Money laundering

Introduction

Money laundering is a process through which the proceeds of criminal activity are disguised to conceal their actual origins. It can damage economies and destroy market confidence.

'Money laundering' is a term that has been used since the 1970s. It covers criminal activities, corruption and breaches of financial sanctions. It includes handling, or aiding the handling, of assets, knowing that they are the result of crime, terrorism or illegal drug activities. Criminal and terrorist organizations generate a lot of physical cash that they need to channel into the banking and corporate financial systems. Once it is there they can readily move it to finance any further activity, usually without drawing attention to themselves.

There are three stages to the money-laundering process:

- placement of 'dirty' money;
- layering of funds;
- integration of the laundered funds back into the economy.

Placement

This is about moving illegal funds into the financial system. This is the stage when criminals are most likely to be detected.

Criminals, drug dealers and terrorists need to break down large volumes of physical cash into small, manageable amounts so that it can be filtered into the banking system without detection. The technique is known as 'smurfing'. It can involve the purchase of traveller's cheques, postal orders and/or any other form of near-cash monetary instruments.

Smurfing is risky, as unusual cash deposits can arouse suspicion and should invite unwanted questions. Funds deposited in banks or negotiable financial instruments purchased should be of low enough value to avoid triggering reporting requirements (see below).

Money can also be laundered by buying valuable assets such as paintings, works of art, gold, silver, precious stones or antiques.

The time of placement is when the criminal is most exposed and vulnerable. However, it is a risk that the criminal must take to gain access to the banking system.

Placement can also involve proceeds derived from high-value frauds, corruption and extortion. As such they may arrive in the form of electronic transfers. These transfers are still considered to be derived from criminal activities and therefore subject to criminal law.

Technological advances and the growth of e-banking with its automation of many financial transactions have opened up new opportunities to money launderers. They are finding new ways to launder money as soon as one channel is closed to them.

Financial institutions and directly or indirectly involved professionals have to be very vigilant at this stage to notice a change or a pattern, otherwise they become vulnerable. This is particularly the case for the informal financial sector, which consists of parallel or alternative banks. These informal financial organizations cash cheques for people, issue money orders, wire money or conduct money-transfer operations. Because of its informal nature, it is open to exploitation by criminals and others attempting to get around government reporting requirements.

After the cash has been smurfed it has to be layered.

Layering

This is the process of moving laundered money through a number of transactions, each designed to cover its trail back to source. The more numerous and complex the layers, the more difficult it is to locate and identify them and to trace the source of the cash.

Bank drafts, cashier's cheques, traveller's cheques and any other near-cash instrument can be used as they are capable of becoming bearer instruments and are easily transferred to third parties and lodged in a bank account.

The small size of each transaction makes banks and other issuers of monetary instruments vulnerable because generally the transactions will not be large enough to attract attention. The transactions can usually only be picked up if a pattern is noticed.

The layering stage is the point where illegal cash gets buried in the financial system. On successful layering, the cash enters the banking system as clean money – this process is known as 'integration'.

Integration

The integrated funds will appear as the legitimate earnings of an individual or the legitimate profits of a company. It becomes very hard to identify laundered money at this stage of the process, and the consequence is very harmful.

When the proceeds of crime are integrated into the financial system, criminal society becomes enriched. It also distorts the economies of many countries, making economic forecasting and the development of economic policy very difficult because the extent of the black economy is unknown.

Underground and invisible economic activity can destabilize an economy and create volatility of capital flows and exchange rates. It can have an adverse influence on the banking system and financial services market.

Criminal organizations can control business sectors or businesses in particular geographic locations, which can lead to monopolistic price fixing.

Developing nations are particularly vulnerable to money launderers because they usually have less well-regulated financial systems. These provide the greatest opportunities to criminals.

Legislation

Many countries have laws in place to fight money laundering. The European Union's Money Laundering Directives, issued between 1991 and, most recently, 2007, have led to member states' ratification in the form of:

- The First Money Laundering Directive (1991), which concentrated on combating the laundering of drugs proceeds through the traditional financial sector. This imposed obligations on financial sector firms, which included requirements relating to maintaining systems for customer identification, staff training, record keeping and reporting of suspicious transactions.
- The Second Money Laundering Directive (2001) amended the 1991 Directive to introduce changes in two main areas:
  - It expanded the scope of predicate offences for which suspicious-transaction reporting was mandatory, from drug trafficking to all serious offences;
  - It extended the scope of the Directive to a number of non-financial activities and professions including lawyers, notaries, accountants, estate agents, art dealers, jewellers, auctioneers and casinos.
- The Third Money Laundering Directive (2007) replaced the First Money Laundering Directive (as amended by the Second). The main purpose is to provide a common EU basis for implementing the revised Financial Action Task Force (FATF: see later)

Recommendations on Money Laundering (issued in June 2003). It also takes account of the new risks and practices that have developed since the previous Directive.

For further information regarding EU/UK implementation see **http://www. fsa.gov.uk**.

Outside the EU

US federal law related to money laundering is implemented under the Bank Secrecy Act of 1970 as amended by anti-money laundering acts up to the present.

Under the Bank Secrecy Act, anti-money laundering (AML) and anti-terrorist financing (ATF) are classified into two different categories when financial institutions file suspicious activity reports (SAR) to the Financial Crimes Enforcement Network (FinCEN), a US government agency.

In Canada, FINTRAC (Financial Transaction and Reports Analysis Centre) is responsible for investigation of money-laundering and terrorist-financing cases that originate in or are destined for Canada. The financial intelligence unit was created by the amendment of the Proceeds of Crime (Money Laundering) Act in December 2001 and created the Proceeds of Crime (Money Laundering) and Terrorist Financing Act.

China's top legislature adopted in 2007 an anti-money laundering law that broadens the definition of money-laundering crimes to include accepting bribes. The definition of money laundering has been expanded to include corruption and bribe taking, violating financial management regulations and financial fraud.

Previously, the law only identified drug trafficking, organized crime, terrorist crimes and smuggling as money-laundering crimes. China's officials and analysts believed the coverage was too narrow. They called for efforts to be stepped up to combat money laundering, which has risen in recent years along with activities such as embezzlement, drug trafficking and other smuggling.

The law demands financial and some non-financial institutions to maintain records on clients and transaction records, and to report large and suspect transactions. The People's Bank of China, or central bank, is the nerve centre of the anti-money-laundering campaign. Its provincial branch offices are authorized to investigate suspect fund transfers of financial institutions.

The level at which such legislation and required reporting become necessary does vary from country to country. For example; in the USA a deposit of US$10,000 or more requires a CTR (currency transaction report). In the EU it is €15,000, and in Switzerland it is CHF25,000. In some countries there is no CTR requirement.

Suspicion of money-laundering activity in the USA requires the submission of an SAR, while in Switzerland an SAR will only get filed if that activity can be proved. As a result, thousands of SARs are filed daily in the USA, while in Switzerland the rate is much lower.

Although aimed at those operating on the wrong side of the law, exporters, bankers, lawyers, accountants and others, such as bureau de change, money-transmission agents and cheque cashers, can innocently and unwittingly fall victim to its powers by not exercising due diligence. This is because these, and other professions, are involved directly or indirectly in international financial activities.

Whatever the nature of the business, anti-money-laundering procedures need to be in place. Many companies appoint a properly trained money-laundering reporting officer, and train their staff to report suspicious transactions.

A suspicious transaction is one that is outside the normal range of trans-actions undertaken by the client. This can include:

- unusual payment settlement;
- unusual transfer instructions;
- secretiveness;
- rapid movements in and out of accounts;
- numerous transfers;
- complicated account structures.

Any and all of the above should be considered suspicious.

Money laundering offences and penalties

There are five main offences:

Assisting
A crime is committed if a person suspects someone is engaged in
    criminal activities, or is enjoying the proceeds of criminal activity,
    and assists them to retain or control these proceeds. This includes
    participating in any arrangement that helps the suspected person
    make investments or acquire property.

Acquisition
Acquiring or using property that is known to be, or to have been
    purchased with, the proceeds of crime is an offence.

Concealing
Involves the concealment or transfer of the proceeds of crime to avoid
    prosecution or to help any other person to avoid prosecution. It includes
    concealing or disguising the property, and converting and transferring
    it elsewhere. It also includes concealing and transferring the proceeds
    of crime to avoid the enforcement of a confiscation order.

Failure to disclose
The offence of failing to disclose knowledge or suspicion of money
laundering usually only applies to suspicion of drug trafficking and
terrorism. A person is obliged to disclose information that comes to
their attention in the course of their trade, profession, business or
employment, and which leads to them discovering or suspecting that
someone is engaged in laundering the proceeds of drug-related or
terrorism activities. An offence is also committed if suspicions are not
reported to the authorities as soon as possible after they arise.

Tipping off
Tipping off means telling someone who is suspected of money
laundering that they are under suspicion.

The financial penalties globally are normally unlimited and prison sentences of
five years are common for not reporting reasonable suspicions, or for tipping
off a suspected offender. For actual involvement in money laundering, even
higher penalties of up to 14 years in prison are imposed.

All international traders need to be aware of the issues and potential
dangers, particularly as launderers exploit differences in controls and regulations that exist between different countries. Funds are channelled into
sophisticated instruments or assets, and into countries that have weaker
controls, strict secrecy laws or where few questions are asked.

PART NINE
New horizons

28
ICT and export documentation

SITPRO

The most important organization in the UK charged with developing systems for the electronic production of export documents is SITPRO Limited, formerly The Simpler Trade Procedures Board. Set up in 1970 as the UK's trade facilitation agency and reconstituted as a company limited by guarantee in April 2001, SITPRO is one of the non-departmental public bodies for which the Department of Trade and Industry has responsibility. It receives a grant-in-aid from the department.

SITPRO's primary objectives are to reduce the costs of trading, particularly to business, and to help the UK meet the challenges of globalization. Its activities range from grass-roots problem solving on behalf of UK businesses to high-level policy input in support of broad government and business objectives in the worldwide trade facilitation domain.

SITPRO's mission is to 'make international trade easier' by:

- influencing the simplification of international trade procedures;
- promoting best trading practices;
- developing and promoting international standards for trade documentation;
- working towards better border regulations and the removal of international trade barriers;
- remaining the world's premier trade facilitation agency.

It offers a wide range of services, including advice, briefings, publications and checklists covering various international trading practices, and champions the 'single window' concept, both nationally and internationally.

It also manages the UK-aligned system of export documents and licenses the printers and software suppliers who sell the forms and export document software.

For further information contact SITPRO Ltd, Kingsgate House, 66–74 Victoria Street, London SW1E 6SW: **http://www.sitpro.org.uk**.

Equivalent organizations working and cooperating on similar issues exist in many countries, for example:

- Germany: EFA (Europäisches Forum für Aussenwirtschaft, Verbrauchsteuren und Zoll E.V.).

- France: ODASCE (Office de Développement par l'Automatisation et la Simplification du Commerce Extérieur).

- Trade facilitation bodies around Europe come together under the EUROPRO umbrella.

- USA: NCITD (National Committee on International Trade Documentation).

- Canada: COSTPRO.

- Japan: JASTPRO.

Please note: As part of the UK budget cuts in the latter half of 2010, SITPRO will eventually be closed and its activities absorbed into BIS.

The background

Electronic Data Interchange

In simple terms, EDI can be described as 'the transfer of structured data by agreed message standards from one computer system to another, by electronic means'.

In essence, EDI is a means of paperless trading and was a natural evolution from paper documents as data carriers to computer and telecommunication systems as automatic carriers and processors of data. In traditional business processes, such as ordering and invoicing, paper documents contain structured information in various 'boxes'. In EDI this information is mapped into a structured electronic message. In operation EDI is the interchange of these agreed messages between trading partners to ensure speed and certainty and better business practice in the supply chain.

EDI allows the electronic transmission of a wide range of information between businesses that would otherwise be paper based. Since its introduction in the late 1970s its use as a replacement for paper-based systems has increased dramatically. The concept involves defining a standard format for the transmission of data between two businesses, which allows the whole transaction process to be automated. Thus, the actual applications at each end (eg accounting software) need not be identical.

The differences between EDI and other types of e-business is that while e-business can be thought of as the exchange of electronic information in any format, EDI is done through a standardized format. This makes it especially useful for large volumes of repetitive documents such as purchase orders and order acknowledgments and, increasingly, standard documents used in international trade, eg invoices, certificates of origin, transport documents, customs declarations.

UN EDIFACT

The United Nations EDIFACT (Electronic Data Interchange for Administration, Commerce and Transport) is the international EDI standard. The work of maintenance and further development of this standard is done through the United Nations Centre for Trade Facilitation and Electronic Business (UN/CEFACT) under the UN Economic Commission for Europe.

EDIFACT has been adopted by the International Organization for Standardization (ISO) as the ISO standard ISO 9735.

The EDIFACT standard provides:

- a set of syntax rules to structure data;
- an interactive exchange protocol (I-EDI);
- standard messages that allow multi-country and multi-industry exchange.

In addition, the American National Standards Institute (ANSI) has a group of basically compatible EDI standards called 'X12'. These standards can be customized for use within specific industries. ANSI ASC (Accredited Standards Committee) X12 is widely used in North America.

Trends and developments

The main reason for using EDI is that it provides a standardized rigid format for exchanging data. However, this is also a disadvantage in that it is relatively inflexible. Setting up ad hoc relationships cannot normally be done as relationships and data formats have to be formally agreed before any transactions can take place.

Traditional EDI is now being replaced by newer technologies based on Extensible Markup Language (XML). XML is the world standard platform for electronic business transactions.

The key benefits of XML are:

- it can be read by both humans and computers;
- it facilitates the optimal structuring of data;
- it can be extended to accommodate future needs;
- it is free and/or inexpensive;
- it is widely available;

- it is easy to learn;
- it is supported by all major software vendors.

XML-based EDI allows the transfer of data between companies without the format of the data having to be rigidly pre-defined; therefore companies can carry out e-business with new trading partners much more easily. XML-based technology is well suited to use over the internet, which has a much lower cost than the value-added networks of conventional EDI.

The most notable progress in terms of international trade has been the development of UneDocs, internationally agreed standards for producing aligned paper, EDI and XML international trade documents and messages developed within UN/CEFACT.

Some other important developments include:

Bolero.net.
International trade has traditionally been fraught with financial, logistic and time inefficiencies, costing world business hundreds of billions of dollars every year. Created by the world's logistics and banking communities, Bolero.net is getting rid of these inefficiencies by moving world trade onto the internet, allowing documents and data to be exchanged online between all parties in the trade chain. See **www.Bolero.net**.

Export documentation software
SITPRO licenses a network of approved suppliers to produce and supply the UK Aligned Series of Export Documents, which is based on a global template that would be familiar in many parts of the world. Printed forms can be purchased to complete manually but the norm would be to use software provided by SITPRO licensees and others that will produce completed documents. For a full list of SITPRO licensees see **http://www.sitpro.org.uk/documents/licensees.html?type=ALL**.

In addition, there are a number of other commercial providers of software packages designed to produce all the documents that an international trader might require and much more besides. For example, a Google UK search for 'export documentation software' produces about 187,000 results.

A selection of the main providers in the UK would include (with a brief description of their product in their own words):

AEB (International) Ltd
www.aeb-international.co.uk; e-mail: **info@aeb-international.co.uk**.
For over 30 years, AEB has developed highly innovative and adaptable supply-chain management solutions as well as cost-effective and secure solutions for global trade management. Our integrated modular software system is designed to facilitate and streamline business processes in supply-chain visibility and supply-chain execution. Companies operating globally optimize their processes with our

solutions package, making their business interactions more secure and efficient throughout. AEB's software suite offers comprehensive functionality via a wide range of modules including warehouse management, freight management, transport management, customs management, monitoring and alerting, and risk management.
We are proud to have over 5,000 customers worldwide supported by our offices in the UK, Germany, Singapore and the USA.

Man Sys Ltd

www.mansys.net; e-mail: **sales@mansys.net**. International trade, export management and documentation software. ManSys is a complete business support system for those dealing in physical goods such as chemicals, electricals, engineering parts, foodstuffs, military supplies, pharmaceuticals or tools. In some organizations it is a departmental system supporting the procurement team or the export department. For other organizations, ManSys manages, tracks and reports on every aspect of the business from enquiry through order processing to shipment and documentation production. Functions include sourcing, quotations, sales orders, purchase orders, invoicing, stock control, shipping, product history, client history and reporting.

Precision Software

E-mail: **info@precisionsoftware.com**. Established in 1984, Precision Software is a division of QAD Inc (QADI), a publicly traded company headquartered in Santa Barbara, CA. Precision provides industry-leading transportation and global trade management software for businesses around the world. The Precision suite of products is designed with open architecture and integrates with leading enterprise resource planning, warehouse-management systems and legacy applications to reduce transportation costs, avoid delays at trans-border crossings and mitigate the risks associated with dynamic trading environments. Precision Software's customers span multiple verticals (including life sciences, consumer packaged goods, electronics, retail, industrial products, food and beverage and third-party logistics providers) and benefit from end-to-end visibility, centralized control of their multimodal (parcel, LTL, TL, rail, ocean and air) transportation requirements and compliance with global trade regulations.
For more information, see **www.precisionsoftware.com**.

Exportmaster Systems Ltd

www.exportmaster.co.uk; e-mail: **info@exportmaster.co.uk**.
Exportmaster has been a significant provider of software for exporters since 1985. It offers not only export documentation software but also a wide range of modules from which much more comprehensive export sales, shipping and management systems can be built. It is generally integrated with corporate processing systems, but can be installed stand-alone where appropriate. Special features

include calculation of export margins, quotations, maintenance of freight and shipping rates, distribution cost calculation, tracking, progress chasing and straightforward facilities for users to design their own documents and reports. For traders, it offers product sourcing, purchasing and goods-received facilities. Exportmaster is true 32-bit software for Windows PC and network platforms.

Similar provision exists in most trading countries and, in fact, a similar search for US providers of export documentation software results in over 14 million results.

Conclusion

There is no doubt that the concept of 'the paperless export office', which has been a topic of discussion since the 1970s, is technically well advanced and many examples of paperless trading exist throughout the world.

However, if you were to go into any shipping agent's office or a department of a bank dealing with documentary letters of credit, or a section of a Chamber of Commerce dealing with document certification, you would find mountains of 'bits of paper'. The fact is that the majority of international trade procedures are still very much paper based. The differences in the type and number of documents required by various controlling authorities around the world, differing legal environments, the need for an absolute global standard of trade documentation, the language used and the differing levels of technological development all contribute to the fact that the global paperless export office is still a dream to be achieved.

29
EU governance

The competencies of EU institutions are conferred upon them by the various treaties and according to the principle of subsidiarity. The basis of this principle is that action should only be taken by the EU where an objective cannot be achieved sufficiently by the member states alone. Law made by the EU institutions is passed in a variety of forms but primarily comes into direct force and must be passed in a refined form by national parliaments.

Legal acts of the EU come in three forms: regulations, directives and decisions. Regulations become law in all member states as soon as they come into force without implementing measures and override conflicting domestic provisions. Directives issued by the EC require member states to achieve a specified result, allowing discretion to the member states as to how the result may be achieved.

The European Union was established by the Maastricht Treaty of 1992, which consolidated the three previous European communities: the European Atomic Energy Community (EURATOM); the European Coal and Steel Community (ECSC); and the European Economic Community (EEC). By envisaging progress towards a European constitution, the Maastricht Treaty introduced an enhanced political dimension and set in train the process that culminated in the Lisbon Treaty of 2009.

Along the way, the draft constitution of which the former French president Valéry Giscard d'Estaing was the architect, was presented to the Council of the European Union and referred to member states for approval by a series of referendums. The draft constitution foundered when it was rejected by the French and Netherlands electorates. Most of the provisions of the constitution were then redrafted in the form of a treaty, which each national government was required to approve in parliament.

When Czech President Vàclav Klaus signed the Lisbon Treaty in November 2009, he completed a long and tortuous process that has seen the treaty almost wrecked in Ireland and the Czech Republic and vilified by many in the UK.

However, with the final obstacle removed, all member states have now ratified the text, and the treaty entered into force on 1 December 2009.

Prominent changes included more qualified majority voting in the Council of Ministers, increased involvement of the European Parliament in the legislative process through extended co-decision with the Council of Ministers, and the creation of a President of the European Council with a term of two and a half years, and a High Representative of the Union for Foreign Affairs and Security Policy to present a united position on EU policies. The Treaty of Lisbon will also make the union's human rights charter, the Charter of Fundamental Rights, legally binding.

The immediate consequences of the treaty were the creation of a permanent presidency of the European Council to replace the previous six-monthly rotation by member states, and of the new office of EU High Representative in Foreign Policy, to be held by a member of the European Commission.

Outcomes of the 2009–10 recession

It is too early to forecast with any degree of certainty in what economic shape and when the constituent members of the EU will emerge from the current recession, although the WTO has made some predictions in its March 2010 report for resumed growth in international trade; these are summarized in Chapter 30.

Meantime, commentary is restricted to the headline economic results of 2009 for the EU as a whole with some analysis of where individual member state economies stand.

GDP

After falling approximately 4 per cent in 2009, the EU's nominal GDP was €11.8 trillion (US$16.5 trillion) for the year. Converted to international purchasing power parity (PPP; see below), GDP translates to US$14.8 trillion for comparison purposes.

Purchasing power parity (PPP)

Allows the comparison of the standard of living between countries by taking into account the impact of their exchange rates. The concept is founded on the fact that a US dollar exchanged and spent in India will buy more haircuts than a dollar spent in the USA. PPP takes into account this lower cost of living and adjusts for it as though all income was spent locally. In other words, PPP is the amount of a certain basket of basic goods that can be bought in the given country with the money it produces.

Big Mac index

An example of a simpler form of PPP is the Big Mac index popularized by the *Economist* in the UK, which looks at the prices of a Big Mac burger in McDonald's restaurants in different countries. If a Big Mac costs US$4 in the USA and £3 in the UK, the PPP exchange rate would be £3 for $4. The Big Mac index is useful because it is based on a well-known good whose final price, easily tracked in many countries, includes input costs from a wide range of sectors in the local economy, such as agricultural commodities (beef, bread, lettuce, cheese), labour (blue and white collar), advertising, rent and real estate costs, transportation, etc.

Recovery in the early part of 2010 has been patchy, with a return to GDP growth at 1.4 per cent forecast for the euro area on the assumption that there would be no double-dip recession and before the debt crisis of Greece had fully emerged. Similar levels of 2010 growth are forecast for the UK and Denmark, with perhaps 2.1 per cent for Sweden. Among the three largest economies of those members which were admitted in 2004, the GDP of Poland is also forecast to recover by as much as 2 per cent, with the Czech Republic at less than 1 per cent and Hungary remaining in recession.

GDP per capita

There is a wide variance in GDP per capita (converted to PPP), the most useful measure for comparing relative wealth and poverty. Based on the EU average as 100, the ranking in descending order is detailed in Table 29.1.

TABLE 29.1   Ranking of EU members by GDP at PPP (2008) and contributions to EU GDP (2009)

	GDP per capita (at PPP) %	Contribution to EU GDP %
EU average	100	
Luxembourg	276	0.3
Ireland	135	1.6
Netherlands	134	4.7
Austria	123	2.3
Denmark	120	1.9

TABLE 29.1   Continued

	GDP per capita (at PPP) %	Contribution to EU GDP %
Sweden	120	2.7
Finland	117	1.5
UK	116	15.3
Germany	116	19.8
Belgium	115	2.7
France	108	15.4
Spain	103	8.8
Italy	102	12.6
Cyprus	96	0.1
Greece	94	2.0
Slovenia	91	0.3
Czech Republic	80	1.1
Portugal	76	1.3
Malta	76	0.1
Slovakia	72	0.4
Estonia	67	0.1
Hungary	64	0.8
Lithuania	62	0.3
Latvia	57	0.2
Poland	56	2.4
Romania	42	1.0

TABLE 29.1   Continued

	GDP per capita (at PPP) %	Contribution to EU GDP %
Bulgaria	41	0.3
Candidates for EU membership		
Croatia	63	
Turkey	46	
Macedonia	31	
States outside the EU		
Norway	191	
Switzerland	141	
Iceland	121	

Wikipedia 6 May 2010

Member state contributions to EU GDP

The second column of Table 29.1 details the percentage GDP contribution of each member state in 2009 to total EU GDP. The two sets of data support the following conclusions:

- All of the pre-2004 EU15 members except for Portugal and Greece enjoy PPP per capita GDP above the EU average.
- The EU15 members contributed 92.8 per cent of the community's GDP in 2009.
- Of these, Germany, France, the UK and Italy accounted for 63.1 per cent.
- All of the 12 post-2003 members have PPP per capita GDP below the EU average.
- The 12 post-2003 members contributed only 7.2 of EU GDP in 2009.
- Of these, Poland and the Czech Republic together accounted for 3.5 per cent.

Further EU expansion

The three official candidate countries are Croatia, Macedonia and Turkey. Both Croatia and Macedonia are well placed to qualify for EU membership but Turkey has made only limited progress with its application.

Albania, Bosnia-Herzegovina, Iceland, Montenegro and Serbia have also gained the status of potential candidates. Kosovo could be a potential candidate but is not included in the European Commission's (EC's) list because some member states do not recognize it as an independent country from Serbia.

Iceland has always resisted joining the EU, mainly because it was never willing to risk opening its traditional fishing grounds to vessels from the member states.

The recent economic crisis seems to have changed its mind, however, as its banks have been harder hit than most and as the protection offered by accession to the union has begun to look like an increasingly good idea. In July 2009 its parliament voted in favour of presenting an application for EU membership.

Iceland has already spent 15 years as a member of the European Economic Area (EEA), the organization that allows it, together with Liechtenstein and Norway, to enjoy the benefits of freedom of movement of goods, workers and capital in exchange for applying the union's single-market legislation. It also has a bilateral free trade agreement (FTA), established in 1972 with the then European Economic Community (EEC).

More recently, in January 2010 Serbia submitted a formal application for membership and is said to have broad popular support. As with previous applications, the process will take several years. Serbia will have to work with the EC to align its laws with EU legislation and demonstrate a commitment to EU principles concerning justice and human rights in order to satisfy the EC that it is ready for membership. In the meantime, Serbia will receive significant EU funding as it prepares for accession and demonstrates that it is a functioning market economy, capable of sustaining trade within the internal market.

30
Global trading trends

In the first part of Chapter 3 we examined the history of world trade from 1870 to the end of the 20th century, with particular emphasis on the post-war period from 1945 to the millennium. In the second part of the chapter we reviewed the more uneven pattern of world trade over the first nine years of the 21st century and the new phase of global uncertainty as Western economies strive to repair the ravages of the 2008 debt crisis and the subsequent recession.

There are four elements in the current business climate of 2010:

- the global economic slowdown after 2008;
- lack of progress in the evolution of the WTO;
- increased political risk;
- the rise of China as an economic superpower.

This chapter focuses in turn on the likely impact of each of these key factors and on the prospects for further steady growth in international trade.

The global economic slowdown after 2008

Outcomes for 2008 and 2009

World exports of goods and services combined topped $19.8 trillion in 2008 but declined to less than $15.5 trillion in 2009. The early reports of recovery in the USA and most of the EU in 2010 give some reassurance that growth in international trade will resume.

Looking in more detail at the top trading nations and the eurozone in total, Table 30.1 is a brief summary of individual country current account balances over the last two years:

TABLE 30.1   Current account balances of selected economies

| | Current account balance (+) / deficit (−) | |
	2008 $ billion	2009 $ billion
USA	−728	−575
China	+384	+167
Japan	−12	+6
India	−97	−77
Russian Federation	+156	+94
Brazil	−1	+1
Germany	+217	−40
UK	−98	−89
France	−79	−60
Netherlands	+50	+48
Italy	−27	−18
Spain	−95	−37
Eurozone (total)	−215	+54

WTO

One rather contradictory conclusion is that the USA and some countries in Europe (UK, France, Italy and Spain) actually improved their current account balances as a result of reduced merchandise trade, and therefore lower trade deficits, in 2009. The same was true for India, whose merchandise trade activity was lower in the first half of the year, and for Japan, which succeeded in reversing its deficit in commercial trade services.

Conversely, a reduction in its trade account surplus to $68 billion and an increase in the deficit on commercial services resulted in Germany registering a current account deficit in 2009 of $40 billion against a surplus of $217 billion in 2008. The Netherlands held its own.

Again, the contrast between China and the USA is striking. Chinese exports fell by about 40 per cent in the first five months of 2009 but recovered strongly throughout the rest of the year so that, although the surplus on merchandise trade was reduced to $196 billion for 2009 from $396 billion in 2008 and the deficit on commercial services increased by $17 billion, China maintained an overall current account surplus of $167 billion.

The outlook for 2010 and 2011

A revival in world trade to 2008 levels, which would require an increase of almost 28 per cent, is clearly not achievable in 2010. The current WTO forecast in May 2010 is for expansion of 9.5 per cent this year with no prediction for 2011. This is considerably more optimistic than the World Bank forecasts of January 2010 for growth of only 4.1 per cent and 6.2 per cent. The implied compound rate of 10.6 per cent over two years falls far short of recovery.

Moreover, GDP growth is a necessary precondition for improvement in merchandise trade, and there is a variety of forecasts for what may happen in 2010 and 2011. In Table 30.2, World Bank forecasts of January 2010 for 2010 and 2011 are set against 2009 performance and May forecasts for 2010.

TABLE 30.2   Current account balances of selected economies

	2009	2010 World Bank	Coface	2011 World Bank
USA	−2.5	2.5	2.7	3.2
China	8.4	9.0	8.7	9.0
Japan	−5.4	1.3	1.8	1.8
India	6.0	7.5	8.5	8.0
Russian Federation	−8.7	3.2	3.5	3.0
Brazil	−0.1	3.6	5.5	3.9
Germany	−2.2	1.0	1.8	1.7
UK	−4.5	1.0	1.2	1.8
France	−2.3	1.6	1.3	1.9
Euro area	−3.9	1.0	n.a.	1.7
World	−2.2	2.7	n.a.	3.2

World Bank and Coface

In the case of the UK, HM Treasury and the British Chambers of Commerce (BCC) both produced forecasts in April 2010 for the two years. The Treasury forecasts range from 0.8 to 1.0 per cent growth for 2010 and 1.0 to 3.2 per cent for 2011 against 2.3 to 2.1 per cent from the BCC for 2011. On the evidence of all these forecasts it will take much longer to regain the 2008 level of international trade.

Additional elements of risk

For Europe the outlook was thrown further into uncertainty by the Greek sovereign debt crisis, which forced the EU to introduce its €110 billion three-year rescue plan. However, other debt-ridden eurozone economies were infected by the Greek crisis, notably Portugal, Spain and Italy, with the prospect of Ireland and even the UK suffering from loss of global market confidence and unwillingness to purchase their government bonds. For Germany, its €22 billion loan contribution to support Greece was immediately unpopular, causing plans to reduce taxes and for health reform to be delayed and Chancellor Merkel's coalition to lose its majority in the German upper house (Bundesrat).

Greece's dilemma exposed a basic flaw in the European Monetary Union that will make it more difficult for Greece to regain economic health. As a member of the eurozone, it is unable to devalue its currency in order to improve international competitiveness, unless it withdraws from the euro and returns to the drachma as its currency. If other eurozone members go the same way as Greece, the EU inter-trade of all members will be affected adversely. The UK, with its unsustainable public debt to GDP ratio, is also vulnerable, as are the UK and US banks, which hold more than $1 trillion in European debt.

In response to these looming threats, the EU finance ministers agreed on 9 May to add €60 billion to the 'stability mechanism' (already €50 billion) to assist members with balance of payment difficulties. At the same time, the members of the eurozone agreed to set up a larger safety net of €440 billion – underwritten by eurozone governments – for the use of the 16 members of the eurozone only. In addition, the European Central Bank (ECB), previously criticized for being slow to introduce quantitative easing, has agreed to become a purchaser of members' government bonds to pre-empt another liquidity crisis. For the time being, these measures have restored market confidence and averted the crisis.

Evolution of the WTO

The Uruguay round (UR) of negotiations was concluded at the end of 1993 and a single undertaking summarizing the results of the multilateral negotiations was signed at the Marrakesh Ministerial Conference in April 1994 by all its members. The UR had been a remarkable achievement, with 120 countries agreeing on a myriad of rules and disciplines covering old and new trade sectors and issues. It also ushered in the WTO on 1 January 1995, which provided a clearer framework than GATT and a more effective dispute-settlement mechanism with the addition of an appellate body that has been tested to the limit in the nine years since.

The Doha round

Further ministerial conferences were held in Singapore (1996), Geneva (1998) and Seattle (1999). The achievements of the first two of these conferences were modest, although there was increased focus on addressing the problems for developing countries in implementation of the UR at Singapore. At Geneva, the beginning of the movement against globalization was orchestrated by civil society and non-government organizations (NGOs), with demands that the WTO sanction environmental and labour transgressions.

   This movement reached a crescendo at the Seattle Conference under US chairmanship, which was called to launch a new millennium round of negotiations. The meeting was a political and diplomatic failure due to the eruption of violent, globally televised anti-globalization demonstrations. The purpose of the meeting was frustrated. However, the developing countries firmly opposed the inclusion of the issues of child labour, violation of workers' rights and environmental degradation, championed by the demonstrations, on the grounds that they would serve protectionist ends and take away their comparative economic advantage. The USA opposed a demand from the EU, Japan and South Korea for the issues of trade and investment and trade and competition to be included in the agenda for a new round.

   Two years later, in November 2001, the next ministerial conference was held in Qatar, where the current Doha round was launched. The Doha meeting was remarkable in taking place barely two months after the terrorist outrage of 9/11 at the World Trade Centre, New York. It also approved the admission of the Republic of China and Chinese Taipei (Taiwan) as 143rd and 144th members of the WTO, which has proved a milestone in the expansion of international trade. The meeting negotiated on the agenda for the Fifth Ministerial Conference under the WTO in Mexico in September 1993 and on implementation of the Agreement on Trade Related Intellectual Property Rights (TRIPS) in its application to pharmaceutical products, so as to support public health. The ministers also agreed to launch tariff-cutting negotiations on all non-agricultural products, 'in particular on products of export interest to developing countries'. At the same time, a negotiating deadline of 1 January 2005 was set for the new round of services negotiations initiated in 2000, and working groups were set up to address the trade and competition and trade and investment relationship issues first raised at the Singapore meeting, and the issues of trade facilitation and transparency in government procurement.

The Cancun Ministerial Conference

The ministerial conference in Cancun, Mexico, in September 1993, was ultimately unproductive, ending in failure to achieve consensus on key issues. This was a disappointment, particularly after an apparent breakthrough in late August when member governments seemed to have broken their deadlock over TRIPS and public health.

There were a number of factors in the collapse of the meeting, but disagreement on agriculture was a root cause. There were several strands to the disagreement, starting with the EU's failure to agree on a Common Agricultural Policy (CAP) reform to reduce supports for agriculture, and complicated by the US post-Doha implementation of the Farm Bill to increase substantially federal support for agriculture. Japan's refusal to compromise on exceptionally high tariffs on rice and other specific agricultural products was a third strand. Ahead of the Cancun meeting, the EU and the USA succeeded in framing a joint approach to agriculture, with limited cuts to the most trade-distorting subsidies and some reduction in the high tariffs affecting developing country farm exports. However, the developing countries rejected this proposal and insisted on product-specific reductions of domestic support and the total elimination of export subsidies.

One result of the unsatisfactory Cancun outcome is that the May 2005 deadline for completion of the Doha Development Agenda (DDA) had to be extended. In its aftermath, negotiators met again in Geneva (2004) and Paris (2005) before a Sixth WTO Ministerial Conference was held in Hong Kong in December 2005, which did not produce results but led to further meetings in Geneva (July 2006), Potsdam (June 2007) and a further Ministerial in Geneva (2008), all of which collapsed.

Agriculture remains the key issue of the agenda for both developing and developed countries in further negotiations. Two other outstanding issues involve a review of provisions giving special and differential treatment to developed countries and the problems that developing countries experience in implementing current trade obligations.

For the time being, the WTO's effective role is as an umpire and court of appeal for disputes between countries, particularly the USA, the EU and China regarding their current membership commitments.

Increased political risk

The assessment of international political risk is outside the remit for this book. Since the beginning of the century, the risks from the permanent threat of terrorism from Al-Qaeda, the Taliban and other factions have accelerated with the second Iraq war, the ongoing war in Afghanistan and the open wound of the Palestinian–Israeli conflict. The uncertainties resulting from Iran's and North Korea's nuclear programmes have created uncomfortable environments for the development of international trade, particularly in the Middle East.

Buoyancy in international trade for the medium term will probably be confined to Asia Pacific, North America, Europe as it recovers from recession, and those parts of Latin America that benefit from the strong demand for raw materials. The emerging countries of North Africa and sub-Saharan Africa, where China has taken the lead in infrastructure investment as a trade-off for oil-supply contracts and concessions, also offer a brighter long-term outlook.

Living with China

China's economy is now a major engine of the world economy. GDP growth faltered only in the first half of 2009, when it was feared it would fall below the 6 per cent level at which Chinese employment is sustainable. However, export-led industrial activity recovered sharply in the remainder of the year to reach 8.4 per cent for the full year. For 2010 and 2011 China's GDP growth is forecast to be the highest among major economies, followed by India from a lower base.

In most other respects the Chinese economy is strong. In 2010 public sector debt is forecast to be no more that 3.3 per cent of GDP, with a current account surplus of 5 per cent and foreign debt at 7.7 per cent of GDP.

We should view this strength as a positive stimulus to international trade rather than a threat to US and European exports. The challenge for China now is to encourage domestic consumption to take over from exports as the main engine of GDP growth, and the government seems to be moving in that direction. Of course, a continuing strong flow of exports will remain necessary to fund China's massive imports of oil and gas and other raw materials.

The most serious issue in dealing with China is the foreign exchange indebtedness of the USA and, to a much lesser extent, the EU. Reducing these imbalances will take time and requires China to resume the revaluation of its currency by more than token removal of the peg to the US dollar.

As Chinese manufacturing moves inexorably up the added-value chain, Western manufacturers will have to raise their game by maintaining a lead in technology in order to grow exports to China – but that is a reasonable challenge.

The rise of China as a major economy is now accompanied by the rise of the three other BRIC countries, Brazil, Russia and India, which may be joined in the medium term by South Africa. These four economies will be the main source for a new upward trend in global trade for the medium term to eclipse over time the 2008 level.

APPENDIX 1
Websites for exporters

Government

UK Trade and Investment: **https://www.uktradeinvest.gov.uk**
USA: **http://www.export.gov/about/index.asp**
France, Ministry for Foreign Trade: **http://www.exporter.gouv.fr/exporter/**
Germany, Trade and Invest: **http://www.gtai.de/**
Market Access database: **http://mkaccdb.eu.int/**
UK Office for National Statistics: **www.statistics.gov.uk**
UK Revenue and Customs: **www.hmrc.gov.uk/**
UK Business Link (for local contact): **www.businesslink.gov.uk**
Euro info centres: **www.euro-info.org.uk**

International

European Commission: **http://ec.europa.eu/index_en.htm**
EU Information in the UK: **www.cec.org.uk/directry/index.htm**
TARIC; EU tariff regulations: **http://ec.europa.eu/taxation_customs/dds/
    tarhome_en.htm**
International Chamber of Commerce: **http://www.iccwbo.org/**
ICC Bookshop, UK: **http://www.iccbookshop.com/**
ICC Bookshop, USA: **http://store.iccbooksusa.net/**
US trade services: **www.worldtrademag.com**
US virtual trade library resource: **www.logisticsworld.com**
International Trade Centres: **www.intracen.org**
Overseas Chambers: **www.worldchambers.com**
World Trade Organization: **www.wto.org**
International Monetary Fund: **www.imf.org**
NATO: **www.nato.int**
United Nations: **www.un.org**

Country information: **www.internetgeographer.co.uk**; **http://www.imf.org/external/country/index.htm**

Statistics

International agencies: **www.census.gov/main/www/stat_int.html**

CIA World Fact Book: **https://www.cia.gov/library/publications/the-world-factbook/**

Economist Intelligence Unit: **www.eiu.com**

Credit insurance

Atradius (Gerling NCM): **www.atradius.co.uk**

Coface: **www.coface.com**

Euler Hermes: **www.eulergroup.com**

General information

Web index: **http://www.webcrawler.com/webcrawler203/ws/index**

European importers/exporters: **www.europages.com**

Marketing library: **www.knowthis.com**

Mintel: **www.mintel.com**

Kompass: **www.kompass.com**

Press clippings: **www.publist.com**; **www.thepaperboy.com**

APPENDIX 2
Further reading from Kogan Page

Business and management

Austin, M (2010) *Mobile Business: the essential guide to putting your business on the mobile web*

Booth, C (2010) *Strategic Procurement: organizing suppliers and supply chains for competitive advantage*

Hopkin, P (2010) *Fundamentals of Risk Management: understanding, evaluating and implementing effective risk management*

Jolly, A (ed) (2010) *The Growing Business Handbook: inspiration and advice from successful entrepreneurs and fast-growing UK companies*, 13th edn

Reuvid, J (ed) (2010) *Managing Business Risk: a practical guide to protecting your business*, 7th edn

Business law

Cushway, B (2010) *The Employer's Handbook: an essential guide to employment law, personnel policies and procedures*, 7th edn

Institute of Directors, Pinsent Masons (2010) *The Director's Handbook: your duties, responsibilities and liabilities*

Institute of Directors (2009) *The Handbook of International Corporate Governance: a definitive guide*

Finance and investment

Arundale, K (2007) *Raising Venture Capital Finance in Europe: a practical guide for business owners, entrepreneurs and investors*

Becket, M and Essen, Y (2009) *How the Stock Market Works: a beginner's guide to investment*, 3rd edn

Bloomfield, S (2008) *Venture Capital Funding: a practical guide to raising finance*, 2nd edn

Davidson, A (2009) *How the Global Financial Markets Really Work: the definitive guide to understanding international investment and money flows*

Davidson, A (2010) *How the City Really Works: the definitive guide to money and investing in London's Square Mile*, 3rd edn

Plummer, T (2009) *Forecasting Financial Markets: the psychology of successful investing*, 6th edn

Reuvid, J (2008) *Mergers and Acquisitions: a practical guide for private companies and their UK and overseas advisers*

Reuvid, J (ed) (2010) *The Business Guide to Credit Management: advice and solutions for cash flow control, financial risk and debt management*

Human resources

Comfort, J and Franklin, P (2010) *The Mindful International Manager: how to work effectively across cultures*

Reuvid, J (ed) (2008) *The Corporate Guide to Expatriate Employment: an employer's guide to deploying and managing internationally mobile staff*

Intellectual property

Jolly, A (2010) *The Innovation Handbook: how to profit from your ideas, intellectual property and market knowledge*, 2nd edn

Jolly, A (ed) (2010) *The Handbook of European Brand Rights Management: how to develop, manage and protect your trademarks, domains, designs and copyrights*

Jolly, A and Philpott, J (eds) (2009) *The Handbook of European Intellectual Property Management: developing, managing and protecting your company's intellectual property*

International business

Dayal-Gulati, A and Jain, D (eds) (2010) *Winning Strategies for the Indian Market*

Jolly, A (ed) (2009) *Business Insights: Europe: a practical guide to company formation, employment law and taxation across the EU*

Reuvid, J (ed) (2010) *Business Insights: China: practical advice on operational strategy and risk management*, 2nd edn

Sales and marketing

Cambie, S and Ooi, Y-M (2009) *International Communications Strategy: developments in cross-cultural communications, PR and social media*

Cheverton, P (2008) *Global Account Management: a complete action kit of tools and techniques for managing key global customers*

Transport and logistics

Dent, J (2008) *Distribution Channels: understanding and managing channels to market*

Lowe, D (2010) *Lowe's Transport Manager's and Operator's Handbook*, 41st edn

Rushton, A and Walker, S (2007) *International Logistics and Supply Chain Outsourcing: from local to global*

Waters, D (2010) *Global Logistics: new directions in supply chain management*, 6th edn

Please visit **www.koganpage.com** for online resources and for more information on these and other titles from Kogan Page.

INDEX